T0155737

IT Security Controls

A Guide to Corporate Standards and Frameworks

Virgilio Viegas
Oben Kuyucu

Apress®

IT Security Controls: A Guide to Corporate Standards and Frameworks

Virgilio Viegas
Doha, Qatar

Oben Kuyucu
Doha, Qatar

ISBN-13 (pbk): 978-1-4842-7798-0
https://doi.org/10.1007/978-1-4842-7799-7

ISBN-13 (electronic): 978-1-4842-7799-7

Managing Director, Apress Media LLC: Welmoed Spahr
Acquisitions Editor: Susan McDermott
Development Editor: Laura Berendson
Coordinating Editor: Shrikant Vishwakarma
Copy Editor: Kim Burton

Cover designed by eStudioCalamar

Cover image designed by Pexels

Distributed to the book trade worldwide by Springer Science+Business Media LLC, 1 New York Plaza, Suite 4600, New York, NY 10004. Phone 1-800-SPRINGER, fax (201) 348-4505, e-mail orders-ny@springer-sbm.com, or visit www.springeronline.com. Apress Media, LLC is a California LLC and the sole member (owner) is Springer Science + Business Media Finance Inc (SSBM Finance Inc). SSBM Finance Inc is a **Delaware** corporation.

For information on translations, please e-mail booktranslations@springernature.com; for reprint, paperback, or audio rights, please e-mail bookpermissions@springernature.com, or visit http://www.apress.com/rights-permissions.

Apress titles may be purchased in bulk for academic, corporate, or promotional use. eBook versions and licenses are also available for most titles. For more information, reference our Print and eBook Bulk Sales web page at http://www.apress.com/bulk-sales.

Printed on acid-free paper

To my wonderful daughters, Joana and Carolina

—Virgilio Viegas

To my beloved wife, Burcu, dearest daughter, Dünya, all my family, and everyone who raised, taught, and inspired me in life

—Oben Kuyucu

Table of Contents

About the Authors

Virgilio Viegas, CISSP, CCSP, CISM, CISA, CRISC, CEH, has more than 25 years of experience in the banking sector, having worked in Europe, Asia, and the Middle East. Currently, he is the group head of international IT security at one of the largest financial institutions in the Middle East and Africa, with a strong presence across Europe, Africa, and Asia.

Virgilio previously worked for more than 20 years for a major Portuguese financial institution, where he participated in the design and implementation of an Internet services reference platform and later developed an information security reference architecture.

While working in Asia, Virgilio developed projects related to information security, compliance, and retail, such as Internet banking, ATM and POS network implementation, issuing and acquiring international card schemes, anti-money laundering, and customer fingerprint authentication. He also supported projects with significant impact in the Timor-Leste financial sector, such as the definition of the country's International Bank Account Number (IBAN) standard, the implementation of the real-time gross settlement system (RTGS), and the national ATM and POS switch.

Oben Kuyucu, CISSP, CISA, has 15 years of experience in IT security, cybersecurity, governance, risk, compliance, and PCI DSS, as well as other international standards and regulations. Currently, he is an IT Security Governance and Oversight Senior Analyst at one of the largest financial institutions in the Middle East and Africa.

Oben previously worked as a Senior Information Security Expert and PCI Qualified Security Assessor (QSA) at a leading information security company in Turkey. He was the first PCI 3DS Assessor and one of the first PCI QSAs in Turkey, and he carried out more than 150 IT security-related engagements, mainly related to PCI DSS and ISO 27001 internal audits.

Throughout his career, Oben has performed PCI DSS auditing, system administration, design, penetration testing, security analysis, consulting, pre-sales activities, and post-sales support for companies in Europe, Asia, and the Middle East. He also has made a significant contribution to many information security projects, including providing support to a PCI SSC Approved Scanning Vendor portal and transforming it into a governance, risk, and compliance vulnerability management tool.

About the Technical Reviewers

Vitor Ventura is a Cisco Talos security researcher and manager of the EMEA and Asia Outreach team. As a researcher, he investigated and published various articles on emerging threats. Most of the day, Vitor is hunting for threats, investigating them, and reversing code while also looking for the geopolitical and/or economic context that better suits them. Vitor has been a speaker in conferences such as Virus Bulletin, NorthSec, Recon, DEF CON's Crypto and Privacy Village, and BSides Lisbon.

Prior to his current position, Vitor was an IBM X-Force IRIS European manager. He was a lead responder on several high-profile organizations affected by the WannaCry and NotPetya infections, helping determine the extent of the damage and defining the recovery path. Vitor also did penetration testing at IBM X-Force Red, where he led flagship projects such as connected car assessments and oil and gas ICS security assessments, and custom mobile devices, along with other IoT security projects. Vitor holds a BSc in computer science and multiple security-related certifications, including GREM (GIAC Reverse Engineer Malware) and CISM (certified information security manager).

Onur Arıkan has been working in the information security area for more than 25 years. He co-founded Biznet, one of the well-known cyber security companies in Turkey. Onur had direct responsibility for the consultancy and penetration testing team, and he also managed the sales department as the VP of sales and marketing. His company was acquired and merged with other security companies in 2018.

ABOUT THE TECHNICAL REVIEWERS

Onur is an experienced assessor and consultant in the payment security area and assisted many merchants, service providers, and banks to comply with international security standards and regulations. Since 2020, Onur has been a partner of Secureway, an information security company in payment security. He holds CISSP, CISA, CISM, CCSP, PCI QSA, and ISO 27001 LA security certifications.

Acknowledgments

We would like to thank the reviewers (Vitor Ventura and Onur Arıkan) for accepting the challenge, the Apress team (Susan, Rita, Shrikant, Laura, and the production team) for their professional contributions, and Alex Constantinidis and our colleagues for their endless support.

—Oben and Virgilio

I would like to personally thank friends (especially Fatih Tuna) and colleagues at my previous company for accompanying me for more than eight years and directors and managers for providing me tremendous opportunities for my development in my career. Many thanks to my mother, Şenel, for always being by my side. Finally, I am grateful for the immeasurable love and support from my wife, Burcu, and daughter, Dünya, throughout this long journey.

—Oben

Thanks to all my colleagues who supported my personal and professional development and all the people who stood by my side and inspired me to do the right things throughout my life in particular, Nuno Félix, Eduardo Baleiras, Rui Pereira, João Azevedo, Eduardo Brás Duarte and Fernando Torrão Alves. Special thanks to Graça, my parents, and my daughters for their amazing support.

—Virgilio

Introduction

Having dealt with a significant number of frameworks and standards during our careers we have realized that, although different in the way they are organized and presented, most frameworks recommend the implementation of very similar security controls and processes. This book intends to be a reference guide for IT security practitioners to summarize the major standards and frameworks and present an architecture to meet their requirements. The book covers identifying and describing the necessary technical security controls and processes to be implemented to secure every organization infrastructure and several follow-up metrics to monitor the effectiveness of those controls.

The security professionals should note that implementing these technical controls and processes does not guarantee each organization's information security. As in every aspect of life, the human factor is determinant; this is also addressed by some of the standards in this book. User awareness, employee vetting and training are only a few examples of how to increase security, besides technology and processes.

It must always be taken into account that every organization is as strong as the weakest link in the chain. Information security is ultimately the responsibility of every employee within the organization—top to bottom.

To provide some perspective, several well-known real case studies are presented to explain what went wrong on some of the biggest hacks of the last decades and what could have been done to prevent them.

Finally, this book presents a list of well-known security tools to support the readers.

Most organizations' structure and governance model, where physical security, human resources, business continuity, audits, and compliance have organizational units distinct from the information security department, which can be autonomous, integrated in the risk department or IT department. This book focuses on technical controls and processes directly related to information security. It does not underestimate the importance of the remaining areas to protect each organization's information confidentiality, integrity, and availability.

This book was written as a reference guide for chief information security officers, information security managers, IT security practitioners, and IT security auditors.

Please check our GitHub page

Reference Library
IT Security Controls Checklist
High Level Architecture Diagram

https://github.com/IT-Security-Controls/IT-Security-Controls

CHAPTER 1

The Cybersecurity Challenge

Types of Threats

More than two decades ago, computer users were terrified that a destructive and undetected virus called CIH might be present in the memory of their computers and become active on April 26 and delete programs in hard drives, flash the BIOS, and brick the motherboard. The date was chosen as it is the anniversary of the Chernobyl nuclear meltdown. Back then, IT support staff informed users not to open their PCs on that date so that it would not be activated. All the leading antivirus companies at the time developed fixes for that virus, and it was estimated that the virus caused damage equivalent to $250 million[1] to $1 billion.[2] Not long after that, an email arrived at users' mailboxes with the subject "ILOVEYOU" and containing a Visual Basic Script attachment (Figure 1-1). This email used social engineering to trick users into opening the attachment. When opened, it exploited a Microsoft Outlook vulnerability, changed the file name extensions, and spread via email using the infected computer contacts. The ILOVEYOU worm infected 50 million computing systems with some impact on many government bodies, intelligence agencies, and military institutions.[3]

---

[1] www.zdnet.com/article/cih-one-year-later/

[2] https://en.wikipedia.org/wiki/CIH_(computer_virus)

[3] https://en.wikipedia.org/wiki/ILOVEYOU

© Virgilio Viegas and Oben Kuyucu 2022

V. Viegas and O. Kuyucu, *IT Security Controls*, https://doi.org/10.1007/978-1-4842-7799-7_1

Figure 1-1. *An email with an attachment that has ILOVEYOU worm*

Compared to today, these incidents were relatively simple and focused on only one technology or one attack surface. Those were static viruses that had limited spread. With the introduction of broadband networks, the Internet, and emails, viruses or worms were no longer confined to floppy drives or CD-ROMs and quickly spread through emails or popular but unprotected websites. Network-based viruses and trojans were starting to be seen in the wild. These may have had more impact or more victims than static viruses. However, the impact was random because they were directionless. The attackers were not so innovative.

Then the era of ransomware and command and control concepts began, with sophisticated and well-written malware that made it more difficult to detect or protect the network against them. Cyberattackers understood that they could monetize unauthorized access by exploiting vulnerabilities present in a targeted organization network. Their methods were also getting more and more complicated. Traditional rule-based processes were no longer suitable. As IT security professionals build up more defenses, they keep finding new methods to infiltrate networks (e.g., kill chain, privilege escalation, and internal C&C systems). IT and security professionals were searching for solutions that would minimize, if not eliminate, the threat and at the same time deliver the services or products in the intended time frame. The security solutions added to the enterprise network should not slow down the business processes, and additional security processes should not make it difficult for employees to do their job.

One enterprise-grade malware concept is *advanced persistent threats* (APTs). These are highly sophisticated custom-built threats for very specific targets, particularly VIP individuals or large enterprises. The threat actors have a specific objective instead of creating a greater impact on the general public. APTs can be used to steal corporate data or cause service interruptions on infrastructure, including IT systems or industrial control systems. Several APT groups can be seen from FireEye's APT list.[4]

As digital transformation progresses, new attack surfaces are inevitable. In the center of digital transformation, there is data. Everything physical is now transforming into something digital. We used to have commodities for trading, then precious stones, coins, and banknotes evolved. Now, with cryptocurrencies, money is digitized. Like in ancient times, when there is something valuable, there is always someone trying to steal it. In this case, it is data. Data has become the most important commodity in the digitized world. Moreover, digital transformation helped (!) our "data" to be stored in any digital media. Thus it created a new attack surface.

Cybercriminals are now aiming to acquire this data, wherever and however it is stored; external or internal sources, structured (e.g., databases), semi-structured (e.g., XML or JSON files), or unstructured (e.g., MS Excel). Although the detection mechanisms got more intelligent to discover malicious behavior, malware became more intelligent to hide. Encrypted or oligomorphic, polymorphic, or metamorphic methods can obfuscate the code or the behavior. These require more expertise and substantial resources to create and make it possible to work.

Most of the threats are to the information technology devices such as our PCs, mobile devices, servers, and so forth. That said, operational technology (OT) or industrial control systems (ICSs) are not so invulnerable to these attacks. In 2010, a worm called Stuxnet caused damage to nuclear facilities by targeting the underlying supervisory control and data acquisition (SCADA) systems and programmable logic controllers (PLCs).[5] This was the turning point for the cyberattacks to become a weapon for cyberwarfare. After the discovery of Stuxnet, Flame[6] was found for the sole purpose of targeted cyberespionage.

---

[4] www.fireeye.com/current-threats/apt-groups.html

[5] Kushner, David. "The Real Story of Stuxnet." *IEEE Spectrum*.

[6] Wikipedia. "Flame (malware)." https://en.wikipedia.org/w/index.php?title=Flame_(malware)&oldid=1020516460. (April 29, 2021.

One other example that shows the eagerness of cybercriminals to start exploiting the vulnerabilities as soon as they are announced is WannaCry. May 2017 was a bad month for a significant number of Windows users who missed the March 2017 Microsoft Patch Tuesday advisory (Figure 1-2) and had not patched their systems. In less than two months, cyberattackers successfully impacted personal computers, hospitals, financial institutions, telecom operators, universities, and government institutions.[7]

The WannaCry or WannaCrypt ransomware, which started to spread with a phishing email on May 12, 2017, affected more than 300,000 machines from more than 150 countries. The cryptoworm targeted Microsoft Windows operating systems and used an exploit that was stolen from the U.S. National Security Agency.

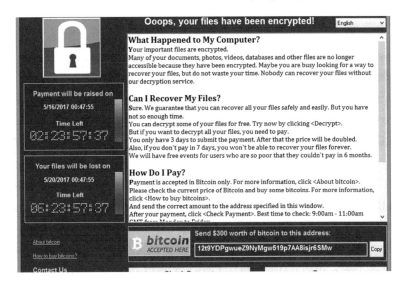

Figure 1-2. *WannaCry message after your files are encrypted*

Who Are These People?

The people behind most of these incidents are still a mystery. It is only possible to identify the name of the group that created the malware by observing their modus operandi, also known as tactics, techniques, and procedures (TTPs). When researchers dive into the malicious code, they sometimes identify certain groups' habits, which

---

[7] Wikipedia. "WannaCry ransomware attack." https://en.wikipedia.org/w/index. php?title=WannaCry_ransomware_attack&oldid=1023190294. May 14, 2021.

helps associate the attack to a particular hacker group. It should also be noted that conventional national borders are meaningless as the attackers can be in a different country from the victim. They can compromise systems around the world without leaving their rooms.

Some threats are for the small prize. They do not have a specific agenda or a specific target. Commodity threats are opportunistic threats, and their impact is typically low because most security devices are now capable of detecting, if not blocking, those threats. They could be observed in IPS logs, where there is a great deal of "nonsense" traffic from a certain IP address throughout the day or a bot performing a simple port-scanning activity. Although their impact is relatively low, they should still be considered because they can be the start of a more threatening attack.

Then there are hacktivists. These individuals/groups want to make a statement or draw attention to their cause by targeting an individual, a company, or a state actor. They can use readily available tools and techniques to discover something exploitable. Notable examples are Anonymous[8] and Lulzsec.[9]

Criminal groups that engage in cybercrime (a cyber-assisted, cyber-enabled, or cyber-dependent crime) are organized crime actors. They are involved in various cybercrimes, including fraudulent activities, financial attacks, hacking, malware/spear-phishing tools creation and distribution, distributed denial-of-service (DDoS) attacks, and blackmailing. They also target intellectual properties such as personally identifiable information (PII) data (e.g., credit card numbers, financial and health data, passports, and voter registration identifications) or a software's corporately owned source code. These actors generally sell wholesale data and earn as much as possible. As a quick example, it is possible to find millions of stolen credit card information on the dark web (Figure 1-3 and Figure 1-4). They range between $1 for credit cards and $10 for medical records or Internet banking accounts.

---

[8] https://en.wikipedia.org/wiki/Anonymous_(hacker_group)
[9] https://en.wikipedia.org/wiki/LulzSec

Figure 1-3. *EchoSec Beacon[10] is a tool to search breached data on the dark web*

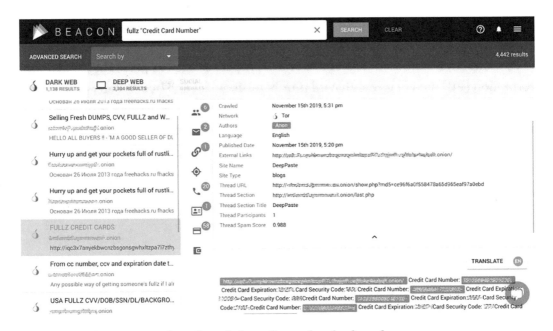

Figure 1-4. *Some samples of card data from the dark web*

---

[10] www.echosec.net/darknet

Cybercriminals often clean up after themselves or cover their tracks to prevent the attack from being detected by using intrusion detection techniques to hide the red flags and other thresholds. They can design their attacks to leave a minimal trace or digital footprint, hide their scripts or malicious code, or even disable auditing by using other exploits.

Another threat actor that takes cybercrime to the next level is cyberespionage actors. These actors try to obtain secret information without the knowledge or authorization of the data owners or custodians to gain personal, economic, political, or military advantage. These virtual spies are not famous for their cocktail recipes but for their talent to create hidden malicious codes that would help them to exfiltrate confidential information such as trade secrets or proprietary information from individuals, corporations, and even governments. It is not a mystery that state-sponsored actors are also involved in cyberespionage. The famous WannaCry, which was attributed to North Korea, resulted from an NSA-crafted malicious code known as EternalBlue,[11] which was leaked by a hackers group called Shadow Brokers to infiltrate systems for more than five years. Most cyberespionage techniques require a certain complexity and, when analyzed, the attacks are created by a group that "is likely government-sponsored."[12,13]

Cyberespionage is used for stealing sensitive data, whereas cyberwar focuses on damaging it. In 2007, the first cyberwar[14] started when several Estonian governmental, commercial, financial, and communications websites were inaccessible for nearly three weeks after a DDoS attack on more than a million computers originated from a country that Estonia disagreed with in some matters.[15] Estonia considered this attack an act of war, resulting in the creation of the NATO Cooperative Cyber Defense Centre of Excellence (CCDCOE)[16] in Estonia. In addition, most of the military now considers cyberspace as the fifth domain of warfare, following land, sea, air, and space.[17]

---

[11] https://en.wikipedia.org/wiki/EternalBlue

[12] "Report APT1: Exposing One of China's Cyber Espionage Units." February 18, 2013.

[13] www.fireeye.com/blog/threat-research/2013/02/mandiant-exposes-apt1-chinas-cyber-espionage-units.html

[14] www.nytimes.com/2007/05/28/business/worldbusiness/28iht-cyberwar.4.5901141.html?smid=url-share

[15] https://en.wikipedia.org/wiki/2007_cyberattacks_on_Estonia

[16] https://ccdcoe.org/

[17] Lynn, William J. III. "Defending a New Domain: The Pentagon's Cyberstrategy", *Foreign Affairs*, Sept/Oct. 2010, pp. 97–108.

How Do Cyberattacks Happen?

Although most cyberattacks are opportunistic, many hackers and cybercriminals are motivated to infiltrate the system, gain unauthorized access, or overload the system to cause a denial of service.

Verizon annually publishes a "Data Breach Investigations Report" (DBIR)[18] that provides a good analysis and statistics[19] of information security incidents and breaches throughout the world. According to a 2021 report,[20] social engineering is still the most widely used attack type, and 85% of the breaches involve a human element. It would not be incorrect to say that hackers still rely on the psychological aspect rather than the technical approaches. Eavesdropping, shoulder surfing, and dumpster diving can be identified as methods for social engineering. Phishing is the most common. Typically, a cybercriminal sends an email that appears to be legitimate; however, it is fake and asks the recipient for personal information, to click a link, or to execute a file. The primary goal of a phishing email is to cause panic or create an emergency situation so that the victim cannot think thoroughly before falling for the phishing attack. There are also various types of phishing, such as smishing, where an SMS is sent, spear phishing, or whale phishing, where the attackers create phishing emails especially designed and crafted for the executives, VIPs, or companies.

The human element is still the weakest link, and the threat surface is increasing daily with the new technologies brought by the challenges we encounter, such as the COVID-19 pandemic. Five years ago, online video conferencing tools were "nice to have" technologies, whereas we cannot live without them now. Therefore it is inevitable that new vulnerabilities would emerge from online conferencing tools. Indeed, the number of found and reported Common Vulnerabilities and Exposures (CVEs) has doubled in 2020 and 2021 compared to the pre-COVID-19 era for the most popular online video collaboration tools (Figure 1-5).

---

[18] www.verizon.com/business/resources/reports/dbir/

[19] https://github.com/vz-risk/dbir/tree/gh-pages/2021

[20] www.verizon.com/business/resources/reports/dbir/2021/masters-guide/summary-of-findings/

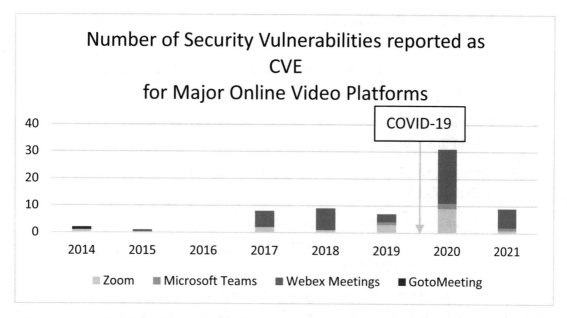

Figure 1-5. *Number of security vulnerabilities reported as CVE for major online video platforms*[21,22]

Cyber threat attack modeling techniques include Schneider's attack tree[23] or Open Web Application Security Project (OWASP) cyberthreat model,[24] kill chain,[25] and many others.[26] The major ideas behind these models are to understand the environment and related threats as much as possible, prepare and reinforce yourself with the most powerful tools designed for your environment, and use them effectively.

Kill chain analyzes the threats from the perspective of the dark side.

- **Reconnaissance**: Identify and understand the victim or the environment, make in-depth research on the target and possible exploitable points.

- **Weaponization**: Prepare the weapon (or payload) to be used for the exploitation. It can be a zero-day payload.

---

[21] www.cvedetails.com

[22] 2021 as of end of May

[23] Schneier, Bruce. "Attack Trees." *Dr Dobb's Journal*, v.24, n.12. December 1999

[24] https://owasp.org/www-community/Threat_Modeling

[25] www.lockheedmartin.com/en-us/capabilities/cyber/cyber-kill-chain.html

[26] Shostack, A. *Threat Modeling: Designing for Security*. Wiley, 2014.

- **Delivery**: Arm the weapon or send the payload. This can be through USB drives, email attachments, and websites.

- **Exploitation**: The weapon starts the action. The payload is exploiting the vulnerability.

- **Installation**: The weapon creates the foothold so that the attacker can infiltrate further.

- **Command and control**: The weapon establishes communication with the attacker.

- **Actions on objectives**: The attackers can finally act—encryption in ransomware attacks, data exfiltration in espionage, or data destruction in hacktivism.

Another famous cyber-adversary behavior model is the MITRE Adversarial Tactics, Techniques, and Common Knowledge (MITRE ATT&CK) framework that includes the tactics, which are the attackers' goals, and their techniques used for these tactics (Figure 1-6). It is currently used in many red and blue team exercises.

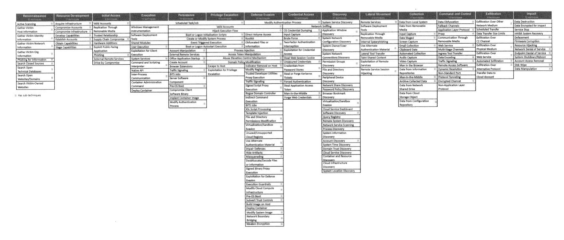

Figure 1-6. *MITRE ATT&CK Framework v9 for enterprise*

The following are the most common attack types in cyberspace.

- Malware such as botnets, worms, Trojans, ransomware

- Unwanted programs such as adware and spyware

- Identity theft

- Phishing/ spear phishing

- DNS spoofing

- Man-in-the-middle attack

- Keylogging

- Denial-of-service attack (includes DDoS)

- Session hijacking (broken authentication)

- Injection flaws (SQL, Code, OS, LDAP injection, etc.)

- Pass-the-Hash/Pass-the-Ticket (for Kerberos)

- Zero-day exploit

- Cross-site scripting

- DNS tunneling

- Drive-by attack

- Password cracking: brute force or dictionary

- Eavesdropping attack

- Cryptojacking

- IoT-based attacks

What Can We Do?

The answer to this question lies within the answers of why they succeed. Although IT security budgets are becoming "must have" from a "nice to have" when compared to 20 years ago, there are still gaps in the environment that require security hardening or change of perspective. Earlier, it was "it can't happen here" or "it won't happen to me," which made many companies suffer from cyberattacks due to the lack of investment in technologies, people, and processes that protected them. Even though there is increased budgeting, some companies still think that they are protected if they purchase enough equipment (software and hardware) and tend to forget that security is an ongoing process where there is no golden tool that provides 100% protection. Additionally, companies are now struggling with the complexity of their architectures and struggle to adapt the existing security controls to new technologies such as mobility, work from home, or the Internet of Things (IoT).

In addition, if related departments (primarily IT and IT security) are not in continuous and effective communication, or preventive controls are failing, or detective controls are not working or are not properly implemented, there will be gaps in the security posture, which yield incidents or breaches.

The following are the top 10 common mistakes in cybersecurity.

1) **Presuming that a single line of defense is sufficient**

   A secure enterprise architecture can only be achieved by implementing multiple layers of defense (defense-in-depth), where each layer deals with a different threat. Multiple lines of defenses (1LoD: operational management (i.e., users, custodians); 2LoD: risk monitoring and oversight (i.e., administrators, IT security professionals); 3LoD: auditors) must be taken into consideration.

2) **Not knowing or understanding your environment, people skills, and technology you are/will be using**

   You cannot protect an asset that you are not aware of. You cannot harden a server equipped with a technology you do not understand. You must know your capabilities and limits to efficiently secure your environment. Hackers are still targeting the weakest link of all—humans. Therefore, end-user education and awareness are key to establishing a good security posture. In addition, security professionals must continuously train themselves and diversify their skills for the new and emerging technologies for better protection.

3) **Disabling everything for the sake of security**

   Although it might work in a prison, it would not work for a functioning enterprise. When your approach to the security problem is to disable everything, businesses cannot function, and there will be resistance to the security controls, which will create the temptation to avoid them.

4) **Considering only software/hardware to achieve security**

Remember that security consists of technology, people, and processes. If you invest only in technology, but not in people, inevitably, there will be security gaps.

5) **Disregarding physical security**

Kevin Mitnick once said, "If you have physical access to the network, 90% of the obstacles are removed."[27]Always consider the physical access controls to data centers, buildings, branches, sensitive areas, server rooms, and so forth.

6) **Using weak authentication mechanisms and not following the principle of least privilege**

Think one step ahead. If your authentication systems are bypassed, how can you still protect your environment? If one account is compromised, how can you ensure it cannot move laterally through the network? Make sure to implement the least privileges with a valid and approved business need that is provided to the individuals.

7) **Not having enough visibility on the perimeter**

Things can get messy if you have a backdoor that you are unaware of. Periodically perform external vulnerability scans to your external perimeters, not only to the IP addresses you know but to the IP address ranges enterprise own and the domain names. If possible, subscribe to Threat Intelligence feeds or Attack surface management platforms.

8) **Failed communication between departments**

If the IT department is opening external ports without the knowledge of IT security, most likely, these ports are not monitored and hardened enough for the overall security of the enterprise.

---

[27] Allsopp, W. *Unauthorized Access: Physical Penetration Testing for IT Security Teams.* Wiley, 2009.

9) **Receiving too many alarms**

Although getting the event data from everywhere may provide good visibility, you become lost in the vast number of logs. Without proper correlation between systems, you may lose some of true positive incidents or breaches.

10) **Focusing on security controls for minor incidents**

Use the Pareto Principle (80% of the problems are caused by 20% of the defects)[28] to help prioritize security controls. Risk-based prioritization of patches can help to significantly decrease the overall risk in the environment.

To achieve cybersecurity in a corporate environment, every aspect of the threats should be covered. Companies should focus not only on the network or perimeter security, but application security, data security, endpoint security, business continuity planning (BCP)/disaster recovery, incident detection and response, IoT security, cloud security, and if it is used, OT security. And there are many more areas. Enterprises need to establish preventive controls, detective controls, and audit controls for each area. Reflecting on all aspects of the security to the architecture can be exhausting. Luckily, there are many established, industry-accepted best practices or very mature frameworks and standards that would significantly help security professionals to ensure the highest security posture of their enterprises (Table 1-1).

---

[28] www.juran.com/blog/a-guide-to-the-pareto-principle-80-20-rule-pareto-analysis/

Table 1-1. *Most Known Cybersecurity Standards and Frameworks and Their Domains*

CIS Controls v8[29]	NIST 800-53 v5.1[30]	ISO 27001 and 27002 v2013[31]	CISSP Certification Domains[32]
• Inventory and Control of Enterprise Assets	• Access Control	• Information security policies	• Security and Risk Management
• Inventory and Control of Software Assets	• Awareness and Training	• Organization of information security	• Asset Security
• Data Protection	• Audit and Accountability	• Human resource security	• Security Architecture and Engineering
• Secure Configuration of Assets, Network Infrastructure, and Applications	• Assessment, Authorization, and Monitoring	• Asset management	• Communication and Network Security
• Account Management	• Configuration Management	• Access control	• Identity and Access Management (IAM)
• Access Control Management	• Contingency Planning	• Cryptography	• Security Assessment and Testing
• Continuous Vulnerability Management	• Identification and Authentication	• Physical and environmental security	• Security Operations
• Audit Log Management	• Incident Response	• Operations security	• Software Development Security
• Email and Web Browser Protections	• Maintenance	• Communications security	
• Malware Defenses	• Media Protection	• System acquisition, development, and maintenance	
• Data Recovery	• Physical and Environmental Security	• Supplier relationships	
• Network Infrastructure Management	• Planning	• Information security incident management	
• Network Monitoring and Defense	• Program Management	• Information security aspects of business continuity management	
• Security Awareness and Skills Training	• Personnel Security	• Compliance	
• Service Provider Management	• Personally Identifiable Information Processing and Transparency		
• Application Software Security	• Risk Assessment		
• Incident Response Management	• Systems and Services Acquisition		
• Penetration Testing	• Systems and Communications Protection		
	• Systems and Information Integrity		
	• Supply Chain Risk Management		

[29] www.cisecurity.org/controls/v8/

[30] https://csrc.nist.gov/Projects/risk-management/sp800-53-controls/release-search#!/families?version=5.1

[31] www.iso.org/isoiec-27001-information-security.html

[32] www.isc2.org/Certifications/CISSP

Cybersecurity frameworks provide blueprints for a successful, sustainable information security program to manage IT security and cybersecurity risks. Most frameworks are divided into functional areas, mainly called *families*, *domains*, or *categories*, for easy readability and applicability. Security professionals can use these frameworks to assess their environment's cybersecurity maturity, where they can prioritize their missing gaps to minimize the risk. Most of them provide evaluation guidance in the form of scoring or checklists. These frameworks and standards include security controls to

- Detect the vulnerability

- Prevent exploitation

- Eliminate or reduce the probability of the risk or the severity

- Manage the incident

- Help restore the business after the incident

Summary

Since the "birth" of computing systems, information security threats have always been with us, sometimes in the form of viruses sent by emails with intriguing subjects or in the form of very sophisticated and nearly undetectable attacks that encrypt all your documents for a ransom. For every new technology that makes your life one step closer to digital transformation, there will always be hackers trying to gain access to sensitive information.

To help organizations and government institutions protect themselves against the increased attack surface and sophistication of cyberattacks, several standards and frameworks were created and kept being developed with security controls and processes. The following chapters of this book explain the most significant of these standards and frameworks and accompanying security controls and processes, a suggested approach to implement them, tools to test those controls, and some case studies where those controls could have prevented major information security incidents.

CHAPTER 2

International Security Standards

Organizations must increasingly demonstrate to their customers that they have sufficient protection, security, resilience, and privacy of their information, assets and systems, based on best practices. International information security standards applicable for all organizations such as ISO 27000 series or industry-specific information security standards such as PCI DSS and SWIFT were created for that reason. When organizations show their compliance to these standards, their customers acknowledge that they understand their risks, perform risk mitigation actions, create baseline security, and manage the risk on their systems. This does not mean that compliant organizations are free of risks or vulnerabilities, but they certainly have a better security posture than non-compliant organizations.

This chapter covers the main international standards related to information security that were created to be implemented worldwide, like ISO27001, ISO27002, or across certain industries like the Payment Card Industry Data Security Standard and SWIFT Customer Security Controls Framework.

© Virgilio Viegas and Oben Kuyucu 2022
V. Viegas and O. Kuyucu, *IT Security Controls*, https://doi.org/10.1007/978-1-4842-7799-7_2

ISO 27001 and ISO 27002

ISO standards are issued by the International Organization of Standardization and can be purchased at the ISO website (www.iso.org).

The current edition of ISO 27001 *Information Technology, Security Techniques, Information Security Management Systems: Requirements*[1] was issued in 2013 and superseded the first edition issued in 2005,[2] which preceded British Standard BS 7799 published by the British Standards Institution (BSI) in 1995.

According to ISO 27001, each organization should implement an *information security management system* (ISMS) and promote continuous improvement. This system should be designed according to each organization's context considering internal and external aspects, business risks, interfaces, and dependencies.

Top management of each organization needs to be fully committed to the ISMS implementation by promoting and assuring that information security policies are aligned with the organization's strategic objectives, internal processes, and needs to ensure the availability of the necessary resources through a properly documented and communicated information security policy. It is simply defined as "leadership and commitment" in the standard. In addition, top management must assign roles, responsibilities to ensure compliance with ISO 27001 requirements and report the ISMS performance.

You may also wonder about the definition of *top management*. It varies depending on the organizational structure, size, and responsibilities. In general, it should include the executive members responsible for taking strategic steps and deciding on behalf of the whole organization. In a significant number of countries with highly regulated markets, top management is also legally accountable for implementing an effective ISMS. Therefore, and considering that ISO 27001 is certifiable, as part of top management goals, organizations should certify their ISMS through an independent and accredited certification organization called a *certification body*.[3] Additionally, ISO 27001 certification is becoming a requirement for many major organizations as part of their third-party risk assessment processes.

---

[1] www.iso.org/standard/54534.html

[2] www.iso.org/standard/42103.html

[3] www.iaf.nu/articles/Accreditation_Body_Members_by_Name/52

The organization must also delineate a security risk assessment process with established risk acceptance and performance criteria, and consistent, valid, measurable, and comparable results. You may also consider adding "improvable" to those criteria for continuous progress of the security posture in the organization (Figure 2-1). This risk assessment process identifies information security risks related to the potential loss of confidentiality, integrity, and availability, identifies each risk owner, its potential impact, and likelihood so its treatment can be prioritized.

The information security risk treatment process must select the appropriate treatment options considering the risk assessment results by determining all the needed controls, matching them with the ISO27001 Annex A reference control objectives and controls, and establish a risk treatment plan approved by the risks owners. The information security risk assessment and treatment process should be aligned with ISO 31000 - Reference control objectives and controls.

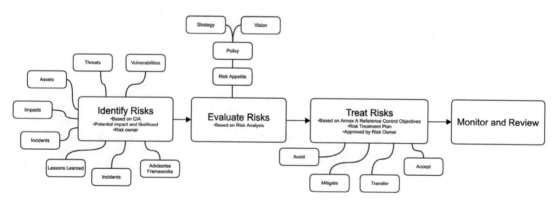

Figure 2-1. *ISO 27001 Risk management process*

Each organization must implement and document the necessary in-house and outsourced processes to meet the information security objectives and requirements, ensure that these processes are executed as planned, control all planned changes, foresee the impact of unwanted changes, and take the appropriate mitigation actions to avoid potential negative impact.

In addition to processes, the organization should produce and maintain the following mandatory documents and records.

- Scope of the ISMS (clause 4.3)

- Information security policy and objectives (clauses 5.2 and 6.2)

- Risk assessment and risk treatment methodology (clause 6.1.2)

- Statement of applicability (clause 6.1.3 d)

- Risk treatment plan (clauses 6.1.3 e, 6.2, and 8.3)

- Risk assessment report (clauses 8.2 and 8.3)

- Definition of security roles and responsibilities (clauses A.7.1.2 and A.13.2.4)

- Inventory of assets (clause A.8.1.1)

- Acceptable use of assets (clause A.8.1.3)

- Access control policy (clause A.9.1.1)

- Operating procedures for IT management (clause A.12.1.1)

- Secure system engineering principles (clause A.14.2.5)

- Supplier security policy (clause A.15.1.1)

- Incident management procedure (clause A.16.1.5)

- Business continuity procedures (clause A.17.1.2)

- Statutory, regulatory, and contractual requirements (clause A.18.1.1)

- Records of training, skills, experience and qualifications (clause 7.2)

- Monitoring and measurement results (clause 9.1)

- Internal audit program (clause 9.2)

- Results of internal audits (clause 9.2)

- Results of the management review (clause 9.3)

- Results of corrective actions (clause 10.1)

- Logs of user activities, exceptions, and security events (clauses A.12.4.1 and A.12.4.3)

Considering its ISMS capabilities, each organization must adopt the best way to store and maintain these documents. It can vary from having hard-copy paper records (not very environment-friendly) to having a governance, risk, and compliance-vulnerability management tool managed by a team.

ISO 27001 performance evaluation is done by implementing monitoring, measurement, analysis and evaluation, internal audit processes, and management review.

The organization assesses its ISMS performance and effectiveness by determining what should be monitored and measured. Chapter 7 presents metrics that measure an organization's security controls effectiveness. However, each metric threshold must be defined according to each organization's risk appetite.

The organization determines the following.

a) What needs to be monitored and measured, including information security processes and controls

b) The monitoring, measurement, analysis, and evaluation methods to guarantee valid results

c) The monitoring and measuring frequency and schedule

d) Who is accountable for monitoring and measuring

e) When the results from monitoring and measurement are analyzed and evaluated

f) Who is accountable for analyzing and evaluating the monitoring results

ISO 27001 establishes 14 control domains or areas under the management of an ISMS.

- Information Security Policies

- Organization of Information Security

- Human Resource Security

- Asset Management

- Access Control

- Cryptography

- Physical and Environmental Security

- Operations Security

- Communications Security

- System Acquisition, Development, and Maintenance

- Supplier Relationships

- Incident Management

- Business Continuity Management

- Compliance

Information Security Policies (Clause A.5)

This clause provides management guidance and support according to business requirements and applicable laws and regulations where the organization's management must define and approve their information security policies. These policies must be published and disclosed to the organization's employees and significant third parties (clause A.5.1.1).

These policies must be frequently reviewed according to established intervals or to ensure the policies' effectiveness and suitability after major changes (clause A.5.1.2).

Organization of Information Security (Clause A.6)

This clause is composed of five controls and creates the management structure to begin the organization's information security controls implementation and operation. Therefore, in regards to internal organizational structure, each organization must implement the following measures.

- Information security roles and responsibilities must be defined and internally assigned.

- The organization must implement a segregation of duties to reduce the risk of undesired changes in the organization's systems.

- The organization must identify and maintain the appropriate channels with the authorities and special interest groups, like local CSIRT, relevant stakeholder's collaborative information sharing initiatives (e.g., www.cybersechub.hk).

- Information Security must be considered in all the organization's projects.

The organization must also secure all remote access (telework) and mobile devices through the definition of a policy and the appropriate controls to protect the stored and processed information remotely accessed by their employees.

Human Resource Security (Clause A.7)

Organizations must implement appropriate processes to ensure the suitability of their employees and contractors to the roles before they are hired, during their engagement with the organization, and upon termination.

Before Hiring

The organization must implement an appropriate vetting process before hiring an employee by conducting background checks, such as criminal records, previous education and employment records, and reference checks, according to the perceived risk of the role.

The employment terms should also be presented to the future employee and contractors before hiring. These terms should include information security responsibilities and acceptable usage policy, including termination or reassignment.

Employees

The organization must also ensure that employees and contractors know their obligations by implementing an information security awareness and training program to advertise the related policies and procedures.

Employees must also be aware of the disciplinary actions for non-compliance with these policies and procedures.

Termination and reassignment

Employees and contractors must keep their information security responsibilities upon termination or reassignment. These responsibilities should be formally acknowledged during the onboarding process. The organization must have well-defined termination and reassignment processes to avoid situations like accumulation of privileges or terminated employees with active user accounts.

Asset Management (Clause A.8)

The purpose of this clause is to implement a suitable asset management system by identifying and classifying the organization's assets, assigning responsibilities over those assets, and defining media handling procedures.

First, each organization must identify its assets and define and assign ownership and responsibilities by creating and maintaining an inventory of assets with the relevant information.

According to each asset classification, information and related assets' acceptable use rules must be defined, documented, implemented, and disclosed across the organization. If applicable, employees and contractors must return the asset in their possession upon termination of their relationship with the organization.

Another important part of asset management is *information classification.* Organizations must classify and label their information, and the assets that process and store this information according to legal requirements and its value, criticality, and sensitivity. Organizations must also apply the security controls accordingly, including media handling controls and procedures like media transfer or disposal procedures.

Access Control (Clause A.9)

Organizations must implement physical and logical access controls to limit access to their information.

Primarily, organizations must establish an access control policy based on their specific context. This policy must be documented and frequently reviewed, considering the organization's business and information security requirements.

All access to corporate resources like networks, systems, and applications must be granted on a "need to have" basis. Therefore, organizations must control access to networks and network services so their users can only access the resources they were explicitly authorized to use through user access management. To ensure the proper access rights assignment and revocation to all systems and services, these users must be formally onboarded and decommissioned through a user access provisioning process.

The assignment of privileged access to users must be restricted, monitored, and controlled.

User secret authentication information like passwords and soft and hard tokens must be controlled through a formal management process.

All user access rights must be periodically reviewed and removed upon termination or adjusted upon reassignment.

During the onboarding or reassignment process, users must acknowledge their responsibilities and be responsible for their authentication information according to the organization's practices in using secret authentication information.

The organization's access control policy must define how a secure logon procedure controls systems and applications.

Likewise, the organization must also define a password policy and implement a password management system to enforce the policy. The password policy must define password complexity, length, maximum age, minimum age, and reusability.

The use of programs that can override the systems and application controls must be limited and its use controlled.

Finally, organizations must also restrict and control access to their source code of programs.

Cryptography (Clause A.10)

Organizations must define a cryptography policy and define standards on the related controls to protect information confidentiality, authenticity, and integrity. This policy must also consider that some countries have specific cryptographic standards that need to be complied with, like the following.

- Qatar National Cryptographic Standard from Qatar Ministry of Transport and Communications

  (https://www.qcert.org/sites/default/files/public/
  documents/qatar_national_cryptographic_standard_-
  _version_1.0.pdf)

- The National Cryptographic Standards (NCS) from the Saudi Arabia National Cybersecurity Authority

  (https://nca.gov.sa/en/pages/ncs.html)

- NIST Cryptographic Standards and Guidelines (https://csrc.nist.
  gov/Projects/cryptographic-standards-and-guidelines)

Key management standards and procedures must also be defined to process cryptographic keys during their life.

Physical and Environmental Security (Clause A.11)

Organizations must implement several controls to avoid unauthorized physical access, deliberate or unintentional damage, or destruction of information and systems.

Physical security perimeters must be established to secure areas with critical and sensitive information and implement access control mechanisms and procedures to ensure that only authorized staff is allowed access. These perimeters must also be protected against other external threats like natural disasters, fire, floods, or power supply problems, among others.

In the same way, the remaining facilities must also be secured.

Exterior access points where external persons might enter the organization facilities, like delivery and loading areas, also have the appropriate access controls and, whenever possible, be separated from the processing facilities.

Access points such as delivery and loading areas and other points where unauthorized persons could enter the premises should be controlled and, if possible, isolated from information processing facilities to avoid unauthorized access.

Similar controls must also be implemented to protect equipment and assets and avoid operations disruptions. Access to equipment must be controlled to prevent unauthorized access. Well-maintained equipment must be protected from environmental threats, supported by well-designed power and data cabling protected against interception, interferences, and destruction. These assets cannot leave the organization's facilities without previous authorization. When that happens, the organizations must also ensure that those assets are protected.

The organization must also implement controls and procedures to ensure that sensitive information and licensed software are not present when the assets are disposed of or reused.

Users have an important role in protecting the organization's assets by ensuring that the assets are protected before leaving them unattended (e.g., log out or lock screen before leaving their workstations) and removing all items from their desks. These measures must be defined by a "clear screen and clear desk policy" that all employees and contractors must acknowledge.

Operations Security (Clause A.12)

To ensure reliable and secure operations of information processing facilities, organizations must document their operating procedures and ensure that users have access to them if they need to.

Business process, system, and facility changes must be approved, documented, and controlled. Resources must be monitored and their usage forecasted to adjust their capacity to maintain the desired performance.

The organizations must also have distinct development, test, and production environments to prevent unauthorized access, modification of the production environment, and disclosure of production data. Development and test environments should not be populated with production data.

Systems must be protected against malware by implementing several combined anti-malware controls in conjunction with adequate user awareness programs.

Communications Security (Clause A.13)

To ensure the security of data in transit, the organization's networks must be managed and controlled. The necessary security mechanisms must be identified and implemented and service levels and management requirements regardless of whether these services are assured by organization resources or by third parties.

Networks should be segregated, and information exchange between the organization and third parties must be regulated by established agreements between the parties and in compliance with the organization-related policies and procedures. These agreements must address the organization's confidentiality and nondisclosure requirements.

System Acquisition, Development, and Maintenance (Clause A.14)

Organizations must ensure that their security requirements are met by the acquisition, development, and maintenance processes. Information security is a core part of information systems during their life cycle, including systems or services provided over public networks.

These information security requirements must be considered in all new information systems and major changes to existing systems.

When the organization's services or applications use public networks, the organization must implement the appropriate security controls against fraudulent activity, unauthorized access, disclosure of information, and conflicting situations with the service provider.

The organization must take the appropriate measures to avoid their applications or services transactions being illegitimately or accidentally misrouted, changed, disclosed, duplicated, or replayed.

Information security requirements must be integrated into the development process (security by design) by defining a software and system secure development and change policy (and security baselines) applied across the organization. This is done by implementing change control procedures to ensure that all changes are reviewed and tested before going live.

Acceptance criteria must be defined, and new systems or applications, new versions, and major changes must be tested before going live. Security functionalities must be tested during the development process.

Test data must be carefully prepared, and development systems should not be populated with production data.

Software package changes should be avoided or limited to strictly necessary and be formally approved and documented.

Outsourced development must be managed and monitored.

Supplier Relationships (Clause A.15)

Information accessed by suppliers must be protected through the definition and implementation of information security requirements that should be documented in an agreement with the supplier that must clearly state what can be accessed, processed, stored, and communicated by the supplier. The supplier service delivery must be monitored and frequently reviewed, and audited.

Any changes to supplier services must be managed and the risks re-assessed considering the information criticality and the related systems and processes.

Incident Management (Clause A.16)

Organizations must implement information security incident management processes and procedures and establish responsibilities for a fast and effective response to those incidents that should include their expedited reporting through the appropriate channels.

All the organization users, including external parties, must report any potentially suspect action or weakness through the appropriate channels. All information security events (reported or automatically generated) should be evaluated and eventually classified as information security incidents according to the organization's criteria. Documented procedures, such as incident playbooks, must be established to effectively respond to information security incidents.

The information security management procedures must ensure that any information that might be used as evidence is identified, acquired, collected, and preserved.

The "lesson learned" during the resolution of each information security incident should be used by the organization to decrease the probability and effect of similar future incidents.

Business Continuity Management (Clause A.17)

Organizations must ensure their information security in any adverse situation where the organization's information is kept secure during a contingency. Therefore, the organization's business continuity management process must include information security requirements through established, documented, and maintained processes, procedures, and redundant controls, and their effectiveness frequently verified.

Compliance (Clause A.18)

To ensure compliance with legal and contractual requirements, organizations must conform to all matters related to information security with their legal and contractual obligations. To do that, organizations must identify all applicable legislative and contractual requirements, including intellectual rights, and define and document the best approach to meet those requirements for each system and software product.

The organization must protect all records from being lost, destroyed, falsified, accessed, or released without authorization, in compliance with the law, agreements with third parties, and business requirements. The organization must also enforce privacy and protect all personally identifiable information.

Cryptographic controls must be used in accordance with the law and other obligations, and all information security policies, controls, processes, and procedures must be subject to internal compliance reviews. Additionally, independent compliance reviews must be conducted regularly or after major changes.

Information systems compliance with the organization's policies and standards must also be regularly attested.

ISO 27002

ISO/IEC 27002 provides additional guidance for ISO 27001 relevant controls implementation by helping organizations select and implement adequate security controls and develop their information security management guidelines.

ISO 27002 contains 14 security controls clauses from ISO 27001 in 35 main security categories and 114 controls. Each category contains control objectives, goals, control, or controls to be applied, and objective, description, and implementation guidance (Table 2-1).

Table 2-1. *ISO 27001 Security Controls Clauses*

Clause/Category	Security Control
A.5	**Information Security Policies**
A.5.1.	**Management direction for information security**
A.5.1.1.	Policies for information security
A.5.1.2.	Review of the policies for information security
A.6	**Organization of Information Security**
A.6.1.	**Internal organization**
A.6.1.1.	Information security roles and responsibilities
A.6.1.2.	Segregation of duties
A.6.1.3.	Contact with authorities
A.6.1.4.	Contact with special interest groups
A.6.1.5.	Information security in project management
A.6.2.	**Mobile devices and teleworking**
A.6.2.1.	Mobile device policy
A.6.2.2.	Teleworking
A.7	**Human Resource Security**
A.7.1.	Prior to employment
A.7.1.1.	Screening
A.7.1.2.	Terms and conditions of employment
A.7.2.	**During employment**
A.7.2.1.	Management responsibilities
A.7.2.2.	Information security awareness, education, and training
A.7.2.3.	Disciplinary process
A.7.3.	**Termination and change of employment**
A.7.3.1.	Termination or change of employment responsibilities
A.8	**Asset Management**

(continued)

Table 2-1. *(continued)*

Clause/Category	Security Control
A.8.1.	**Responsibility for assets**
A.8.1.1.	Inventory of assets
A.8.1.2.	Ownership of assets
A.8.1.3.	Acceptable use of assets
A.8.1.4.	Return of assets
A.8.2.	**Information classification**
A.8.2.1.	Classification of information
A.8.2.2.	Labeling of information
A.8.2.3.	Handling of assets
A.8.3.	**Media handling**
A.8.3.1.	Management of removable media
A.8.3.2.	Disposal of media
A.8.3.3.	Physical media transfer
A.9	**Access Control**
A.9.1.	**Business requirements of access control**
A.9.1.1.	Access control policy
A.9.1.2.	Access to networks and network services
A.9.2.	**User access management**
A.9.2.1.	User registration and de-registration
A.9.2.2.	User access provisioning
A.9.2.3.	Management of privileged access rights
A.9.2.4.	Management of secret authentication information of users
A.9.2.5.	Review of user access rights
A.9.2.6.	Removal or adjustment of access rights
A.9.3.	**User responsibilities**

(continued)

Table 2-1. (*continued*)

Clause/Category	Security Control
A.9.3.1.	Use of secret authentication information
A.9.4.	**System and application access control**
A.9.4.1.	Information access restriction
A.9.4.2.	Secure logon procedures
A.9.4.3.	Password management system
A.9.4.4.	Use of privileged utility programs
A.9.4.5.	Access control to program source code
A.10	**Cryptography**
A.10.1.	**Cryptographic controls**
A.10.1.1.	Policy on the use of cryptographic controls
A.10.1.2.	Key management
A.11	**Physical and Environmental Security**
A.11.1.	**Secure areas**
A.11.1.1.	Physical security perimeter
A.11.1.2.	Physical entry controls
A.11.1.3.	Securing offices, rooms, and facilities
A.11.1.4.	Protecting against external and environmental threats
A.11.1.5.	Working in secure areas
A.11.1.6.	Delivery and loading areas
A.11.2.	**Equipment**
A.11.2.1.	Equipment siting and protection
A.11.2.2.	Supporting utilities
A.11.2.3.	Cabling security
A.11.2.4.	Equipment maintenance
A.11.2.5.	Removal of assets

(*continued*)

Table 2-1. (*continued*)

Clause/Category	Security Control
A.11.2.6.	Security of equipment and assets off-premises
A.11.2.7.	Secure disposal or reuse of equipment
A.11.2.8.	Unattended user equipment
A.11.2.9.	Clear desk and clear screen policy
A.12	**Operations Security**
A.12.1.	**Operational procedures and responsibilities**
A.12.1.1.	Documented operating procedures
A.12.1.2.	Change management
A.12.1.3.	Capacity management
A.12.1.4.	Separation of development, testing, and operational environments
A.12.2.	**Protection from malware**
A.12.2.1.	Controls against malware
A.12.3.	Backup
A.12.3.1.	Information backup
A.12.4.	**Logging and monitoring**
A.12.4.1.	Event logging
A.12.4.2.	Protection of log information
A.12.4.3.	Administrator and operator logs
A.12.4.4.	Clock synchronization
A.12.5.	**Control of operational software**
A.12.5.1.	Installation of software on operational systems
A.12.6.	**Technical vulnerability management**
A.12.6.1.	Management of technical vulnerabilities
A.12.6.2.	Restrictions on software installation

(*continued*)

Table 2-1. (*continued*)

Clause/Category	Security Control
A.12.7.	**Information systems audit considerations**
A.12.7.1.	Information systems audit controls
A.13	**Communications Security**
A.13.1.	**Network security management**
A.13.1.1.	Network controls
A.13.1.2.	Security of network services
A.13.1.3.	Segregation in networks
A.13.2.	**Information transfer**
A.13.2.1.	Information transfer policies and procedures
A.13.2.2.	Agreements on information transfer
A.13.2.3.	Electronic messaging
A.13.2.4.	Confidentiality or nondisclosure agreements
A.14	**System Acquisition, Development, and Maintenance**
A.14.1.	**Security requirements of information systems**
A.14.1.1.	Information security requirements analysis and specification
A.14.1.2.	Securing application services on public networks
A.14.1.3.	Protecting application services transactions
A.14.2.	**Security in development and support processes**
A.14.2.1.	Secure development policy
A.14.2.2.	System change control procedures
A.14.2.3.	Technical review of applications after operating platform changes
A.14.2.4.	Restrictions on changes to software packages
A.14.2.5.	Secure system engineering principles
A.14.2.6.	Secure development environment

(*continued*)

Table 2-1. (*continued*)

Clause/Category	Security Control
A.14.2.7.	Outsourced development
A.14.2.8.	System security testing
A.14.2.9.	System acceptance testing
A.14.3.	**Test data**
A.14.3.1.	Protection of test data
A.15	**Supplier Relationships**
A.15.1.	**Information security in supplier relationships**
A.15.1.1.	Information security policy for supplier relationships
A.15.1.2.	Addressing security within supplier agreements
A.15.1.3.	Information and communication technology supply chain
A.15.2.	**Supplier service delivery management**
A.15.2.1.	Monitoring and review of supplier services
A.15.2.2.	Managing changes to supplier services
A.16	**Incident Management**
A.16.1.	**Management of information security incidents and improvements**
A.16.1.1.	Responsibilities and procedures
A.16.1.2.	Reporting information security events
A.16.1.3.	Reporting information security weaknesses
A.16.1.4.	Assessment of and decision on information security events
A.16.1.5.	Response to information security incidents
A.16.1.6.	Learning from information security incidents
A.16.1.7.	Collection of evidence
A.17	**Business Continuity Management**
A.17.1.	**Information security continuity**

(*continued*)

Table 2-1. (*continued*)

Clause/Category	Security Control
A.17.1.1.	Planning information security continuity
A.17.1.2.	Implementing information security continuity
A.17.1.3.	Verify, review and evaluate information security continuity
A.17.2.	**Redundancies**
A.17.2.1.	Availability of information processing facilities
A.18	**Compliance**
A.18.1.	**Compliance with legal and contractual requirements**
A.18.1.1.	Identification of applicable legislation and contractual requirements
A.18.1.2.	Intellectual property rights
A.18.1.3.	Protection of records
A.18.1.4.	Privacy and protection of personally identifiable information
A.18.1.5.	Regulation of cryptographic controls
A.18.2.	**Information security reviews**
A.18.2.1.	Independent review of information security
A.18.2.2.	Compliance with security policies and standards
A.18.2.3.	Technical compliance review

PCI DSS

Have you ever thought of an internationally accepted standard that is a list of security controls? Well, PCI DSS is *that standard*. The Payment Card Industry Data Security Standard (PCI DSS) is a set of security controls released in 2004 by PCI SSC, founded by the major payment brands—Visa, MasterCard, Discover Financial Services, JCB International, and American Express. The fundamental goal of this standard was to secure cardholder data through numerous security controls to protect the data.

Card theft and fraud are always the main concerns of acquirers, issuers, and, of course, payment brands. The rise of the Internet in the 1990s and e-commerce already amplified those concerns. To protect card data, before PCI DSS, payment brands had their own compliance schemes—a list of security controls like Visa's Cardholder Information Security Program, MasterCard's Site Data Protection, or American Express's Data Security Operating Policy with very similar goals: force merchant and payment service providers to have protection over the cardholder data and their environment. Although they had similar goals, the security controls they imposed were different. Instead of making the life of merchants easier, they became an obstacle to the progress of card transactions. Merchants had to comply with each compliance program of the payment brands in order to accept their cards.

Considering these constraints, the major payment brands aligned the compliance programs and policies into one standard to rule them all—PCI DSS.

The first version (v1.0) of PCI DSS was introduced at the end of 2004. All merchants accepting credit cards, as well as other payment processing organizations, were required to comply with the new standard. Later, the payment brands saw the need to establish governance of the standards, and they formed the PCI Security Standards Council. PCI SSC is now a global forum to maintain, develop and promote PCI standards to protect cardholder data. It is now led by a policy-setting executive committee, composed of representatives from the founding payment brands and strategic members, such as UnionPay. The standards are formed and developed with the help of feedback from several sectors. The board of advisors, which comprises representatives across the payment world like big merchants, major financial institutions, processors, and "participating organizations," can provide feedback to the standards published by PCI SSC within the life cycle of the standard. With this feedback, PCI DSS v3.2.1 was published in May 2018 and v4.0 in 2022.

Although the PCI SSC has no legal authority to enforce compliance, it is the de facto requirement for any business that processes, stores, or transmits card transactions. Many, if not all, monetary authorities and banking regulation agencies mandate PCI DSS compliance for financial institutions and service providers and require merchants to be compliant.

Initially, it may seem that PCI DSS is a very hard standard to achieve and fully comply with. However, as mentioned earlier, PCI DSS does a good job establishing an objective standard on the security controls that fit nearly all environments. For example, many of the security frameworks that you find in this book only say, "create a password policy," and leave the details to you, making it very subjective. In contrast, PCI DSS mandates that your passwords should be "at least seven characters." For that reason, a more technical-oriented security professional would not have to struggle to understand the requirements.

There are many PCI DSS-related resources available online. The most useful would be the *PCI DSS Quick Reference Guide*,[4] where you can have an overview of the standard, some details regarding the requirements, and some security tips. Another available resource is *PCI DSS: an Integrated Data Security Standard Guide*[5] by Jim Seaman, which provides a detailed description of the history and evolution of PCI DSS and the security requirements.

PCI DSS has 12 main requirements, categorized into six main goals.

- Build and maintain a secure network.

    - Requirement 1: Install and maintain a firewall configuration to protect cardholder data.

    - Requirement 2: Do not use vendor-supplied defaults for system passwords and other security parameters.

- Protect cardholder data.

    - Requirement 3: Protect stored cardholder data

    - Requirement 4: Encrypt transmission of cardholder data across open, public networks

- Maintain a vulnerability management program.

    - Requirement 5: Use and regularly update antivirus software.

    - Requirement 6: Develop and maintain secure systems and applications.

- Implement strong access control measures.

---

[4] `www.pcisecuritystandards.org/documents/PCI_DSS-QRG-v3_2_1.pdf`

[5] Seaman, Jim. *PCI DSS: An Integrated Data Security Standard Guide*. Apress, 2020.

- Requirement 7: Restrict access to cardholder data by business need-to-know.

- Requirement 8: Assign a unique ID to each person with computer access.

- Requirement 9: Restrict physical access to cardholder data.

- Regularly monitor and test networks.

  - Requirement 10: Track and monitor all access to network resources and cardholder data.

  - Requirement 11: Regularly test security systems and processes.

- Maintain an information security policy.

  - Requirement 12: Maintain a policy that addresses information security.

Goal 1: Build and Maintain a Secure Network

The purpose of this main goal is the protection of your outer perimeter. It contains requirements about firewall and router configuration (backups, having only stateful firewalls and anti-spoofing measures, NATing, etc.) and the proper change management mechanism of rules. It also contains requirements about the accuracy of your network diagram and all the data flows in the PCI DSS scope. You must know your environment well enough to ensure its safety and security.

Firewalls must be in place between any untrusted zones (including wireless networks) and cardholder data environment, and they should only allow business-need traffic to ensure a "layered defense" mechanism.

This requirement also mandates the presence of personal firewalls in portable computing devices (personal or company-owned) with connectivity to the Internet when outside the corporate network.

The second objective is to ensure the security of the system components (such as servers, databases, workstations, network devices, et al.). Apart from the mandate to change the vendor-defaults on the systems and applying hardening to the components, the standard also accepts that the organization may use an insecure implementation, such as having a legacy system that, if patched, the "nuke codes" will be revealed, or an ancient Java implementation that cannot establish a secure channel between two peers.

However, in this case, the organization needs to implement "additional security features" to any insecure required service, such as encrypting the data itself while transferring it in a cleartext channel or implementing a *network access control* (NAC) solution that prevents an unauthorized device that may sniff the environment. It should be noted that this latter example is not valid for external networks but only internal networks that you have control over.

The second part of "know your environment well" refers to the inventory of the devices in the PCI DSS scope. The organization needs to maintain an up-to-date asset inventory. It would be very useful to keep track of the hardware and software, as the organization needs to take action on any end-of-life/end-of-support hardware and software.

It should also be noted that this requirement aims to minimize the risks and effects of compromise by instructing to only enable the necessary services, protocols, daemons and implementing one primary function per server. For example, consider a server that hosts both web applications and the database. If somehow the web server is compromised, it will be only a matter of minutes, if not seconds, to infiltrate the database. Whereas in a three-layered structure (e.g., front webserver, application server, database server), it may not be so easy to gain access to the data itself, if you have implemented additional security features, of course.

Goal 2: Protect Cardholder Data

Data-at-rest and data-in-transit protection are mentioned in this goal. The main objective of this goal is to safeguard the cardholder data, wherever it is stored or transferred to any untrusted location. The easiest method you may think of should be straightforward. ***Do not store cardholder data unless it is a must for you or your business***.

Organizations that do not store cardholder data often get "not applicable" or "not tested" in many assessments, which is perfectly fine at the end of the day. However, if you are not sure if you are storing card data received from a defined or an unintended channel,[6] you can use various tools to discover cleartext card data in many formats.

---

[6] PCI SSC has an FAQ on card data received from unintended channels. https://pcissc.secure.force.com/faq/articles/Frequently_Asked_Question/What-should-a-merchant-do-if-cardholder-data-is-accidentally-received-via-an-unintended-channel All related PCI DSS requirements are also applicable to those card data that are somehow stored in your system.

According to requirement 3.1, you should use these tools to perform discovery checks every quarter to make sure that no cardholder data is stored beyond its retention period. However, it is up to the organization to define a retention period based on business or legal requirements. Most financial institutions, such as banks, have five to ten years' retention periods legally defined by their primary regulator. Whereas some service providers can choose to have card data not be stored in any of their systems so that related requirements become "not applicable."

Most of the solutions can discover card data stored in a large number of different storage formats, including office documents, email clients, zip files, databases, file servers, shadow volumes, memory, audio files, and scanned files using *optical character recognition* (OCR).

The following are some of the tools used to discover card data.

- Data loss prevention: Discovery tools such as ForcePoint[7], Symantec,[8] McAfee,[9] Netskope,[10] Proofpoint,[11] Digital Guardian[12]

- GroundLabs Card Recon[13]

- Spirion[14]

- Memoryze[15]

---

[7] www.forcepoint.com/product/dlp-data-loss-prevention

[8] www.broadcom.com/products/cyber-security/information-protection/data-loss-prevention

[9] www.mcafee.com/enterprise/en-us/products/total-protection-for-data-loss-prevention.html

[10] www.netskope.com/products/capabilities/data-loss-prevention

[11] www.proofpoint.com/us/products/information-protection/enterprise-dlp

[12] https://digitalguardian.com/products/data-discovery

[13] www.groundlabs.com/card-recon/

[14] www.spirion.com/products/sensitive-data-platform/sensitive-data-finder/#

[15] www.fireeye.com/services/freeware/memoryze.html

If you must store the cardholder data for any reason, such as one-click payments, recurring transactions, fraud detection, chargeback issues, or others, then you should maintain cardholder data security which can be several ways. The standard suggests using the following.

- One-way hashes based on strong cryptography (hash must be of the entire Primary Account Number (PAN))

- Truncation (hashing cannot replace the truncated segment of PAN)

- Index tokens and pads (pads must be securely stored)

- Strong cryptography with associated key management processes and procedures.

One-way hashing uses a representative alphanumeric phrase for that card number. It can be used in instances where there is no need to retrieve the original number because one-way hashes are irreversible (Table 2-2). It is not required but recommended to use a "salt" value, which is a random value added before the hashing. It reduces the feasibility of recovering the PAN from that hash and, consequently, exposure to rainbow attacks. Please keep in mind that all hashes (and encrypted phrases) are outputs of mathematical operations, and they can eventually be cracked. The primary consideration is to increase the time required to crack the hash (or password). Salt values add more entropy to the hash so that brute force attacks may crack it in billions of years, which is not very practical for a hacker (Table 2-3).

Table 2-2. *Hashing Function*

5555123456780004	Original PAN
+	
SHA-512	Hashing algorithm
=	
f3ee23b6658e09a621b62346e3af7975 2e42e551bb4ad34b86f935b7de5df8ff 8c260a0dcd692d9ff6c541ec97aab628 359aae9cce501fb66ebc6d0d1adbcf54	Hashed value

Table 2-3. *Hashing Function with Salt*

5555123456780004	Original PAN
+	
1amA5@LT	Salt
+	
SHA-512	Hashing algorithm
=	
4c4ef099af7ca33007eed77de996a3a7 e8ae3f3d48c5b59c075c086855065901 d9a5b2ee1079943f07ca33056cbd6dac 8a35eac60827e4eb6524ffb4b6ac45a3	Hashed value

The long string starting with f3ee23 can be cracked quickly, even with a home PC, if you have the rainbow table for SHA512 for all possible values. The preparation of the rainbow table would be pretty easy, considering that the original PAN is a 16-digit phrase. Whereas, if you add a "salt" to the PAN, it would take one octillion (10^{48}) years to brute force this hash.

Hashing mechanisms can be used for fraud detection, where the fraud analyzer tool only needs a representation of the cardholder data, not the data itself. In the same way, the hashing can validate if the user has entered the correct PAN. The stored hash value is compared with the hash value of the user input if they match. *Voilà.*

Truncation gets rid of the middle six digits of a card number. The standard allows organizations to store a maximum of the first six and last four digits of the card, which gives an idea of who the issuer is and which customer has that card (Table 2-4).

Table 2-4. *Truncation*

555512	******	0004
Issuing network (a.k.a. payment brand), IIN, and type of the card (debit, credit, or prepaid)	Truncated part	To distinguish the customer

The first six digits contain the issuing network (a.k.a. payment brand), the Issuer Identification Number (IIN), sometimes referred to as the Bank Identification Number (BIN), and the type of the card (debit, credit, or prepaid). The last four digits give a good idea of who the customer is to the issuer bank. Although mathematically possible, there should not be two different individuals having two different cards with the same bank and same card type and ending with the same last four digits.

It is worth noting that hashed and truncated values should not be in the same environment (as per requirement 3.4.e), as it is quite trivial to find the actual card data even with the first digits of the hash data.[16]

Tokenization is substituting a sensitive data element with a non-sensitive equivalent, referred to as a token, which has no meaningful value for attackers. Unlike encryption, the tokenization process is not based on mathematical encryption algorithms with keys and such. It depends on the token vault (or card data vault), where the original card data is stored and mapped to the token. Of course, to secure the data in the token vault, the sensitive card data can be encrypted, but this is apart from the tokenization process.

In most use cases, tokens can be used one-to-one with the card data. Most card data fields accept only 16-digit numerical characters, so the tokens can also be adjusted to be 16 digits. The advantage of tokenization over encryption is that it can be decrypted if you have a large enough set of encrypted data (since it is a mathematical process). Whereas, there is no mathematical connection to the real sensitive data they represent for tokenization.

PCI SSC released an information supplement for tokenization[17] that describes its implementation and security considerations.

Encryption is the process of using a mathematical algorithm to transform plaintext into a non-readable form called *ciphertext*. An algorithm and at least one key are required to encrypt and decrypt the information. Keys can be for data encryption (DEK) and key encryption (KEK).

---

[16] https://github.com/obenkuyucu/panconstructor

[17] www.pcisecuritystandards.org/documents/Tokenization_Guidelines_Info_Supplement.pdf

The primary points for encryption and cryptographic key management are to provide the best security for the card data (Table 2-5). The encryption should be at least the following algorithms and key lengths.[18]

- AES – 128 bits or higher

- TDES/TDEA – triple-length keys

- RSA – 2048 bits or higher

- ECC – 224 bits or higher

- DSA/D-H – 2048/224 bits or higher

Table 2-5. *Encryption*

5555123456780004	Plaintext
+	
1amAs3cR3tK3yPCI	Secret Key
+	
AES-128	Algorithm
=	
32iAkH4dNhdw25E0A/phoH34Fx62U1Fj69+N952fb8A=	Ciphertext in Base64

The "secret key" is the most crucial element in this process, so it can also be encrypted by a *key encrypting key* (KEK) to protect it further. A KEK should be at least as strong as the data-encrypting keys they protect. Both data-encrypting keys and key-encrypting keys should only be accessed by individuals having business needs: key custodians. They are responsible for managing the encryption of the environment. They must sign a formal document stating that they fully understand and accept their key management responsibilities. The access to the cryptographic keys must be restricted to reduce the possibility of a compromise. The keys must be stored within a secure

---

[18] Based on definition of "Strong Cryptography" of PCI SSC Glossary, see `www.pcisecuritystandards.org/pci_security/glossary#Strong%20Cryptography`

cryptographic device, typically a *hardware security module* (HSM) or PTS-approved point-of-interaction device POS devices. Their distributions need to be secure; they should not be distributed in the clear and should only be distributed to key custodians.

Key management also includes the *key management cycle*, meaning that every key must have a *cryptoperiod*. The "life" of a key ends at the end of a cryptoperiod or when it is compromised or suspected of being compromised. In both cases, encrypting data with those keys must be ceased, and new keys must be generated to encrypt new data. The old keys must be securely archived with a KEK to access or verify old data.

In cryptoperiods, the lifespan of a key is typically based on many factors such as key length, block size, algorithm, the volume of data encrypted, and the threat. NIST Special Publication 800-57 has a helpful recommendation document[19] for key management and cryptoperiods. Key custodians (or key managers) should decide on the cryptoperiods based on their needs and the environment.

The second part of the goal is to ensure confidentiality in transit of the card data. When card data is transmitted over open, public networks, secure versions of protocols (i.e., TLSv1.1 or above) with only trusted keys and certificates should be used. This ensures that the card data remains confidential if traffic is intercepted or sniffed. Open networks can be the Internet, any wireless technologies, including 802.11 and Bluetooth, cellular technologies, such as Global System for Mobile communications (GSM), code-division multiple access (CDMA), General Packet Radio Service (GPRS), and satellite communications. For example, if POS devices are connected to the Internet through 4G/5G, either the channel should be TLSv1.1 or above, or the data itself is encrypted per requirement 3. In general, both are applied to POS devices; that is, the data itself is encrypted with trusted acquirer keys, and most of the POS devices, if not all, support TLSv1.1 or above.

Another apparent example would be ecommerce merchants that accept card data. Their secure acceptance page (HTTPS) should be TLSv1.1 or above. To change the registry encryption settings on Windows servers, organizations can use IIS Crypto.[20] One popular online tool to analyze the strength of the TLS Certificate is Qualys SSLLabs[21] (Figure 2-2). For offline needs, Wireshark[22] can sniff the network interface and analyze the strength of the certificate. More examples can be found in Chapter 9.

---

[19] https://nvlpubs.nist.gov/nistpubs/SpecialPublications/NIST.SP.800-57pt1r5.pdf
[20] www.nartac.com/Products/IISCrypto
[21] www.ssllabs.com/ssltest/
[22] http://www.wireshark.org/

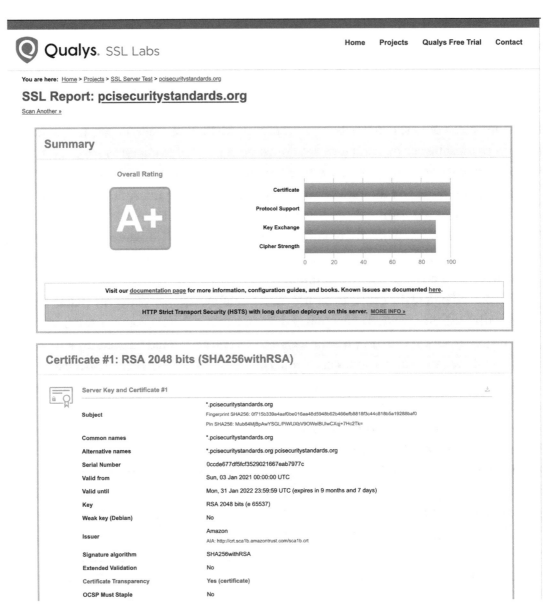

Figure 2-2. *Qualys SSLLabs report of pcisecuritystandards.org*

If the organization uses wireless communication in internal networks and is included in the scope, then the same strong cryptography principles must be applied. Weak encryption, such as SSL or WEP, should not be used as a security control for authentication or transmission.

The last part of the requirement disallows sending card data via end-user messaging technologies such as emails, chat, and instant messaging. These technologies are very susceptible to packet sniffing, and therefore card data can be compromised. If a business needs to transmit card data via those channels, card data must be secured (i.e., encrypted, hashed, truncated, or tokenized). In addition, there must be written policies and procedures to prohibit sending data in the clear.

The standard gives flexibility for the users of legacy POS devices, where TLSv1.1 or above is not possible for the channel encryption to use SSL or early TLS if it can be verified that these devices are not susceptible to any known SSL/TLS exploits. Organizations need to fill Appendix A2 of the PCI DSS, in this case.

Goal 3: Maintain a Vulnerability Management Program

This set of requirements is about protecting PCI DSS scope systems against malware and managing antivirus software or programs. The standard requires that antivirus software should be installed and kept updated on all systems that can be commonly affected by malware, viruses, worms, ransomware, Trojans, rootkits, and so forth. The "commonly affected" systems are susceptible to malware. In the past, it was thought that this impacted only Windows devices, however, now that is not the case. Organizations must consider having antivirus or anti-malware solutions for Linux, Mac, Android, and POS devices. There was recently discovered malware that exploits critical vulnerabilities on those devices. Security professionals should perform annual risk evaluations on their environment and systems, whether their systems are susceptible to malicious software or not.

They should also follow vendor security notifications, released CVEs, and security groups to determine whether the systems are at risk. Five to ten years ago, an AV solution would not be required for an Android mobile device. However, currently, there are more than enough evolving threats to these devices to consider installing an antivirus app on your personal mobile device as well.

The standard also considers that antivirus solutions should be capable of detecting, removing, and protecting against malicious software. Antivirus software and its definitions must be kept current and updated and generate logs as per the logging requirements. In addition, it should not be altered or disabled by users. Organizations may consider using *endpoint detection and response* (EDR) tools to proactively detect and stop malicious behavior. They are not dependent on signatures but behavioral analytics, machine learning, and heuristics. Their primary working mechanism collects data, analyzes processes, detects anomalies, and stops them before they can move horizontally through the network. EDR tools can also be very helpful for forensics and threat hunting purposes. They collect a significant amount of relevant information to detect the anomaly and notify IT security staff to investigate in detail.

Conventional signature-based AV solutions can also be applied to comply with the requirement. However, in that case, signatures need to be kept current to somehow overcome "zero-day" attacks, need to perform periodic scans, and as always, produce logs. The easiest approach to maintain those tools would be through centralized management. Security professionals keep track of the AV versions, signatures, online/offline status of the AV agent, and collect logs.

The second part of the goal is to develop and maintain secure systems and applications, focusing on vulnerability and patch management and secure software development.

Whenever you have sensitive (or valuable) data, you become the target of malicious actors. Those actors always try (and sometimes succeed) to exploit every vulnerability they find to infiltrate into systems, exfiltrate sensitive data or cause a disruption. This is what makes timely patching essential to the overall security posture of the Cardholder data environment. Security vulnerabilities that are not patched in a timely manner can cause ingress points for hackers, or worse, possible paths for lateral movement through the network. The standard mandates that the organization must have an accurate and efficient vulnerability management program that identifies the vulnerability classifies the risk, remediate, or apply patches in appropriate periods of time, having retests for the finding and keeping the systems up-to-date.

The same principle applies to developed software applications. The standard mandates that all internal and external applications be securely developed, following the industry-accepted best practices and security as an indispensable part of the Software Development Life Cycle (SDLC).

In all major system development techniques (Waterfall, Rapid, Joint, Extreme, Agile, Scrum, etc.), the software is constructed into phases, and security should always be a part of those phases.

- Requirements need to be planned or investigated. Although this is particularly for the function of the application, security needs to be incorporated into this phase. PCI DSS has requirements for protecting the card data and transmission of data. These requirements must be reviewed before the design.

50

- The blueprint or design of the application must be in line with the security requirements.

- During development, secure coding guidelines must be followed with proper change control processes, such as impact analysis, sign-offs, verification of tests, and back-off procedures.

- Common coding vulnerabilities (addressed in PCI DSS 6.5.x) must be addressed, and code reviews are required. Developers can choose to use only mature libraries and review the Open Web Application Security Project (OWASP)[23] guidelines to overcome most known issues.

- Testing must include test cases to measure the effectiveness of the security controls on the sensitive cardholder data. The application can be run in production only after ensuring the security controls are in place.

Even if the whole process contains security, there are always new threats. The standard also acknowledges that and mandates using a web application firewall or periodically reviews or tests the systems via automated or manual web application vulnerability assessment solutions. Web application vulnerability assessment is different from penetration testing because web application vulnerability is more focused on web application–related attacks, whereas penetration testing can be done on all systems.

The following are some web application testing tools.

— Tenable.io	— AppSpider
— Qualys	— WebInspect
— Netsparker	— Acunetix
— AppScan	— Burp Suite

---

[23] www.owasp.org/index.php/Main_Page

Web application firewalls are security devices that filter or block non-essential traffic at the application layer and monitor the actual web traffic for potential application-layer attacks. Regular firewalls typically have rulesets that allow HTTP or HTTPS web traffic to pass through to web servers without any inspection of the request. Conversely, web application firewalls can inspect the request (or payload) and detect if it contains any malicious code such as cross-site scripting (XSS), injection attacks (such as those using SQL), or forged HTTP requests that do not conform with IETF specs.[24] Most web applications can also react to certain issues, such as providing a false web server name or hiding it completely to somehow increase the efforts of malicious intent.

The following are some web application firewall tools.

• Barracuda[25]	• AppTrana[26]
• F5[27]	• StackPath[28]
• Imperva[29]	• Sucuri[30]
• Fortinet[31]	• Qualys[32]

Goal 4: Implement Strong Access Control Measures

In this goal, the primary idea is to provide proper identity management for users and ensure that only authorized users with a valid business need are accessing the card data (logically and physically) to minimize the risk of compromise.

---

[24] www.w3.org/Protocols/HTTP/1.0/spec.html

[25] www.barracuda.com/products/webapplicationfirewall

[26] www.indusface.com/web-application-firewall.php

[27] www.f5.com/products/security/advanced-waf

[28] www.stackpath.com/products/waf

[29] www.imperva.com/products/web-application-firewall-waf/

[30] https://sucuri.net/website-firewall/

[31] www.fortinet.com/products/web-application-firewall/fortiweb

[32] www.qualys.com/apps/web-app-firewall/

As a principle, card data should only be accessed by individuals having a valid and approved business "need to know." To achieve that, first, we need to properly identify the users by making sure that everyone uses a unique ID and a strong password that is difficult to crack. This also applies to the non-logical world, where we use badges, locks, and keys. Physical access to systems that store, transmit, or process card data should only be allowed to users with a business need by using either CCTV cameras or access control mechanisms (or both). PCI DSS does not disallow visitors, but all visits must be logged with identifiable information, and visitors must be distinguishable from on-site personnel, for example, by wearing a different colored badge, and they have to be escorted.

When assigning privileges to users, the least privilege approach should be used, where only necessary rights should be given, and for others, it should be "deny all."

The testing procedures in requirement 8 (identify and authenticate access to system components) are the essentials of a proper identity management program that defines the following.

- – Proper user-authentication mechanisms (something you know, something you have, something you are)

- – Minimum password length

- – Password complexity (e.g., containing alphanumeric characters)

- – Password lockout conditions and duration

- – Password age and rotation requirements

- – Idle session timeouts

- – User verifications when providing new credentials

- – Random and unique first-time passwords and obligation to change them after first use

- – Strong cryptography for password storage and transmission

In addition, this requirement mandates that user accounts should be immediately revoked for terminated users, and they should be disabled if they are not active for 90 days.

One other highlight of this requirement is *multi-factor authentication* (MFA). The organization needs at least two of the three proper user-authentication mechanisms for any non-console administrative activity, either remote or on-premises. It should be noted that using one factor twice is not MFA. PCI SSC has comprehensive guidance on MFA[33] published right after version 3.2 introduced a new requirement to use MFA on administrative activities in corporate networks.

The last part of this goal is physical security. It mandates that any physical media containing cardholder data, including backups, must be secured during use, accounted for, and securely destroyed when no longer needed. Protection of devices that capture card data, such as POS devices or PIN PADs, must also be maintained. For example, an accurate inventory must be present and proper training should be given to the users on detecting tampering.

Goal 5: Regularly Monitor and Test Networks

The fifth goal is to make sure that the systems, components, in-house built software are tested and monitored for any malicious activity that would compromise the system. The difference between this goal and goal 3 is the amount of manual work involved.

The first section contains the logging requirements for the environment. Organizations should build up a logging mechanism that would monitor all required activities so that breach attempts can be identified, tracked, notified, analyzed, and, if breached, the root cause can be found. After finding the root cause, appropriate security measures can be set up to prevent further cases.

In line with the previous goal, the primary approach is to accurately map individuals to their actions. When an event is investigated, security analysts occasionally ask these questions.

- Who did the action?

- What was the action?

- When was the action?

---

[33] www.pcisecuritystandards.org/pdfs/Multi-Factor-Authentication-Guidance-v1.pdf

- Was the user successful or failed on the action?

- Where did the action begin?

- What are the systems affected?

Similarly, PCI DSS logging requirements demand these fields be included in the events. Security professionals must implement the proper mechanisms to record these audit trail entries without any modifications.

- User ID

  - It answers the question, "Who did the action?" For non-repudiation, it is essential to use unique usernames or at least have the ability to precisely correlate them with the users.[34]

- Event type

  - Examples include simply logging on to the system, accessing a card data in a database, a privilege escalation command, adding/deleting a user or a system-level object,[35] an attempt to crack the password by brute force, or stopping/initializing/pausing of audit logs.

- Date and time

  - Organizations need to ensure the time is correct and consistent using a time-synchronization technique. NTP is the most common one. Time data is required to be protected from unauthorized modifications. It is a privileged action in most operating systems, so it creates an audit log when the time is changed.

---

[34] The use of generic usernames should be avoided as per requirement 8.5, however, some PAM tools are using these generic usernames on-the-fly. It is transparent to the user, but in the event logs, it generally shows the generic username. The PAM tool itself associates the individual's PAM account with these generic user logins. Organizations using such processes need to make sure that they can identify the actual user.

[35] www.pcisecuritystandards.org/pci_security/glossary#System-level%20object

– Indication of success or failure

- Failures are as important as successes. It can be a good indicator for possible brute force attempts if multiple failures of logins are received for a particular username in a specific period of time.

– The source of the event

- It can identify the root cause of the problem. Generally, this would be patient-zero in most cyberattacks.

– The identity of the data, system component, or a resource that was affected

- To measure the extent of the compromise, it is essential to detect the impact of the incident.

Organizations are required to ensure the integrity of the logs by using *file integrity monitoring* (FIM) or a change-detection tool. As mentioned, one of the first things that hackers do is try to cover their trail. This can be effortlessly achieved by erasing or changing the logs in an unprotected environment.

The hardest part of this requirement is probably the review of the logs. In an environment where thousands of servers create millions of events per day, it is crucial to implement specific use cases designed for the environment, well-planned thresholds for the events, and experienced security operations employees who have the necessary skills to detect and analyze the incident with proper training. At a minimum, to minimize the risk and exposure time for a possible compromise, organizations need to review at least daily the following.

- All security incidents

- Logs of all system components that store, process, or transmit cardholder data

- Logs of all critical system components

- Logs of all servers and system components that perform security functions[36]

---

[36] For service providers, it is also essential to timely detect any faults and respond in the following security devices: firewalls, IDS / IPS, FIM, antivirus, physical access controls, logical access controls, audit logging mechanisms, segmentation controls

The second part of the goal refers to the analysis of the environment to ensure that possible infiltration points are thoroughly and regularly tested and remediated.

One infiltration method is to somehow connect or attach an unauthorized wireless access point to the network or the system, so the malicious users gain access to the network. Wireless access points broadcast SSIDs, and it is possible to scan the environment for rogue wireless networks and identify the device's location by checking the signal strength and noise levels. This manual approach is time-consuming for most organizations, where a person needs to visit every floor of the buildings in scope with a laptop to list the unknown wireless devices. To solve this problem, automated processes can be implemented. Some wireless access point vendors provide rogue wireless network scanning that lists "other" wireless devices detected in the organization's premises. It is possible to filter out the known ones, which yields only the ones that need investigation. Additionally, to reduce the risk of these attacks, organizations should also install an NAC solution to the environment and disallow any unknown, unauthorized device to be connected to the environment.

Another infiltration threat surface is the external and internal networks. Although goal 3 mandates the implementation of a *web application firewall* (WAF) or perform web application scans, those scans would not find operating system vulnerabilities, and hackers can easily exploit those weaknesses to gain full control of the system. Hence, it is also crucial to run external and internal vulnerability scans at least quarterly and after any significant change in the network or system.

External vulnerability scans need to be performed by Approved Scanning Vendors (ASV)[37] whose scanning solutions are tested and approved by PCI SSC. ASVs are qualified and responsible companies to perform *external vulnerability scanning* in accordance with PCI DSS requirements and the ASV guide.[38] ASV scans are automated scans initiated from the Internet, where some manual review is required for the final quarterly attestation report. ASV scans should not impact the organization's normal operation, and they should not penetrate the environment or change it intentionally. ASVs are also responsible for getting feedback from the organization on the findings or disputed scan results since the scan can produce false positives or findings that require more evidence from inside the network.

---

[37] www.pcisecuritystandards.org/assessors_and_solutions/approved_scanning_vendors
[38] www.pcisecuritystandards.org/documents/ASV_Program_Guide_v3.1.pdf

Moreover, although the scanned organization is ultimately responsible for the scope of the scan, ASVs need to *consult* with the organization if ASV discovers an external component that is not defined as in the scope defined by the organization. ASV scans should be non-intrusive and include host and service discovery with an operating system and service fingerprinting. The scope should be not only the public-facing web applications but also any public-facing system or system components such as firewalls, routers, DNS, and email servers, including their operating systems, POS software, and remote access solutions.

Internal vulnerability scans are important to quickly identify vulnerabilities, as there would be some firewall restrictions to certain ports during external vulnerability scans. In contrast, internal scans should be performed with none or very limited restrictions to the ports, making it easier to detect weaknesses. Many organizations use credentialed (or authenticated) scans to increase the detection rate, where a privileged account is provided to the vulnerability management tool. This tool uses authenticated remote queries (WMI, for example, for Windows machines or remote SSH commands for Linux), and identify exact versions of the services, applications, patches applied can be gathered and compared with the vulnerable versions. Plus, authenticated scans collect more information from the system, such as a list of the processes, users, or listening ports, which provides more information to the tool to detect exposures accurately. This process, however, can be frustrating in large organizations where credentials are mixed and managed by multiple different administrators. Nowadays, with the introduction of host-based vulnerability scanner agents, there is no requirement to enter credentials to address this constraint. It is even possible to scan the systems daily. It should also be noted that most of the vulnerability management vendors now support integration with *privileged access management* (PAM) tools or password vaults, where only access credentials to the vaults are provided, not the credentials to the actual system.

Internal vulnerability scans must be performed by qualified individuals, internal resources, or external third parties. For internal resources, organizational independence is required. To not violate segregation of duties, scans should not be performed by the individuals managing the systems.

In goal 5, there are also penetration testing requirements. Penetration tests are different from automated scans. It is a very manual process yet a more efficient method to find the actual weaknesses in the systems. Automated scans only report the known vulnerabilities, and most of them are signature-based. Whereas, in penetration tests, following specific methodologies, the tester tries many ways to infiltrate the system and hop to another system to make new attacks or exploit any privilege escalation vulnerability to penetrate further into the environment.

PCI DSS mandates the implementation of a penetration testing methodology that covers both application and network layers in the entire cardholder data environment and other connected critical systems. PCI SSC published comprehensive guidance on penetration testing,[39] which can be used as a starting point for creating such a methodology.

Penetration testing methodology should also cover segmentation controls. Although it is not a requirement when isolating cardholder data environment from other non-related networks, it can significantly reduce the PCI DSS scope. Hence, the effort needed to be fully compliant and reduce the risk.

Goal 6: Maintain a Policy That Addresses Information Security

The final goal in PCI DSS mandates the formal establishment of information security policy and relevant documentation. The standard instructs the adoption of the following documents and processes.

- Information security policy

- Risk assessments

- Acceptable usage policies

- Information security roles and responsibilities

- Security awareness program

- Information security perspective of employee vetting and onboarding processes

- Tracking third-party service provider's PCI DSS compliance

- Incident response processes and training for incident response teams

---

[39] www.pcisecuritystandards.org/documents/Penetration_Testing_Guidance_March_2015.pdf

Prioritization

PCI DSS compliance is also considered the best way to safeguard sensitive data and information, thereby helping businesses build long-lasting and trusting relationships with their customers. Compliance with PCI DSS in one shot can be demanding and exhausting, and organizations may now know where to start. To address this, PCI SSC released a guide called *The Prioritization Approach*[40] for companies to start their compliance journey (Table 2-6). The prioritized approach's first goal is to protect data and then gradually increase the organization's security posture.

***Table 2-6.** Prioritization Milestones[41]*

Milestone	Goals
1	**Remove sensitive authentication data and limit data retention**. This milestone targets a key area of risk for organizations that have been compromised. Remember – if sensitive authentication data and other cardholder data are not stored, the effects of a compromise are greatly reduced. If you don't need it, don't store it
2	**Protect systems and networks, and be prepared to respond to a system breach**. This milestone targets controls for access points to most compromises and the processes for responding.
3	**Secure payment card applications**. This milestone targets controls for applications, application processes, and application servers. Weaknesses in these areas offer easy prey for compromising systems and obtaining access to cardholder data.
4	**Monitor and control access to your systems**. Detect the who, what, when, and how concerning accessing your network and cardholder data environment.
5	**Protect stored cardholder data**. For those organizations that have analyzed their business processes and determined that they must store primary account numbers (PAN), this milestone targets key protection mechanisms for stored data.
6	**Finalize remaining compliance efforts, and ensure all controls are in place**. Complete PCI DSS requirements and finalize all remaining related policies, procedures, and processes needed to protect the cardholder data environment.

---

[40] www.pcisecuritystandards.org/documents/Prioritized-Approach-for-PCI-DSS-v3_2_1.pdf

[41] www.pcisecuritystandards.org/documents/Prioritized-Approach-Tool-v3_2_1.xlsx

Note   PCI SSC also publishes other standards such as PCI Payment Application Data Security Standard, PCI PIN Entry Devices Standard, PCI Software Security Standards, and many more. Check out `http://www.pcisecuritystandards.org` for more information.

SWIFT: Customer Security Controls Framework

Society for Worldwide Interbank Financial Telecommunications (SWIFT) provides safe and secure financial transactions for member financial institutions. Each member institution is assigned a unique ID code that identifies the bank name and country, city, and branch. This ID is designated as Bank Identification Code (BIC).

In March 2017, in the scope of their Customer Security Programme (CSP), SWIFT released Customer Security Control Framework 1.0 (Table 2-7), defining a security baseline with 27 security controls (16 mandatory and 11 advisory) to be implemented by member financial institutions. Every time there is a change to the SWIFT connection architecture setup (or annually), each institution must conduct a self-assessment and attestation that all mandatory security controls are implemented and submit it to SWIFT. All member financial institutions had to be fully compliant through 2018.

The CSP covers the following elements.

- **Data exchange**: The data transport layer between the organization back-office and the on-premises SWIFT infrastructure

- **On-premises SWIFT infrastructure**: A group of specific SWIFT components managed by the member financial institution that includes systems, applications, network devices, tokens, removable media, and other related support hardware and software

- **Operators**: The end users or administrators that interact directly with the on-premises SWIFT infrastructure

- **Operator workstations**: The end-user or administrator computers to operate or manage the on-premises SWIFT infrastructure

Table 2-7. *List of SWIFT CSP CSCF v.1.0 Controls*

Control or Section

1. SWIFT Environment Protection

1.1 SWIFT Environment Protection

1.2 Operating System Privileged Account Control

1.3 Virtualization Platform Protection

1.4 Restriction of Internet Access

2. Reduce Attack Surface and Vulnerabilities

2.1 Internal Data Flow Security

2.2 Security Updates

2.3 System Hardening

2.4 A Back-office Data Flow Security

2.5 A External Transmission Data Protection

2.6 Operator Session Confidentiality and Integrity

2.7 Vulnerability Scanning

2.8 A Critical Activity Outsourcing

2.9 A Transaction Business Controls

2.10 Application Hardening

2.11 A RMA Business Controls

3. Physically Secure the Environment

3.1 Physical Security

4. Prevent Compromise of Credentials

4.1 Password Policy

4.2 Multi-Factor Authentication

5. Manage Identities and Segregate Privileges

(continued)

Table 2-7. (*continued*)

Control or Section

5.1 Logical Access Control

5.2 Token Management

5.3 A Personnel Vetting Process

5.4 Physical and Logical Password Storage

6. Detect Anomalous Activity to Systems or Transaction Records

6.1 Malware Protection

6.2 Software Integrity

6.3 Logging and Monitoring

6.4 A Intrusion Detection

7. Plan for Incident Response and Information Sharing

7.1 Cyber Incident Response Planning

7.2 Security Training and Awareness

7.3 A Penetration Testing

7.4 A Scenario Risk Assessment

SWIFT also defined four distinct secure zone architecture categories, types A1, A2, and A3, where the financial institution has variations of on-premises SWIFT infrastructure implementations and type B, where the financial institution has no on-premises ("no local footprint") SWIFT infrastructure. Some controls are not mandatory depending on the type of architecture, being A1 the type with most mandatory controls and type B with the least mandatory controls.

In 2018, SWIFT released SWIFT CSF 2019, also known as version 2. This version introduced the following changes.

- A new total of 29 controls, with 19 mandatory controls and 2 new controls

- New mandatory controls

- 2.6: Security Operator Sessions

- 2.7: Yearly Vulnerability Scanning

- 5.4: Physical and Logical Password Storage

- 10 controls advisory (2 new)

  - new advisory

    - 1.3A: Virtualization Platform Protection

    - 2.10A: Application Hardening

- It also made available information on how guidelines should be interpreted and implemented and other clarifications about the existing controls.

Since then, two other versions have been released: SWIFT CSCF v2021 and v2022. The latest version defines one more reference architecture type, to a total of five. In the new architecture (A4), an application locally installed is used as an interface between the financial institution and the service provider (e.g., service bureau).

This latest version also makes several adjustments and clarifications to the existing controls where most relevant.

- Guidance changes to Internet access

- Extended third-party control to cloud providers, where the users are still accountable for their infrastructure security, and the financial institution must have the assurance from the third parties that the outsourced services and externally hosted infrastructure are compliant with the CSP security controls

- The use of MFA becomes necessary to access any SWIFT service or application operated by a service provider

There are three types of assessments under the CSP (self-assessment, community-standard assessment, SWIFT-mandated assessment) for financial institutions to verify that their attestations correspond with their actual level of security control implementation. Self-assessment may be classified as non-compliant by January 2022. Community-standard assessments should be performed as of 2021, including independent external and internal assessments. Sometimes, the SWIFT CSP Assurance Team mandates financial institutions to have independent cybersecurity companies audit their compliance with CSP as part of the independent assessment framework, or SWIFT-mandated assessments. Those independent companies should have relevant knowledge and expertise to execute a cybersecurity-oriented operational assessment such as PCI DSS, ISO 27001, NIST 800-53, or other CSP assessments and have completed such assessments recently. Although it is not an exhaustive and authorized directory, SWIFT has a list of cybersecurity companies[42] and CSP assessors[43] registered to SWIFT.

Summary

To have a global standard for information security management that can be applied to organizations of any size or any industry, ISO created the ISO 27000 series, which includes legal, physical, and technical controls on managing the information security risks. Organizations can be certified by independent external bodies to demonstrate and validate that they follow the industry-accepted best practices.

For the payment industry, there was the need to have a consolidated standard to protect the card data, merchants, acquirers, issuers, and payment schemes, because each payment brand had its own merchant compliance program. PCI DSS was created to establish security controls for payment providers, and it has many technical requirements from top to bottom, designed to protect cardholder data. In many countries, compliance with PCI DSS is becoming a must for any organization that transmits, processes, or stores card data.

The need to define and comply with similar security baselines was also required for cross-border electronic fund transfers to respond to major incidents in the SWIFT system. For that reason, SWIFT published the CSCF and obliged members to be compliant with the framework to continue working with SWIFT.

It should be noted that these standards are generally accepted across several industries. However, some countries needed to publish their own standards to address specific requirements, which are explained in the next chapters.

---

[42] www.swift.com/myswift/customer-security-programme-csp/find-external-support/directory-cyber-security-service-providers

[43] www.swift.com/node/300831/directory-csp-assessment-providers

CHAPTER 3

Information Security Frameworks

This chapter covers industry-accepted information security frameworks, including NIST frameworks, COBIT, and CIS Controls, which help organizations understand current cyber risks, identify missing security controls that protect from cyber threats, and prioritize mitigative activities. This chapter also discusses select national-level security requirements and frameworks in Qatar, Singapore, Saudi Arabia, Turkey, and India, which organizations in those countries need to comply with.

NIST Frameworks

The National Institute of Standards and Technology (NIST),[1] founded in 1901 and formerly known as the National Bureau of Standards, is a U.S. physical sciences laboratory and a measurement agency that supported the development of many technologies in areas such as nanoscale science and technology, engineering, neutron research, material physical measurement, as well as information technology and information security. Through its publications and guidelines, NIST became *an* influencer of many industries.[2] NIST's major contributions to the industry through its Information Technology Laboratory (ITL) include competitions for a stronger data encryption standard (which helped create the Advanced Encryption Standard (AES) in 2000) and better hash functions (SHA-3 in 2005), the Federal Information Processing Standards (FIPS), the National Vulnerability Database,[3] and NIST's Special Publication 800 series, which are the fundamental documents and catalogs for many NIST frameworks.

---

[1] www.nist.gov/about-nist

[2] www.nist.gov/industry-impacts

[3] https://nvd.nist.gov/

© Virgilio Viegas and Oben Kuyucu 2022
V. Viegas and O. Kuyucu, *IT Security Controls*, https://doi.org/10.1007/978-1-4842-7799-7_3

NIST SP 800-53: Security and Privacy Controls for Federal Information Systems and Organizations

The NIST ITL Computer Security Resource Center publishes many "special publications"[4] that are now considered as the most comprehensive of all industry-accepted standards in information security. The most well-known is the NIST 800 series related to computer security in the U.S. federal government. Among the NIST-800 series publications, "NIST SP 800-53: Security and Privacy Controls for Federal Information Systems and Organizations" is one of the most widely used benchmarks of computing systems that can be used as a catalog for the security and privacy controls of those systems. NIST SP 800-53 was initially released in February 2005 as "recommended security controls for federal information systems" and with time evolved into the baseline for most organizations and vendor products. At the time of the writing of this book, the latest revision of NIST SP 800-53 is Rev. 5.1., even though Rev. 4 was widely used, it was withdrawn in September 2021.

Since it contains some security controls needed for compliance to U.S. presidential executive orders, it might sound like it is mainly meant for U.S. organizations. However, it can be used partially, if not entirely, by almost all organizations worldwide.

NIST SP 800-53 provides a list of operational, technical, and administrative controls and policy, oversight, supervision, manual processes, and automated mechanisms to help build a secure computing system. The controls are categorized into three impact classes: low, moderate, and high.

Security and privacy controls have the following structure: a base control section, a discussion section, a related controls section, a control enhancements section, and a references section (Figure 3-1).

---

[4]https://csrc.nist.gov/publications/sp

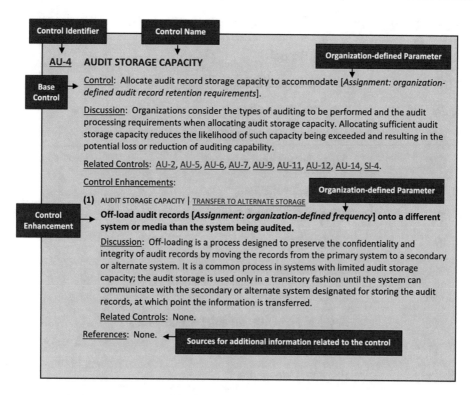

Figure 3-1. *NIST 800-53 control structure[5]*

NIST SP 800-53 has 20 security control families (Table 3-1) to ease the use of the control selection and specification process. Each family is designated by a unique two-character identifier (e.g., AC, AT, AU). NIST SP 800-53 includes control baselines (SP 800-53B) to support specific protection needs. Furthermore, assessors or auditors can use SP800-53A to assess the controls' effectiveness.

---

[5] https://nvlpubs.nist.gov/nistpubs/SpecialPublications/NIST.SP.800-53r5.pdf

Table 3-1. *NIST 800-53 Security and Privacy Control Families*

1. AC	Access Control
2. AT	Awareness and Training
3. AU	Audit and Accountability
4. CA	Assessment, Authorization, and Monitoring
5. CM	Configuration Management
6. CP	Contingency Planning
7. IA	Identification and Authentication
8. IR	Incident Response
9. MA	Maintenance
10. MP	Media Protection
11. PE	Physical and Environmental Security
12. PLP	Planning
13. PM	Program Management
14. PS	Personnel Security
15. PT	Personally Identifiable Information Processing and Transparency
16. RA	Risk Assessment
17. SA	Systems and Services Acquisition
18. SC	Systems and Communications Protection
19. SI	Systems and Information Integrity
20. SR	Supply Chain Risk Management

- **Access Control**: These controls are focused on ensuring that the organization has sufficient access controls in place and only authorized users can access sensitive systems and information through on-premises, wireless, mobile, or remote devices. The AC Control Family also includes security requirements regarding the access logs, segregation of duties and, principle of least privilege.

- **Awareness and Training**: This family of controls is specific to the security training management and procedures, as well as maintaining training records.

- **Audit and Accountability**: These controls focus on the auditing capabilities of the organization to ensure non-repudiation (accountability) of users and their actions. This includes audit policies and procedures, audit logging, audit record reviews, audit report generation, and protection of audit information.

- **Assessment, Authorization, and Monitoring**: This control family is designed to execute security assessments, including penetration testing, authorizations, continuous monitoring, and internal system connections.

- **Configuration Management**: This control family addresses baseline configuration management, change control, and security impact assessments. Additionally, it includes information system component inventories.

- **Contingency Planning**: This control family is specific to the organization's business continuity plan in a cybersecurity incident. This includes contingency plan testing, updating, training, backups, and system recovery.

- **Identification and Authentication**: This control family addresses the organization's identification and authentication policies, including types of authentication methods to be used (MFA, SSO, etc.), encryption, and identities.

- **Incident Response**: This family is designed for the incident response and management controls which also include incident response training, incident handling, monitoring for incidents, and incident handling.

- **Maintenance:** This family aims to ensure that systems are adequately maintained. Controls include maintenance tools, non-local and field maintenance, and maintenance personnel.

- **Media Protection**: This family identifies the specific controls to be implemented for media access, media marking and storage, transportation, and media sanitization.

- **Physical and Environmental Security**: This family identifies the controls to be in place for physical security, such as physical access controls, authorizations, visitor access, overall power equipment, disaster recovery planning, emergency power, emergency lighting, and fire protection, as well as environmental protection.

- **Planning**: This family includes the controls for the security architecture and rules of behavior (acceptable usage policies).

- **Program Management**: This control family is about information security governance, who manages your cybersecurity program and how it operates, as well as a critical infrastructure plan, information security program plan, plan of action milestones and processes, risk management strategy, and enterprise architecture.

- **Personnel Security**: This family is designed with controls regarding personnel screening, termination, transfers, and access agreements.

- **Personally Identifiable Information Processing and Transparency**: This new control family is about PII data handling, consent, privacy notices, and PII data records management.

- **Risk Assessment**: This family specifies how an organizational risk assessment should be performed, policies for performing the risk assessment, and vulnerability scanning.

- **Systems and Services Acquisition**: This family identifies the controls to be considered in the system development life cycle, including development process, standards and tools, acquisition process, and information system documentation, in addition to security and privacy engineering principles.

- **Systems and Communications Protection**: The goal of this control is the mitigation of network-related risks. The controls to be implemented are segregation of networks, boundary protections, protection against denial-of-service (DoS) attacks, cryptographic controls in the network.

- **Systems and Information Integrity**: This control family is responsible for ensuring the integrity of information systems. The controls include malicious code protection, system monitoring, input validation, error handling, spam protection, memory protection, fail-safe procedures, and de-identification.

- **Supply Chain Risk Management Family**: This family of controls addresses the management of risks originated by third parties, suppliers, and others.

NIST SP 800-37: Guide for Applying the Risk Management Framework to Federal Information Systems

Also known as the Risk Management Framework (RMF), NIST Special Publication 800-37, *Guide for Applying the Risk Management Framework to Federal Information Systems is the handbook* for the security and privacy risk management activities in an organization. It is technology-neutral, meaning that it can address any type of information system. It is also flexible since organizations can choose how to carry out each step, provided that they comply with all applicable requirements. The framework defines the risk management activities as a six-step process, plus a preparatory step (Figure 3-2).

1) **Prepare** to execute RMF.[6] Identify roles, responsibilities, strategies, governance structure for the people that manage RMF. The document has nice guidance on the definitions and the responsibilities of the supporting security and privacy-related roles in a typical organization in Appendix D[7] and in RMF Quick Start Guide: Roles and Responsibilities Crosswalk.[8]

---

[6]https://csrc.nist.gov/Projects/risk-management/about-rmf/prepare-step

[7]https://nvlpubs.nist.gov/nistpubs/SpecialPublications/NIST.SP.800-37r2.pdf#%5B%7B%22num%22%3A460%2C%22gen%22%3A0%7D%2C%7B%22name%22%3A%22XYZ%22%7D%2C88%2C700%2C0%5D

[8]https://csrc.nist.gov/CSRC/media/Projects/risk-management/documents/Additional%20Resources/NIST%20RMF%20Roles%20and%20Responsibilities%20Crosswalk.pdf

2) **Categorize** the information systems. Use NIST publications (FIPS 199[9] or SP 800-60[10]) to categorize (or classify) the information systems so that the level of security to each system can be defined.

3) **Select** the security controls. Select the appropriate security controls from the NIST SP 800-53 based on the desired or defined security level from the previous step.

4) **Implement** the security controls. Implement the security control selected in the previous step using related NIST publications.[11]

5) **Assess** the security controls. Assess the implemented security controls to ensure they are working correctly, as intended.

6) **Authorize** information systems. Authorize systems to operate if they have acceptable risk levels.

7) **Monitor** security controls. Monitor the environment, systems, and security controls continuously so that they do not deviate from the intended level. Document any change that may impact the system's overall security and privacy posture.

---

[9] https://csrc.nist.gov/publications/detail/fips/199/final

[10] https://csrc.nist.gov/publications/detail/sp/800-60/vol-1-rev-1/final and https://csrc.nist.gov/publications/detail/sp/800-60/vol-2-rev-1/final

[11] https://csrc.nist.gov/publications/

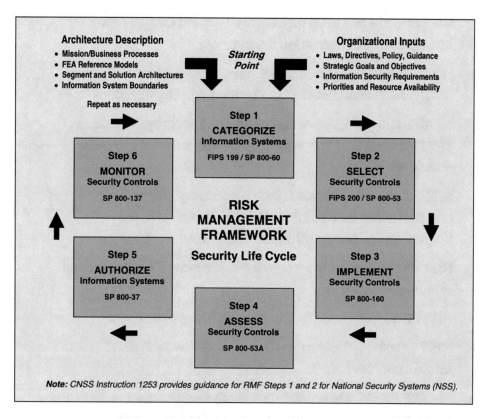

Figure 3-2. *NIST Risk Management Framework*[12]

The RMF also refers to several other supporting NIST publications for better implementation and enhanced information security and privacy posture.

- – Federal Information Processing Standard (FIPS) 199, Standards for Security Categorization of Federal Information and Information Systems[13]

- – FIPS 200, Minimum Security Requirements for Federal Information and Information Systems[14]

---

[12] National Institute of Standards and Technology Special Publication 800-53, Revision 4. April 2013. p8.

[13] https://csrc.nist.gov/publications/detail/fips/199/final

[14] https://csrc.nist.gov/publications/detail/fips/200/final

- NIST SP 800-128, Guide for Security-Focused Configuration Management of Information Systems[15]

- NIST SP 800-137, Information Security Continuous Monitoring (ISCM) for Federal Information Systems and Organizations[16]

- NIST SP 800-137A, Assessing Information Security Continuous Monitoring (ISCM) Programs: Developing an ISCM Program Assessment[17]

- NIST SP 800-160, Volume 1, Systems Security Engineering: Considerations for a Multidisciplinary Approach in the Engineering of Trustworthy Secure Systems[18]

- NIST SP 800-18, Guide for Developing Security Plans for Federal Information Systems[19]

- NIST SP 800-30, Guide for Conducting Risk Assessments[20]

- NIST SP 800-34, Contingency Planning Guide for Federal Information Systems[21]

- NIST SP 800-39, Managing Information Security Risk: Organization, Mission, and Information System View[22]

- NIST SP 800-40, Rev 3: Guide to Enterprise Patch Management Technologies[23]

- NIST SP 800-41, Rev 1: Guidelines on Firewalls and Firewall Policy[24]

---

[15] https://csrc.nist.gov/publications/detail/sp/800-128/final
[16] https://csrc.nist.gov/publications/detail/sp/800-137/final
[17] https://csrc.nist.gov/publications/detail/sp/800-137a/final
[18] https://csrc.nist.gov/publications/detail/sp/800-160/vol-1/final
[19] https://csrc.nist.gov/publications/detail/sp/800-18/rev-1/final
[20] https://csrc.nist.gov/publications/detail/sp/800-30/rev-1/final
[21] https://csrc.nist.gov/publications/detail/sp/800-34/rev-1/final
[22] https://csrc.nist.gov/publications/detail/sp/800-39/final
[23] https://csrc.nist.gov/publications/detail/sp/800-40/rev-3/final
[24] https://csrc.nist.gov/publications/detail/sp/800-41/rev-1/final

- NIST SP 800-61, Computer Security Incident Handling Guide[25]

- NIST SP 800-77: Guide to IPsec VPNs[26]

- NIST SP 800-83, Rev 1: Guide to Malware Incident Prevention and Handling for Desktops and Laptops[27]

- NIST SP 800-92: Guide to Computer Security Log Management[28]

- NIST SP 800-153: Guidelines for Securing Wireless Local Area Networks (WLANs)[29]

- NISTIR 8011, Automation Support for Security Control Assessments: Multiple Volumes[30]

- NISTIR 8062, An Introduction to Privacy Engineering and Risk Management in Federal Systems[31]

- NISTIR 8212, ISCMA: An Information Security Continuous Monitoring (ISCM) Program Assessment[32]

NIST Cybersecurity Framework

After a U.S. presidential executive order in 2013,[33] NIST published the Cybersecurity Framework,[34] which provides a set of cybersecurity guidelines for companies aiming to identify, detect, and respond better to cyber risks. The industry widely accepts this framework because it contains best practices, references to standards, and many

---

[25] https://csrc.nist.gov/publications/detail/sp/800-61/rev-2/final
[26] https://csrc.nist.gov/publications/detail/sp/800-77/rev-1/final
[27] https://csrc.nist.gov/publications/detail/sp/800-83/rev-1/final
[28] https://csrc.nist.gov/publications/detail/sp/800-92/final
[29] https://csrc.nist.gov/publications/detail/sp/800-153/final
[30] https://csrc.nist.gov/publications/detail/nistir/8011/vol-1/final
[31] https://csrc.nist.gov/publications/detail/nistir/8062/final
[32] https://csrc.nist.gov/publications/detail/nistir/8212/final
[33] https://obamawhitehouse.archives.gov/the-press-office/2013/02/12/executive-order-improving-critical-infrastructure-cybersecurity
[34] https://nvlpubs.nist.gov/nistpubs/CSWP/NIST.CSWP.04162018.pdf

applicable recommendations that help organizations improve their cybersecurity posture. It is a risk-based, adaptable, living document with the contributions of many representatives from the information security sector and academia. The framework has a common and accessible language to the security practitioners that use it, and it has been translated to more than five languages.

The Cybersecurity Framework contains three primary components.

- The **Core** is the set of activities, desired cybersecurity outcomes, and hierarchical references aligned to detailed guidance and controls, such as NIST SP 800-53, CIS, CSC, or COBIT for Information Security, to help organizations manage cybersecurity risks. It has five functions, 23 categories, 108 subcategories, and six informative references. Functions are the families for the categories: Identify, Protect, Detect, Respond, and Recover. Categories are the subdivisions of a function into cybersecurity outcomes. Subcategories further divide into more detailed preventive and reactive, operational, technical, or administrative activities. Lastly, informative references provide references from other industry-accepted security frameworks or standards (Figure 3-3).

- **Implementation tiers** provide a qualitative measure of organizational cybersecurity risk management practices. It has four implementation tiers: Partial, Risk Informed, Repeatable, and Adaptive. The tier selection is based on the organization's capabilities and desires, aligned with the organizational goals, objectives, and cost/benefit analysis. All tiers have definitions for risk management process, integrated risk management program, and external participation.

- **Profiles** align the organization's business requirements and objectives, risk appetite, and resources to the framework core components (functions, categories, and subcategories). It can also describe the organization's current state (current profile) and the desired target state (target profile), and the comparison between them shows the gaps to be addressed.

The framework's five core functions and 23 categories are shown in Table 3-2.

Function	Category	Subcategory	Informative References
IDENTIFY (ID)	**Asset Management (ID.AM):** The data, personnel, devices, systems, and facilities that enable the organization to achieve business purposes are identified and managed consistent with their relative importance to organizational objectives and the organization's risk strategy.	**ID.AM-1:** Physical devices and systems within the organization are inventoried	CIS CSC 1 **COBIT 5** BAI09.01, BAI09.02 **ISA 62443-2-1:2009** 4.2.3.4 **ISA 62443-3-3:2013** SR 7.8 **ISO/IEC 27001:2013** A.8.1.1, A.8.1.2 **NIST SP 800-53 Rev. 4** CM-8, PM-5
		ID.AM-2: Software platforms and applications within the organization are inventoried	CIS CSC 2 **COBIT 5** BAI09.01, BAI09.02, BAI09.05 **ISA 62443-2-1:2009** 4.2.3.4 **ISA 62443-3-3:2013** SR 7.8 **ISO/IEC 27001:2013** A.8.1.1, A.8.1.2, A.12.5.1 **NIST SP 800-53 Rev. 4** CM-8, PM-5

Figure 3-3. *Excerpt from NIST Cybersecurity Framework: ID.AM-1 and ID.AM-2*

Table 3-2. *NIST Cybersecurity Framework Core Functions and Categories*

IDENTIFY (ID)	Asset Management (ID.AM)	Develop the organizational understanding to manage cybersecurity risk to systems, assets, data, and capabilities.
	Business Environment (ID.BE)	
	Governance (ID.GV)	
	Risk Assessment (ID.RA)	
	Risk Management Strategy (ID.RM)	
	Supply Chain Risk Management (ID.SC)	
PROTECT (PR)	Identity Management, Authentication and Access Control (PR.AC)	Develop and implement safeguards to ensure delivery of critical infrastructure services
	Awareness and Training (PR.AT)	
	Data Security (PR.DS)	
	Information Protection Processes and Procedures (PR.IP)	
	Maintenance (PR.MA)	
	Protective Technology (PR.PT)	
DETECT (DE)	Anomalies and Events (DE.AE)	Develop and implement the appropriate activities to identify the occurrence of a cybersecurity event.
	Security Continuous Monitoring (DE.CM)	
	Detection Processes (DE.DP)	

(continued)

Table 3-2. (*continued*)

RESPOND (RS)	Response Planning (RS.RP)	Develop and implement the appropriate activities to take action against a detected cybersecurity event.
	Communications (RS.CO)	
	Analysis (RS.AN)	
	Mitigation (RS.MI)	
	Improvements (RS.IM)	
RECOVER (RC)	Recovery Planning (RC.RP)	Develop and implement the appropriate activities to take action against a detected cybersecurity event.
	Improvements (RC.IM)	
	Communications (RC.CO)	

The Cybersecurity Framework can establish or improve an organization's cybersecurity program. The following is the proposed approach.

1) **Prioritize and scope.** Identify cybersecurity objectives, organizational priorities, and critical systems to decide on the framework's strategic implementations of cybersecurity activities.

2) **Orient.** Identify related systems and assets, regulatory requirements, and overall risk approach, as well as threats and vulnerabilities applicable to those systems.

3) **Create a current profile.** Document the current state of the activities.

4) **Conduct a risk assessment.** Analyze and assess the likelihood of a cybersecurity event and its impact on the organization by identifying the emerging risks and using cyber threat information from internal and external sources.

5) **Create a target profile.** Document the desired or target state of the outcomes.

6) **Determine, analyze and prioritize gaps.** Compare the current and target profiles and create an action plan of the gaps, considering organization motives, priorities, costs and benefits, and risks.

7) **Implement the action plan.** Determine the steps needed for the action plan, implement them and monitor progress if target profile is achieved. Repeat the steps as needed.

COBIT 5 for Information Security

Information Systems Audit and Control Association (ISACA) was formed in 1976 by the EDP (Electronic Data Processing) Auditors Associations as an education foundation to conduct research that expands the knowledge and value of the IT governance and control field. Currently, ISACA is formally known only by its acronym to embrace the wide range of IT governance professionals it serves.

The Control Objective for Information Technologies (COBIT) was initially released in 1996 by ISACA as a set of control objectives to support financial auditors with a better understanding of IT-related environments.

COBIT version 5 was published in 2012. It provides a broad framework to support organizations to reach their governance and IT enterprise management objectives helping to create value from IT, improve risk management and optimize resource usage.

COBIT 2019 was released in 2019, increasing the total number of processes from 37 to 40.

Considering that COBIT 5 for Information Security was based on COBIT 5, we focus on COBIT 5 instead of the latest version.

COBIT 5 was developed with the following five principles.

- Meet stakeholder needs.

- Cover the enterprise end to end.

- Apply a single integrated framework.

- Enable a holistic approach.

- Separate governance from management.

Although COBIT 5 was created with a much broader scope, it can be adapted to Information Security. The COBIT 5 for Information Security Professional Guide was developed with that objective. ISACA members can download it from the ISACA website.

COBIT 5 Product Family

- COBIT 5

- COBIT 5 Enabler Guides

  - COBIT 5 Enabling Processes

  - COBIT 5 Enabling Information

  - Other Enabler Guides

- COBIT 5 Professional Guides

  - COBIT 5 Implementation

  - **COBIT 5 for Information Security**

  - COBIT 5 for Assurance

  - COBIT 5 for Risk

  - Other professional guides

Even though information security must be considered holistically, it is specifically addressed by COBIT 5 processes APO13 (manage security), DSS04 (manage continuity), and DSS05 (manage security services) that guide you on how to define, operate and monitor a system for general security management.

According to COBIT 5 for Information Security, you can obtain direction on the following enablers.

- Information security policies, principles, and frameworks

- Processes, including information security-specific details and activities

- Information security-specific organizational structures

- In terms of culture, ethics, and behavior, factors determining the success of information security governance and management

- Information security-specific information types for enabling information security governance and management within the enterprise

- Service capabilities required to provide information security and related functions to an enterprise

- People, skills, and competencies specific to information security

COBIT 5 for Information Security provides details on adjusting each process to information security, incorporating its concepts and requirements, and describing each process's information security goals, metrics, management practices, and related activities.

COBIT 5 for Information Security also provides detailed guidance about the information security organizational structure and governance model and a relevant mapping between COBIT 5 and several international standards, ISO/IEC 27001, ISO/IEC 27001, NIST Special Publication 800-53A, and ISF 2011 Standard of Good Practice for Information Security.

COBIT 5 Process Goals Applied to Information Security

Each COBIT 5 process goal can be applied to information security in the following way.

- **EDM01 Ensure governance framework setting and maintenance.** Information security must have a governance system and be incorporated across the enterprise processes.

- **EDM02 Ensure benefits delivery.** Ensure that information security investments are balanced with their advantages by maximizing the benefits with the minimum cost.

- **EDM03 Ensure risk optimization.** Ensure that the enterprise risk management process includes information security risks.

- **EDM04 Ensure resource optimization.** Ensure the optimization of Information security resources and their alignment with business goals.

- **EDM05 Ensure stakeholder transparency.** Stakeholders have appropriate, accurate, and comprehensive updates on their organization's information security and risks status.

- **APO01 Manage the IT Management Framework.** Effectively implement, communicate and align information security with organization IT and business frameworks.

- **APO02 Manage strategy.** The organization must have an information security policy framework and strategy properly aligned with the IT strategy and the organization's business goals and objectives. This strategy should be cost-effective, adequate, accurate, and achievable.

- **APO03 Manage enterprise architecture.** In addition to the organization's enterprise architecture which should incorporate information security requirements, the organization must also have an official information security architecture that facilitates resource optimization and reutilization.

- **APO04 Manage innovation.** The organization's information security plan should promote innovation, and innovation processes must include information security requirements.

- **APO05 Manage portfolio.** Information security investments are prioritized considering the organization's risk appetite, and any change to the organization's information security plan must be reflected across the organization's processes, services, assets in scope.

- **APO06 Manage budget and costs.** Information security must have a clearly defined budget, and its execution prioritized according to the identified risks and the organization's risk posture.

- **APO07 Manage human resources.** Incorporate information security requirements in HR processes.

- **APO08 Manage relationships.** The organization must assure an effective relationship between the information security function and the remaining stakeholders and that these stakeholders acknowledge the information security function as a business facilitator.

- **APO09 Manage service agreements.** Incorporate information security requirements in the existing or new service-level agreements (SLAs).

- **APO10 Manage suppliers.** Assure that third parties and the established contracts with those third parties are regularly assessed and reviewed, and that suitable risk mitigation plans are established. Third parties should acknowledge information security as a relevant business facilitator.

- **APO11 Manage quality.** Information security quality requirements are defined and integrated into the information security processes.

- **APO12 Manage risk.** The organization's applications, infrastructure, and implemented technologies must have a comprehensive information risk profile. The risk management process is linked with the Information Security incident response process to assure that the risk management portfolio is updated accordingly.

- **APO13 Manage security.** The organization must implement a system that considers and enforces the implementation of information security requirements through a formally accepted and established security plan that should be disclosed across the organization where all the identified needed information security controls are applied and operated.

- **BAI01 Manage programs and projects.** The organization must ensure that all programs and projects include information security requirements.

- **BAI02 Manage requirements definition.** In this process goal, the organization must ensure the identification and implementation of all significant information security aspects related to business functional and technical requirements and the identification and treatment of the related risks.

- **BAI03 Manage solutions identification and build.** Information security must support the business strategy objectives, and information security solutions are accepted, tested, and integrated into all solutions.

- **BAI04 Manage availability and capacity.** The organization's availability, performance, and capacity management plans must include information security requirements and their impact monitored and optimized.

- **BAI05 Manage organizational change enablement.** Assure the effective use of information security alerts and tendencies to influence the organization's transformation processes and culture. As the organization changes through the influence of security awareness, the Information security protocols must also be frequently reviewed and improved.

- **BAI06 Manage changes.** Security impact assessments of processes, applications, and infrastructure changes and emergency changes must consider information security requirements.

- **BAI07 Manage change acceptance and transitioning.** Acceptance tests must include information security tests to identify security issues for immediate resolution and improvement opportunities in future versions or releases.

- **BAI08 Manage knowledge.** The organization must ensure that its staff has adequate Information security knowledge to efficiently exercise their activities and make responsible decisions.

- **BAI09 Manage assets.** All assets must meet information security requirements and assigned roles and responsibilities.

  Security controls must be implemented to prevent unauthorized assets usage.

- **BAI10 Manage configuration.** Approved and maintained security configuration baselines and standards must be implemented.

- **DSS01 Manage operations.** Information security operations must be performed in accordance with a defined information security operational plan consistent with the organization's information security strategy. The organization must identify, define and implement Information security standards.

- **DSS02 Manage service requests and incidents.** The organization must establish and maintain an information security incident plan.

- **DSS03 Manage problems.** The organization must ensure that information security problems are solved efficiently.

- **DSS04 Manage continuity.** The IT continuity plan must assure that Information risks are effectively identified and treated.

- **DSS05 Manage security services.** Network and communication security must meet business needs. Information and data at rest, in transit, while being processed or disposed of must be protected. Users must use a unique identifier and access rights granted according to their roles. Physical security controls must be implemented to prevent unauthorized access, manipulation, or destruction of information while being processed, stored, or transmitted.

- **DSS06 Manage business process controls.** The organization must implement adequate controls to protect its confidentiality, integrity, and availability of its business processes. Adequate controls to oversee Information security processes are implemented and frequently reviewed.

- **MEA01 Monitor, evaluate, and assess performance and conformance.** Regular information security performance monitoring processes must be implemented. Information security and information risk processes must meet internal compliance requirements.

- **MEA02 Monitor, evaluate, and assess the system of internal control.** The organization must implement information security controls monitoring and reporting processes.

- **MEA03 Monitor, evaluate, and assess compliance with external requirements.** Information security and information risk processes must meet external compliance requirements. New or changed external compliance requirements affecting information security must be monitored.

Other Regulatory Frameworks

Many other frameworks sometimes use the previous standards and frameworks as a reference but address specific needs of the context where they are supposed to be implemented, such as the following.

- Requirements for distinct information and cybersecurity policies

- Requirements to hire national citizens for certain roles or positions

- Strict personal vetting for certain roles

- Prohibition to host certain data outside the country

- Customer awareness

- Fraud monitoring

- Customer authentication

- Transaction signing

CIS Controls

Also known as The Center for Internet Security (CIS) Critical Security Controls for Effective Cyber Defense,[35] this set of IT security controls are best practice and defensive guidelines for computer security. It was established to provide a quick, more prescriptive, and prioritized approach to support increasing the security posture of the organization and stopping most of the dangerous ones. The publication was initially developed by the SANS Institute in 2008 and called SANS Top 20. Currently, CIS Controls v8 is used.

Other platforms are more comprehensive, whereas CIS Controls are meant to be simple and can be implemented in any organization. To that end, CIS has guidelines for the size, risk profile, risk appetite, resources, and the security need of the organization, called *implementation groups*.

---

[35] www.cisecurity.org/controls/

There are three implementation groups.

- IG1 provides the simplest cyber hygiene and represents a minimum information security standard for all enterprises. It supports organizations to protect against simple cyber threats, mainly non-targeted ones. Fifty-six cyber defense safeguards are present in IG1.

- IG2 introduces differing risk profiles to several other departments in the organization. It is designed for organizations having more risk exposure and more resources to protect. There are 74 additional safeguards than IG1.

- IG3 supports larger organizations with dedicated IT security professional teams to further increase the security of sensitive data and protection of more complicated cyberattacks. There are 23 more safeguards than IG1 and IG2.

The CIS Controls are grouped into 18 key controls, consisting of 153 cyber defense safeguards.

- Inventory and Control of Enterprise Assets
- Inventory and Control of Software Assets
- Data Protection
- Secure Configuration of Enterprise Assets and Software
- Account Management
- Access Control Management
- Continuous Vulnerability Management
- Audit Log Management
- Email and Web Browser Protections
- Malware Defenses
- Data Recovery
- Network Infrastructure Management
- Network Monitoring and Defense
- Security Awareness and Skills Training

- Service Provider Management

- Application Software Security

- Incident Response Management

- Penetration Testing

The Center for Internet Security also provides additional tools for security professionals to track and prioritize implementations of the CIS Controls, such as CIS Controls Self-Assessment Tool[36] or the Controls Navigator, which shows mapping to other standards or frameworks.[37]

Saudi Arabia Monetary Authority (SAMA) Cybersecurity Framework

The Saudi Arabia Monetary Authority's cybersecurity framework was developed with the following goals.

- Have a common approach to address cybersecurity within the member organizations (financial institutions)

- Achieve appropriate cybersecurity controls maturity level within the member organizations

- Ensure that cybersecurity risks are properly managed throughout the member organizations

SAMA periodically assesses its member organizations' maturity level and evaluates their cybersecurity controls' effectiveness, and compares the results with other member organizations.

SAMA based its cybersecurity framework on its own requirements and other industry cybersecurity standards, like NIST, ISF, ISO, BASEL, and PCI DSS. The document is available on the SAMA website at `www.sama.gov.sa`.

---

[36] `https://csat.cisecurity.org/`

[37] `www.cisecurity.org/controls/cis-controls-navigator/`

Overall, SAMA is a simple yet comprehensive and easily understandable framework with which all financial institutions must comply to operate in Saudi Arabia.

Reserve Bank of India

The Reserve Bank of India (RBI) has published its guidelines on cybersecurity with the release of DBS.CO/CSITE/BC.11/33.01.001/2015-16[38] in June 2016. It is the result of key historical RBI requirements, starting in 2001, with the introduction of guidelines for Internet banking, information security, electronic banking, technology risk management,[39] cyber fraud,[40] and security and risk mitigation measures for electronic payment transactions, mobile banking transactions, and issuing ATM and debit cards.

The following are key points in the Reserve Bank of India's cybersecurity framework.

- Implement a cybersecurity policy for combating cyber threats, approved by the board. This cybersecurity policy should be distinct and separate from the bank's broader information technology or information systems security policy to emphasize the risks from cyber threats and the security controls to mitigate these risks.

- A security operations center[41] should be set up, which ensures continuous security monitoring of the systems and keeping the components of SOC up to date for efficient cyber combat.

- Banks should begin implementing the minimum baseline cybersecurity and resilience framework provided in Annex 1.[42]

[38] www.rbi.org.in/scripts/BS_CircularIndexDisplay.aspx?Id=10435
[39] https://rbidocs.rbi.org.in/rdocs/content/PDFs/GBS300411F.pdf
[40] www.rbi.org.in/Scripts/NotificationUser.aspx?Id=6366&Mode=0
[41] https://rbidocs.rbi.org.in/rdocs/content/pdfs/CSFB020616_AN2.pdf
[42] https://rbidocs.rbi.org.in/rdocs/content/pdfs/CSFB020616_AN1.pdf

- As the owners of personal and sensitive information collected by various services provided. Banks should take appropriate steps in preserving the confidentiality, integrity, and availability of the PII data, wherever it is stored (including on-premises, in customer premises, and third-party vendors' premises.)

- Apart from traditional business continuity plans, a cyber crisis management plan should be immediately prepared and part of the overall board-approved strategy.

- Effective measures to prevent cyberattacks and promptly detect any cyber intrusions should be implemented. It must cover detection, response, recovery, and containment of the incident. These measures should also involve security controls for emerging cyber threats such as zero-day attacks, remote access threats, and targeted attacks like APTs, DDoS, phishing, or ransomware.

- The level of compliance to the cybersecurity framework must be assessed and measured by key risk indicators.

- Banks should promptly report all unusual cyber incidents they face, formatted by Annex 3.[43]

- Banks should provide, by taking appropriate steps, high awareness of cyber threats and the preventive actions to all stakeholders, including customers, employees, vendors, and top management, so that, overall, the bank would have a better cybersecurity preparedness.

The baseline cybersecurity and resilience requirements are categorized as follows.

- Inventory Management of Business IT Assets

- Preventing execution of unauthorized software

- Application Security Life Cycle (ASLC)

- Patch/Vulnerability & Change Management

---

[43] https://rbidocs.rbi.org.in/rdocs/content/pdfs/CSFB020616_AN3.pdf

- Vendor Risk Management

- Removable Media

- Maintenance, Monitoring, and Analysis of Audit Logs

- Audit Log settings

- Metrics

- Forensics

- Environmental Controls

- Network Management and Security

- User Access Control / Management

- Authentication Framework for Customers

- Advanced Real-time Threat Defense and Management

- Anti-Phishing

- Vulnerability Assessment and Penetration Test and Red Team Exercises

- Incident Response & Management

- User / Employee/ Management Awareness

- Customer Education and Awareness

- Secure Configuration

- Secure Mail and Messaging Systems

- Data Leak Prevention Strategy

- Risk-based Transaction Monitoring

As part of the continuous communication between RBI and the banks, CSITE (Cyber Security and Information Technology Examination Cell) provides guidelines and advisories on the current cyber threats.

FIFA World Cup Qatar 2022

Cybersecurity is always an issue in an event as big as the FIFA World Cup. A sponsor, participating, or supporter organization's systems could be affected by hacktivists, fraudulent scammers, or simply by the legitimate increase in the number of viewers of the event. The 2018 World Cup witnessed 25 million cyberattacks during the event.[44] Dozens of websites were also attacked during the 2014 World Cup in Brazil and the 2016 Summer Olympics, also in Brazil, including DoS attacks against websites of the Sao Paulo military police and several Brazil ministries[45] websites. Brazil received 2000 daily attacks[46] during these events.

From the lessons learned, host countries are now building up defenses. The 2018 FIFA World Cup teams raised concerns about cybersecurity threats,[47] including leaking sensitive tactical information. In response, Russia, the host country, initiated steps to reinforce cybersecurity by assessing the overall information security posture of hospitality services, applying modern encryption solutions on data at rest, data in use, and data in transit, and reviewing its incident detection and response capabilities.

Similarly, Qatar, the FIFA World Cup 2022 host nation, took security measures to protect the country's infrastructure and 1.5 million expected visitors. This event means huge publicity, and it increases the attack surface and introduces new attack vectors. To overcome that, Qatar has funded an Interpol initiative, called Project Stadia,[48] to help host countries plan and implement security controls, with the support from global experts.

---

[44] www.telegraph.co.uk/news/2018/07/16/putin-says-russia-targeted-almost-25-million-cyber-attacks-world/

[45] EclecticIQ Fusion Center (2018). EclecticIQ Analysis: FIFA World Cup 2018 Threat Landscape (2nd version).

[46] www.forbes.com/sites/federicoguerrini/2014/06/17/brazils-world-cup-of-cyber-attacks-from-street-fighting-to-online-protest/?ss=Security&sh=30e3589951a8

[47] www.reuters.com/article/us-soccer-england-cyber-idUSKCN1BN1A4

[48] www.interpol.int/How-we-work/Project-Stadia/Stadia-activities

In addition to this initiative, Qatar's Supreme Committee for Delivery and Legacy also issued a cybersecurity framework[49] to provide fundamental cyber competencies and cyber capabilities needed to safeguard supporting services. Aimed at the national level, all governmental and critical sectors, businesses, and institutions were expected to implement and adopt controls defined in the framework by 2022. It consists of three major pillars (**prevention, detection, and response**) separated into 14 cybersecurity capabilities (Figure 3-4) and recommended metrics to support these capabilities.

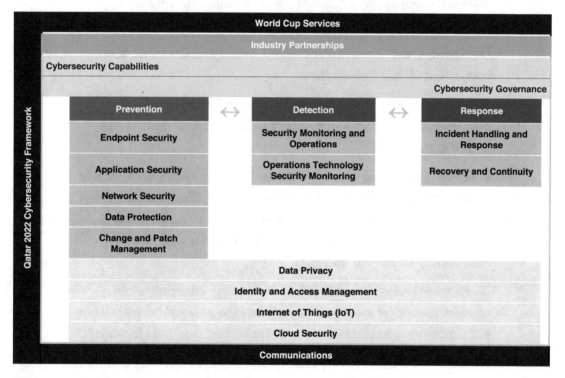

Figure 3-4. *Qatar 2022 cybersecurity framework capabilities*

The following are cybersecurity capabilities.

- **Cybersecurity governance**: Information security governance functionalities, such as risk assessment, internal audit, and training and awareness

---

[49] State of Qatar – Supreme Committee for Delivery & Legacy. (2018). Qatar 2022 Cybersecurity Framework. www.qatar2022.qa/sites/default/files/Qatar2022Framework.pdf

- **Endpoint security**: Protection of all endpoints, including but not limited to servers, desktops, laptops, wireless devices, mobile devices, and Internet of Things (IoT) devices connected to an organization's network

- **Application security**: Protection of applications and the secure development life cycle

- **Network security**: Protection of the IT infrastructure and connected devices

- **Data protection**: Protection of sensitive data and detection and prevention of data leakage/loss

- **Change and patch management**: Ensuring formal change management activities and applying patches in a controlled and secure manner

- **Security monitoring and operations**: Ensuring secure architecture of the organization and continuous monitoring of systems as well as any deviations from expected security posture (major services include vulnerability management, penetration testing, security monitoring, and threat hunting)

- **Operations technology security monitoring**: Ensuring security on mission-critical systems that supports the national critical infrastructure operations such as water, oil and gas, and electricity

- **Incident handling and response**: Managing cybersecurity incidents

- **Recovery and continuity**: Identifying threats, threat landscapes, and their impacts, as well as establishing suitable recovery strategies and tactics

- **Data privacy**: Protection of personal data and ensuring compliance to national (e.g., Qatar Data Protection Law No.13 of 2016[50]) and international data privacy and protection regulations (such as the EU General Data Protection Regulation[51])

---

[50] www.almeezan.qa/LawPage.aspx?id=7121&language=ar (in Arabic)
[51] https://eur-lex.europa.eu/legal-content/EN/TXT/PDF/?uri=CELEX:32016R0679

- **Identity and access management**: Ensuring correct assignment of access privileges to correct users for approved business needs

- **Internet of Things (IoT)**: Prevention, detection, and the response of IoT devices

- **Cloud security**: Protection of resources and information in the cloud

The framework also contains security metrics that support organizations in validating the effectiveness of security controls outlined in the capabilities.

Monetary Authority of Singapore

In January 2021, MAS released the revised Technology Risk Management Guidelines[52] to replace a consultation paper from March 2019. This new version was turned into an official guideline in 2021 to address the growing challenges of financial institutions' rapid digital transformation and adherence to new information technologies and the subsequent changes and increased complexity and exposure to a range of technology risks, including cyber risk.

Each financial institution must understand the context where it operates and exposure to technology risks. They must adopt strong risk management framework to ensure IT and cyber resilience considering the increasingly sophisticated techniques used by threat actors over financial institutions. These techniques would aim to maximize the financial advantages from their activities by carrying out fraudulent financial transactions, sensitive financial data exfiltration and the disruption of IT systems with attacks like ransomware.

This updated version of the MAS Technology Risk Management Guidelines establishes the technology risk management principles and best practices to guide financial institutions to achieve the following goals.

- Establish strong and comprehensive technology risk governance and oversight with the commitment of the board of directors and senior management that should promote a risk culture and the establishment of a technology risk management framework.

---

[52] www.mas.gov.sg/-/media/MAS/Regulations-and-Financial-Stability/Regulatory-and-Supervisory-Framework/Risk-Management/TRM-Guidelines-18-January-2021.pdf

- Maintain cyber resilience by comprehensively adopting the defense-in-depth concept and continuous improvement of the existing IT processes and controls to assure confidentiality, integrity, and availability of data and IT systems.

The following lists some of the requirements tailored for financial institutions in the MAS Technology Risk Management Guidelines.

- Cybersecurity Operations
  - Cyber Threat Intelligence and Information Sharing
  - Cyber Event Monitoring and Detection
- Cybersecurity Assessment
  - Vulnerability Assessment
  - Penetration Testing
  - Cyber Exercises
- Online Financial Services
  - Customer Authentication and Transaction Signing
    - Security of Online Financial Services
    - Customer Authentication and Transaction Signing
  - Fraud Monitoring
  - Customer Education
- Specifications on Application testing
- Mobile Application Security

Overall, except for these requirements, the MAS Technology Risk Management Guidelines can be mapped with major standards requirements like ISO 27001, ISO 27002, and NIST SP 800-53.

BDDK

The Banking Regulatory and Supervisory Authority (BRSA, or BDDK in Turkish) of the Republic of Turkey prepared the Regulation on Banks' Information Systems and Electronic Banking Services,[53] effective since July 1, 2020. This regulation superseded the previous Communiqué on the Principles to Be Considered in Bank Information Systems Management.

This regulation states that the banks' board of directors should consider information security management as a part of their corporate governance practices. They are responsible for allocating necessary financial and human resources to ensure the confidentiality, integrity, and availability of information assets and conducting effective oversight to manage any risks arising from the use of information systems (IS). The board should also approve and establish an IS strategic plan, establish an IS strategy committee, and an IS guidance committee.

As per the regulation, banks should ensure the following.

- Accurate authentication mechanisms (at least two-factor authentication)

- Audit record mechanisms for transactions

- Fraud monitoring

- Network security systems

- A security configuration management program

- A security vulnerability management program

- Cyberattack management and cyber threat information sharing mechanisms

- An information security awareness training program

- An information asset inventory

- An information security management program

---

[53] www.resmigazete.gov.tr/eskiler/2020/03/20200315-10.htm (in Turkish)

- An internal IT audit program

- Restrictions on domestic or cross-border sharing and transfer of client information

- Proper access restrictions are established and maintained for the electronic banking services, including Internet banking, mobile banking, telephone banking, open banking services, and ATM services

The regulation also specifies the requirements for business continuity and high availability management, provided that the primary and secondary systems must be kept in Turkey. Cloud computing (public or private cloud) for banks is allowed as per the regulation; however, it is subjected to BRSA approval if the bank chooses a public cloud provider.

Others

Many other notable frameworks or handbooks are available, including the following.

- NIST Special Publication 800-181 revision 1[54]

- The Workforce Framework for Cybersecurity (NICE Framework) provides the building blocks for the tasks, knowledge, and skills needed to perform cybersecurity work performed by individuals and teams.

- Common Criteria (also known as ISO/IEC 15408—Information technology—Security techniques—Evaluation criteria for IT security—Part 3: Security assurance components)[55]

- RFC 2196 Site Security Handbook[56]

---

[54] https://nvlpubs.nist.gov/nistpubs/SpecialPublications/NIST.SP.800-181r1.pdf
[55] www.iso.org/obp/ui/#iso:std:iso-iec:15408:-3:ed-3:v2:en
[56] www.ietf.org/rfc/rfc2196.txt

- This handbook is prepared by the IETF (Internet Engineering Task Force) for developing computer security policies and procedures for sites that have systems on the Internet.

- SANS Security Policy Resource[57]

- These resources are published by the SANS Institute for the rapid development and implementation of information security policies.

- Health Insurance Portability and Accountability Act (HIPAA)[58]

- The U.S. act for the privacy of individuals' identifiable health information.

- Health Information Trust Alliance Common Security Framework HITRUST CSF[59]

- This is a set of controls with defined objectives that can help to meet the requirements of globally recognized standards, regulations, and business requirements, including ISO, EU GDPR, NIST Frameworks, and PCI DSS. HITRUST CSF has a leveled structure on the controls (L1 to L3) and a useful mapping to all major security frameworks.

Summary

Industry-accepted information security frameworks help organizations build up their defenses and prepare themselves for cyber threats. These frameworks can also be useful to identify and prioritize risk mitigation actions. NIST has several special publications in this regard, including the NIST-800 series publications, which are considered one of the most comprehensive standards in information security. CIS Controls are a useful set of cybersecurity practices that can be applied in most organizations globally.

---

[57] www.sans.org/information-security-policy/

[58] www.hhs.gov/hipaa/index.html

[59] https://hitrustalliance.net/product-tool/hitrust-csf/

Ensuring security and resilience should be the concern of organizations *and* nations. Strengthening defense mechanisms against cyber threats and protecting critical infrastructures is essential to every nation's security and economic well-being. It can only be achieved by shared responsibilities between governments, agencies, and organizations. Many states have developed cybersecurity frameworks and standards for organizations for the better security posture of the whole nation or their critical industries.

CHAPTER 4

IT Security Technical Controls

This chapter lists and explains the technical security controls that organizations must have to secure their assets. These controls implementation should be based on a zero trust[1] model where all users, whether inside or outside the organization, need to be authenticated and authorized, and continuously identified to have access to corporate resources. Although these controls are essential to secure the organization, they are not enough to accomplish it. With these technical controls, organizations must also implement effective management and operational processes and hire qualified resources with the proper skills to implement, administer and operate these controls.

Off-Premises Unmanaged Devices

We have categorized endpoints as off-premises unmanaged devices and managed devices in our approach.

Off-premises unmanaged devices include any Internet-enabled device that the organization has no control over, including anonymous devices, customer devices, mobile devices with corporate mobile applications, partner devices, and employee devices that connect to the organization from the Internet.

Considering that the organization has no control over these devices, it can only protect its resources from these devices. To do that, the organization must implement the following controls.

---

[1] https://nvlpubs.nist.gov/nistpubs/SpecialPublications/NIST.SP.800-207.pdf

© Virgilio Viegas and Oben Kuyucu 2022
V. Viegas and O. Kuyucu, *IT Security Controls*, https://doi.org/10.1007/978-1-4842-7799-7_4

MDM: Mobile Device Management

Mobile device management (MDM) is the concept associated with *bringing your own device* (BYOD), where personal or corporate-owned mobile devices access corporate resources are the most used email.

MDM is frequently confused with *mobile application management* (MAM) and *unified endpoint management* (UEM) since they are relatively similar.

MDM improves security by managing the mobile devices (owned by the organization or by employees) to access the organization's resources and the following.

- Push or remove apps (MAM)

- Manage and encrypt data stored in the mobile devices (MCM)

- Enforce configuration settings

- Disable unused features to minimize the threat surface

- Enforce strong password to access the mobile device

- Control removable media (e.g., microSD cards)

- Manage the device applications, including non-corporate applications (e.g., application whitelisting (MAM))

- Geo location

- Patch management

- Forensics

- Remote wiping of the device

Although MDM is a powerful mechanism that allows organizations to secure mobile devices access to corporate resources, it raises several concerns that must be addressed before any implementation, namely the following.

- **Privacy**: Considering that MDM can have full control (including complete wipe) over mobile devices that the organization might not own, employees must be informed and accept the terms on how their devices are tracked and monitored. The organization must also implement the necessary controls to avoid unauthorized access to employees' devices and data.

- **Acceptable use**: Although devices can be privately owned, employees must be informed and formally accept the organization's acceptable BYOD use policies to remotely access corporate assets.

- **Off-boarding**: The organization must have a process to ensure that all corporate data is removed from the mobile device when the employee leaves the organization or reports a lost device.

- **Data loss**: To avoid data loss, MDM must be configured so that data cannot be copied between the corporate container and the personal space.

- **Infrastructure design**: MDM implementation design must include all security controls (e.g., IDS/IPS, strict access controls, sandboxing).

MAM: Mobile Application Management

MAM solutions securely manage and deploy corporate applications to mobile devices, including BYOD.

MAM solutions can establish the controls over the mobile applications, deliver and configure applications, control application updates, manage software licenses, and track application usage. It can adjust restrictions on applications based on geolocation.

Most MDM solutions can also implement MAM.

NAC: Network Access Control

Network access control acts as a gatekeeper of the corporate network. Its objective is to control the access of all devices and ensure that those devices comply with the organization's security policies, where each device must be authenticated, identified, or cataloged. It is compliance verified before it connects to the network.

NAC is a security control that can automatically detect and respond to potential threats in real time when devices try to connect to corporate networks.

The Institute of Electrical and Electronics Engineers (IEEE) 802.1X[2] is the standard for port-based network access control (PNAC) and the main NAC implementation reference.

---

[2]https://standards.ieee.org/standard/802_1X-2010.html

NAC can also quarantine noncompliant devices and allow them only limited access until they comply with security policies such as installing missing security patches, updating antivirus, renewing certificates, or hardening.

Although NAC must be implemented to avoid unmanaged devices to get unauthorized access to corporate networks, some implementations may allow visitors to access a corporate captive portal, or a landing page to provide them access to the Internet. Through captive portals, some user information can be collected and validated out-of-band (such as an OTP sent to a mobile phone), which may be mandatory in some jurisdictions.

NAC solutions have been integrated with SOAR (Security Orchestration, Automation and Response) technologies in recent deployments. When an unauthorized device is detected, a vulnerability scan is performed to leverage the visibility and ensure this unauthorized device does not impose any threat to the environment.

Multi-Factor Authentication

Access to the corporate environment from unmanaged and untrusted devices is prone to several information security risks. Therefore, organizations must implement all applicable security controls to ensure that threat agents do not impersonate their employees, customers, and partners. One of these mechanisms is multi-factor authentication, where two or more separate factors are used simultaneously for authentication. This provides additional security if one factor is compromised.

The following are authentication factors.

- Factor 1: Something you know

- (e.g., password, PIN, patterns, the name of your favorite pet)

- Factor 2: Something you have

- (e.g., SMS token, push-based OTP, soft-token, hard-token, smartcard, certificates)

- Factor 3: Something you are or something you do

- (e.g., biometrics such as fingerprint, palmprint, face ID, voice, retina or iris, DNA, or handwriting analysis, typing speeds)

Using a password as the first step and a PIN as the second step to authenticate is not multi-factor authentication. Although it uses two authentication elements and the username, these elements are from the same authentication factor (something you know) and not considered MFA.

The terms *multi-factor authentication* and *multi-step authentication* are often used interchangeably; however, it should be noted that they are different. Unlike multi-factor authentication, multi-step authentication may use the same factor as long as it is securely obtained. For example, the one-time password (OTP) token you see in your mobile authenticator app is *something you know*, and when you use it with a password, it is called *multi-step* authentication. Instead, if you have clicked on a notification or approved an authentication request from your mobile device, it would be multi-factor authentication because the device is *something you have*.

One additional important consideration about MFA is that authentication methods used for MFA should not allow access to another direction. For example, if you are receiving an OTP in your email address for the second factor, and if you are using the same username and password to access this email account without MFA, the attacker could access the email account to retrieve the OTP. Hence, preferably, the authentication processes should be *out-of-band*, meaning that they should be distributed over different networks or channels.

RASP for Mobile Applications

Runtime application self-protection (RASP) is a technology built into or linked to an application or runtime environment. It can control the application execution and detect and prevent real-time attacks.

When deploying mobile applications, organizations should include RASP in their applications to create an additional layer of protection on the client side, since the mobile device is run in an insecure, outdated, or compromised operating system.

By implementing RASP technology with their mobile apps, organizations can avoid their apps from running on compromised, rooted, or jailbroken devices.

RASP technology can also prevent the app from debugging, identify potential vulnerabilities, reduce functionalities, or stop the application from running.

Some RASP solutions produce a device fingerprint and relate it to a user or customer account, assigning a risk score to sessions and user or customer profiling.

Secure Connections

Considering that the Internet is a hostile environment and that non-encrypted traffic can be easily eavesdropped on or manipulated, to ensure information integrity and confidentiality, each organization must implement some form of encryption to all connections from the Internet to corporate resources. This includes external partner communications, employee connections to corporate resources, customer or anonymous visitors traffic to corporate websites and mobile applications.

All connections from the outside world to the organization's environment must be secured by encrypting the channel to ensure confidentiality, integrity, authentication, and non-repudiation.

OSI Model

Currently, most network connections are based on the TCP/IP model. However, there are many other communications protocols. To standardize different computer networking methods and protocols developed by different companies since the early days of computer networks, International Organization for Standardization (ISO) developed the Open Systems Interconnection (OSI) model for protocols in the early 1980s. The OSI model is defined by ISO Standard 7498.

The OSI model (Table 4-1) has seven distinct conceptual layers. Each layer is responsible for specific tasks or operations to support the layer above it, and it is supported by the layer below it. Communication between layers is done by standardized protocols.

Table 4-1. *OSI Model Layers and Protocols*

Layer	Protocols	
Application Layer	HTTP	POP3
	FTP	IMAP
	LPD (Line Print Daemon)	SNMP
	SMTP	NNTP
	Telnet	S-RPC
	TFTP	SET
	EDI	
Presentation Layer	American Standard Code for Information Interchange (ASCII)	
	Extended Binary-Coded Decimal Interchange Mode (EBCDIM)	
	Tagged Image File Format (TIFF)	
	Joint Photographic Experts Group (JPEG)	
	Moving Picture Experts Group (MPEG)	
	Musical Instrument Digital Interface (MIDI)	
Session Layer	Network File System (NFS)	
	Structured Query Language (SQL)	
	Remote Procedure Call (RPC)	
	Simplex/Half-Duplex/Full-Duplex	
Transport Layer	Transmission Control Protocol (TCP)	
	User Datagram Protocol (UDP)	
	Sequenced Packet Exchange (SPX)	
	Secure Socket Layer (SSL)	
	Transport Layer Security (TLS)[3]	

(continued)

---

[3] Authors' note: SSL and TLS are located into several layers of the OSI model or the TCP/IP model. TLS runs "on top of transport protocol (e.g., TCP) and encrypts payloads from higher layers. For a good discussion on this matter, please visit https://security.stackexchange.com/ questions/93333/what-layer-is-tls/93338#93338.

Table 4-1. (*continued*)

Layer	Protocols
Network Layer	Internet Control Message Protocol (ICMP)
	Routing Information Protocol (RIP)
	Open Shortest Path First (OSPF)
	Border Gateway Protocol (BGP)
	Internet Group Management Protocol (IGMP)
	Internet Protocol (IP)
	Internet Protocol Security (IPsec)
	Internetwork Packet Exchange (IPX)
	Network Address Translation (NAT)[4]
	Simple Key Management for Internet Protocols (SKIP)
Data Link Layer	Serial Line Internet Protocol (SLIP)
	Point-to-Point Protocol (PPP)
	Address Resolution Protocol (ARP)
	Layer 2 Forwarding (L2F)
	Layer 2 Tunneling Protocol (L2TP)
	Point-to-Point Tunneling Protocol (PPTP)
	Integrated Services Digital Network (ISDN)
Physical Layer	EIA/TIA-232 and EIA/TIA-449
	X.21
	High-Speed Serial Interface (HSSI)
	Synchronous Optical Networking (SONET)
	V.24 and V.35

TCP/IP Model

Unlike the OSI model, the TCP/IP Model (Table 4-2) only has four layers.

---

[4] Although NAT is not a protocol, it is a method that can be implemented in the network layer.

Table 4-2. *Comparison Between TCP/IP Models*

OSI Model	TCP/IP Model
Application	Application
Presentation	
Session	
Transport	Transport
Network	Internet
Data Link	Link
Physical	

TCP/IP is the most used protocol suite and can be found in almost all operating systems and uses several individual protocols (Table 4-3).

Table 4-3. *TCP/IP Model Layer Protocols*

OSI	TCP/IP				
Application	Application	FTP	Telnet	SNMP	LPD
Presentation					
Session		TFTP	SMTP	NFS	X Window
Transport	Transport	TCP		UDP	
Network	Internet	ICMP		IGMP	
		IP			
Data Link	Link	Ethernet	Fast Ethernet	Token Ring	FDDI
Physical					

The TCP/IP network traffic can be secured by encrypting connections with a virtual private network (VPN) between the communicating hosts and ensuring confidentiality, integrity, and authentication. VPNs can be established using the following protocols.

- PPTP: Point-to-Point Tunneling Protocol

- L2TP: Layer 2 Tunneling Protocol

- SSH: Secure Shell

- SSL/TLS: Secure Sockets Layer/Transport Layer Security

- IPsec: Internet Protocol Security

IPsec, SSH, and TLS

The most common ways to secure connections from the Internet to corporate resources are the implementation of the IPsec, SFTP, and TLS.

IPsec

Internet Protocol Security (IPsec) is an Internet Engineering Task Force (IETF) open standard encryption suite that implements encryption between two devices connected through an IP network for data authentication, integrity, and confidentiality. These two devices can be two hosts on a host-to-host communication, two security gateways (network-to-network), or a security gateway and a host (network-to-host). IPsec implements VPNs.

IPsec allows mutual authentication between the two connecting devices at the beginning of each session and the negotiation of cryptographic keys.

The following are IPsec functions.

- **Authentication Header (AH)**: (integrity and non-repudiation) AH provides protection against replay attacks and ensures data integrity, data source authentication (IP datagrams).

- **Encapsulating Security Payloads (ESP)**: (confidentiality and content integrity) ESP provides confidentiality, data integrity, data source authentication, anti-replay attack service (partial sequence integrity), and limited traffic-flow confidentiality.

- **Internet Security Association and Key Management Protocol (ISAKMP)**: This is a framework for authentication and key exchange. It can be implemented by manually configuring pre-shared keys, Internet Key Exchange (IKE and IKEv2), Kerberized Internet

Negotiation of Keys (KINK), or IPSECKEY DNS records. ISAKMP generates the Security Association (SA) with algorithms and parameters needed for AH and/or ESP.

IPsec has the following operation modes (Table 4-4).

- **Transport mode** is where only the payload is encrypted (e.g., peer-to-peer).

- **Tunnel mode** is where the entire packet is encrypted (e.g., gateway to gateway). Each IP packet is encapsulated into another IPsec packet, which may have different source and destination IP addresses from the "inner" packet.

Table 4-4. *IP Packets in IPsec Modes*

Initial IP Packet (Without IPSec)	IP Header	TCP Header	Payload	

Transport Mode:

Transport Mode IPsec Packet	IP Header	IPSec Header	TCP Header	Payload
		Protected		

Tunnel Mode:

Tunnel Mode IPSec Packet	New IP Header	IPSec Header	Original IP Header	TCP Header	Payload
		Protected			

IPsec supports several integrity and encryption algorithms. Before implementing IPsec, each organization must consider that some of the supported algorithms are considered weak (e.g., DES, 3DES, SHA1) and that in some countries, the use of some algorithms is mandatory (e.g., Saudi Cryptographic Standard[5]).

---

[5] https://nca.gov.sa/files/ncs_en.pdf

SSH

Secure Shell (SSH) is a network protocol for secure client-server communication by employing strong password authentication, key pairs, or both. Although SSH connections from the Internet to the organization resources should not be allowed, since it poses several security risks, it can be used between the organizations and partners to exchange files, specifically through Secure File Transfer Protocol (SFTP), including SSH security components.

Like all other processes, it is highly recommended to implement additional security controls like, for example, strong authentication method, source IP whitelisting, scheduled firewall rules.

TLS

Web browsers use Hypertext Transfer Protocol Secure (HTTPS) to encrypt communications with web servers. HTTPS transmissions use SSL/TLS protocol. SSL preceded TLS and was gradually replaced by TLS after Google Security Team found that SSL was vulnerable[6] to POODLE attacks (Padding Oracle ON Downgraded Legacy Encryption).

TLS, first defined in 1999[7], now the current version is 1.3, supports client/server applications to communicate over the Internet and avoid eavesdropping, tampering, and message manipulation, and should be used in all connections to the organization websites and web services (APIs).

TLS version 1.3 is specified by the IETF Request for Comments (RFC 8446) with improvements in performance and privacy compared to previous version 1.2, which also has known vulnerabilities.

- CVE-2012-4929: Compression Ratio Info-leak Made Easy (CRIME)

- CVE-2015-7575: Security Losses from Obsolete and Truncated Transcript Hashes (SLOTH)

---

[6] https://cve.mitre.org/cgi-bin/cvename.cgi?name=CVE-2014-3566
[7] https://datatracker.ietf.org/doc/html/rfc2246

The following are some of the differences between TLS 1.2 and TLS 1.3.

- The TLS 1.2 negotiation mechanism was deprecated.

- Elliptic curve algorithms are part of version 1.3 specifications, and new algorithms like Edwards-curve Digital Signature Algorithm (EdDSA)[8] were included.

- Handshake messages after the ServerHello[9] all encrypted.

- RSA and Diffie–Hellman static cipher suites were removed, and forward secrecy is now provided by all public key–based key exchange mechanisms.

Organizations must ensure that all their web servers and APIs enforce the use of TLS 1.3 and that the downgrading connections to weaker versions like TLS 1.1 or all versions of SSL are disabled. For reference on selecting and configuring TLS implementations, NIST has a nice guideline called SP 800-52 Rev. 2 *Guidelines for the Selection, Configuration, and Use of Transport Layer Security (TLS) Implementations*,[10] which helps organizations configure their TLS implementations according to best practices.

Clean Pipes

Clean pipes concept is an anti-DDoS (distributed denial-of-service) mechanism maintained and managed by the Internet Service Provider (ISP) that protects the organization's Internet connections from well-known bandwidth-consuming denial-of-service attacks. By implementing this mechanism, the organization frees bandwidth for production traffic. This is known as *DDoS deflation*.

DDoS Mitigation

In addition to clean pipes, organizations must also implement on-premises DDoS protection and mitigation mechanisms.

---

[8] https://datatracker.ietf.org/doc/html/rfc8032

[9] Stage of the TLS handshake where, in response to the ClientHello, the server sends a message containing the server's SSL certificate, chosen cipher suite, and server random, and a random string of bytes generated by the server.

[10] https://nvlpubs.nist.gov/nistpubs/SpecialPublications/NIST.SP.800-52r2.pdf

The following are the main types of DDoS attacks.

- Volume-based attacks

- Protocol attacks

- Application layer attacks

Each one of this type requires its own unique mitigation strategy and tool.

Volume-based attacks consist of generating a large volume of requests, overloading network devices or servers so that they cannot respond to legitimate requests. These attacks can be UDP floods, ICMP floods, NTP amplification, among other attacks. Volume-based attacks can be prevented by clean pipes and volumetric anti-DDoS devices that inspect traffic and drop malicious traffic.

Protocol attacks generate requests to exploit network protocol weaknesses like SYN floods, packet fragmentation, or *ping of death*.

Anti-DDoS tools protect the organization's infrastructure by analyzing traffic, identifying, and preventing malicious traffic from reaching the destination target.

Application layer attacks generate a large number of requests to web applications or other application servers, appearing to be generated by legitimate users, and include GET/POST floods, low-and-slow attacks, or attacks that target specific application server limitations or vulnerabilities like Apache or IIS.

Anti-DDoS devices can prevent application layer attacks by analyzing site visitors' behavior and blocking bad requests. Additional protection mechanisms can also be implemented by challenging unrecognized visitors using cookie challenges or CAPTCHAs.

Managed Devices

Directory Service Integration

A directory service is a fundamental tool to organize and unify the management of the organization's users and authentication credentials, computers, printers, and others. Directory services can mirror the organization hierarchy and map the users and other resources to that hierarchy and enforce the relevant policies to those users and resources.

Among several advantages of directory services, we can highlight the following.

- Centralized resource repository

- Centralized security administration

- Enhance single logon to access corporate resources

- Simplified resource location

- Corporate Policies enforcement

- Policies applied according to the organizational structure

Although the most well-known directory service is Microsoft Active Directory (AD), the following alternatives can be considered according to the organization's specific needs.

- Apache Directory Studio

- Open LDAP

- JXplorer

- FreeIPA

- Samba

- 398 Directory Server

- OpenDJ

- Zentyal Active Directory

- Oracle Directory Server Enterprise Edition

- RazDC

It is highly recommended to use strong authentication protocols like Kerberos authentication instead of NT LAN Manager (NTLM), which is vulnerable to several known security vulnerabilities related to password hashing and password salting.

It is also recommended to use security baselines and frequent configuration reviews to confirm compliance with those baseline and other standards (e.g., PCI DSS).

Centralized Endpoint Management

To ensure effective management of their assets, organizations must have *centralized endpoint management*. It is the platform for managing and administering distributed systems running Windows, macOS, Linux, Unix, and other operating systems.

With centralized endpoint management, organizations can provide remote control, patch management, software distribution, operating system deployment, and network access protection, among others. This solution can also play a fundamental role in supporting an effective asset management process. Microsoft System Center Configuration Manager (SCCM) is an example.

TPM: Trusted Platform Module

A Trusted Platform Module (TPM) is a chip in the device's motherboard. TPM manages and stores encryption keys used for full-disk encryption and provides access to those keys to the operating system. If the hard disk is removed and installed in another device, the new device does not have access to the encryption keys.

VPN Client

A VPN client is software that allows a device to establish a secure channel with the organization and access the organization's resources.

Since VPN clients permit direct access to corporate resources, they should only be installed in managed devices, where the organization can install additional security controls. Before connecting to corporate resources, devices that use VPN clients should be checked for the existence of mandatory security controls such as antivirus and up-to-date AV signatures, EDR, up-to-date operating system, hard disk encryption, or disabling print screen option, and if these controls are running the latest versions.

Although it is a widely used solution for remote access, VPN clients raise several security concerns, like data exfiltration. For this reason, organizations should consider implementing alternate, more robust, and secure remote access solutions, like SSL/VPN, where it is possible to access corporate resources through an SSL/VPN portal that does not allow exfiltration of corporate data by blocking the possibility of copying files.

NAC: Network Access Control

NAC agents should be installed on all devices to comply with corporate policies and are properly updated.

Data Classification

Data classification is a crucial element of information security since it allows you to protect data according to its confidentiality, sensitivity, or secrecy, with suitable security controls. Applying the same security controls to data with different types of confidentiality is not cost-effective or does not ensure the proper level of security for confidential information since it treats public and confidential information as the same.

The first step of data classification is to define a classification scheme that allows the organization to group assets or objects in categories according to their value, sensitiveness, risk (impact X likelihood), potential damage or loss, or anything else considered relevant (e.g., cardholder data in PCI DSS or PII in privacy laws).

The scheme must be adjusted to the organization's specific needs and operating context and easily understandable by all employees.

One possible scheme that can be used as a reference is the one used by the US military (Table 4-5).

Table 4-5. *Classification scheme using U.S. military classification scheme as reference*

High	Top Secret	Unauthorized disclosure have drastic effects and cause grave damage to national security
	Secret	Unauthorized disclosure have significant effects and cause critical damage to national security
	Confidential	Unauthorized disclosure have noticeable effects and cause serious damage to national security
	Sensitive but unclassified	Used for internal use and unauthorized disclosure can violate individuals' privacy rights
Low	Unclassified	Disclosure of unclassified data won't compromise confidentiality or cause any material damage

Considering that this classification might be too complex to implement and unsuitable for corporate environments, organizations should consider implementing a more adequate and easier classification scheme with fewer classification levels (Table 4-6), as shown in the following.

Table 4-6. *Simplified corporate classification*

High	Confidential	Private
	Sensitive	Corporate
Low	Public	External

- **Confidential**: The highest classification level to classify extremely sensitive corporate data that could have a significant negative impact on the organization if it was disclosed (e.g., new product specifications or design, corporate formulas or trade secrets like KFC recipes, customer data).

- **Private**: Private or personal data that should only be used internally. Like confidential data, private data can have a significant negative impact on the organization or people if it is disclosed.

- **Sensitive**, **Corporate**: Internal corporate data can harm the organization if disclosed. Examples of sensitive data are internal procedures, accounting, and budget data.

- **Public**: This is the lowest classification level that does not negatively impact the organization if it is disclosed.

The following are other concepts associated with data classification.

- The **data owner** is responsible for classifying information and ensuring that the appropriate security controls are in place.

- The **data custodian** is responsible for implementing the defined security controls for the data according to its classification. The data custodian is also responsible for data backup (and testing those backups), managing storage, and ensuring integrity and availability.

- The **users** are individuals who have limited access to data to perform the necessary tasks according to their job description (least privilege principle).

- The **auditor** reviews and verifies compliance with security and data protection policies and the adequacy of the applied security controls.

Data protection and data classification policy owners are ultimately responsible for ensuring these policies' implementation and approving possible exceptions.

To ensure that all data is classified, organizations must provide end-users tools to classify all documents generated in their workstations. These tools are usually Microsoft Office plug-ins that force users to classify all created documents (Word, Excel, PowerPoint, Outlook email, or modified documents that were not previously classified).

UAM: User Activity Monitoring

User activity monitoring (UAM) allows organizations to monitor and track their users' activities and behavior and generate alerts of potential danger based on the user behavior profile.

UAM can capture all user activities in the operating system and applications, including commands, text entered chosen options, and verify if employees and contractors comply with their assigned tasks or usage profile and pose a potential threat to the organization.

When implementing UAM, organizations must consider the legal implications on the employees' privacy. In some countries, it is not allowed to monitor individual behavior unless informed.[11] In other countries,[12] it is allowed in certain conditions. The key takeaway is that organizations should notify users beforehand of what is tracked and what is not.

---

[11] Bărbulescu v. Romania case. `www.echr.coe.int/Documents/Press_Q_A_Barbulescu_ENG.PDF`.

[12] For example, USA under Electronic Communications Privacy Act of 1986

Endpoint Protection

This section addresses all the security controls present in all the organization endpoints.

Before deploying any of these controls, it must be ensured that the host devices have the needed resources to avoid performance degradation. It should be noted that several EDR solutions in the market currently have all these features except for full-disk encryption.

Phishing Reporting Tool

To provide users with an easy and fast way to report potential email threats, organizations should install a phishing reporting tool on all desktops.

Usually, this tool is an email client plugin (e.g., Microsoft Outlook add-in), which is displayed as a report phishing button that tags and forwards the email to the security operations center for analysis and deletes the original email.

Similarly, this button recognizes the phishing simulation emails that aim to educate users and collect statistics for measuring the program's effectiveness.

Host IPS or EDR

A *host intrusion prevention system* (HIPS) is installed in the organization endpoints and monitors all traffic to and from a host and blocks if an intrusion is detected.

Currently, the concept of HIDS has become outdated, and *endpoint detection and response* (EDR) has become the next generation of HIPS. EDR detects threats and follows up the entire life cycle of the threat, providing useful information about what happened, how the threat got into the system, its location and activity, and how it was stopped.

Some EDR solutions report to cloud-based services, which allow their vendors to provide additional services like response and forensics to support the organization's security operations center.

Desktop Firewall

The desktop firewall feature, or personal firewall, is deployed with most operating systems. However, most of the time, this feature is not enabled or not enforced. Desktop firewalls control network traffic from and to computers, allowing or dropping the packets based on security rules.

Although desktop firewall rule set management can be very complex and create constraints by blocking legitimate network traffic, a limited set of generic rules can be implemented to block traffic that clearly should not be present in the organization networks; for example, certain unused TCP or UDP ports ranges or known malware ports.

Antivirus

Antivirus software is one of the oldest and most well-known endpoint security controls.

Typically, antivirus software detects viruses based on signatures. Therefore, to ensure the effectiveness of this security control, antivirus software must be kept up-to-date and centrally managed, where the signature updates can be pushed to the endpoints, and schedule scan jobs and track detected virus alerts.

End users should not be able to uninstall or stop antivirus software and, scanning exclusions due to performance reasons or others must be properly assessed before being approved.

Most antivirus software currently offers protection against spyware, worms, rootkits, and others.

One of the biggest challenges related to antivirus software and other agent-based security controls is assuring that the software is installed in all endpoints, which must be supported by an efficient and effective IT asset management process.

Antispyware

Spyware is software that monitors user actions, filters relevant information, and transmits them to a remote system. One example of this user information is Internet banking login credentials.

Although in the past, anti-spyware protection was separately licensed, currently, most endpoint antivirus software also offers anti-spyware protection.

Full-Disk Encryption

Full-disk encryption is a security mechanism that prevents the unwanted disclosure of corporate data.

The most frequently shown use case for disk encryption is the loss of corporate laptops with sensitive information that can be prevented with disk encryption. However, there are other cases where disk encryption also prevents the unwanted disclosure of corporate data, like corporate media that is not effectively sanitized before being disposed of or used corporate desktops that are sold without any sanitation.

Full-disk encryption can be implemented using dedicated software or using features provided by the operating system like Microsoft Windows BitLocker. TPM is also used for full-disk encryption.

Application Control and Application Whitelisting

Application control is a solution that controls the applications that can be installed in a device, force certain applications to be installed, and force applications settings. It prevents users from installing or running applications in their workstations and reduces the organization's exposure to potentially malicious software.

Perimeter Security

Firewalls

Firewalls are the most well-known security control name. Almost every person in your organization knows the word *firewall*. However, only a few people know exactly what a firewall is.

Firewalls are software or hardware-based network security systems that control incoming or outgoing traffic between two or more network segments based on a defined ruleset. With firewalls, organizations can establish a barrier between untrusted networks (e.g., Internet, partner, vendor, etc.) and internal networks.

The following are the most common firewall types.

- **Static packet-filtering firewalls** filter traffic by examining message headers and validating source, destination, and port, regardless of the source interface. This type of firewall can be easily tricked since packets can be spoofed.

- **Application firewalls** are also designated *proxy firewalls*. Packets are copied from one network segment to another. Source and destination addresses can be modified to protect certain network segments.

- **Circuit-level gateway firewalls**, designated as *circuit proxies*, manage communications based on the circuit, not on the traffic content, and are used in communications with trusted partners. These firewalls act as the OSI model session layer (Layer 5). SOCKS (Socket service or Socket secure) is a very popular implementation of circuit-level gateway firewalls.

- **Stateful inspection firewalls** are also known as *dynamic packet-filtering firewalls*. These firewalls validate the connection (session) state, inspecting source address, a destination address, destination port, and the relation between the current packet and the previous packet in the same session by keeping track of the session state.

- **Deep packet inspection firewalls** operate at the application level and filter the communication payload content, doing a full packet inspection and identifying domain names, malware, spam, and blocking unwanted traffic.

- **Next-Gen firewalls** are designated all-in-one because they can have several security functions like IPS, SSL/TLS proxy, VPN concentrator, and web filtering.

To increase the misperception of what a firewall does, most vendors provide "all-in-one" solutions in which several security controls (and other functions) are incorporated into a firewall. These include the following.

- An NTP server

- An explicit proxy

- Content filtering

- Antivirus

- A honeypot

- Application control

- A DNS server

- IPS/IDS

- A web application firewall

- A VPN concentrator

- A router

- A remote access platform

  - SSL/VPN

  - VPN

Considering these capabilities, all-in-one firewalls are a very attractive solution for small and medium organizations since they are cheaper and easier to manage. For this reason, all-in-one firewalls can give a false perception of security. To avoid it, IT security teams must have the appropriate training in all the user features to ensure that they are properly configured and updated. These devices can also act as a single point of failure or compromise where a single exploitable vulnerability can compromise all the used features.

We recommend reading the following documents for more information regarding firewall deployment and architecture (Figure 4-1).

- NIST SP 800-125B[13] Secure Virtual Network Configuration for Virtual Machine (VM) Protection

- NIST SP 800-41[14] Guidelines on Firewalls and Firewall Policy

---

[13] https://csrc.nist.gov/publications/detail/sp/800-125b/final
[14] https://nvlpubs.nist.gov/nistpubs/Legacy/SP/nistspecialpublication800-41r1.pdf

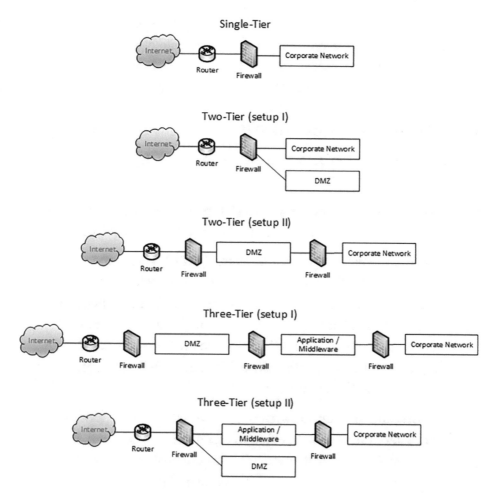

Figure 4-1. *Firewall deployment architectures*

Being one of the most important security controls of an organization, it is important to ensure that these device configurations and policies are fine-tuned and compliant with legal requirements and the organization's policies; otherwise, they give a false perception of security.

Intrusion Detection and Intrusion Protection Systems

An intrusion detection system (IDS) is a passive device that monitors network traffic and generates alerts based on a predefined set of rules with attack signatures. An IDS does not need to be placed inline to monitor traffic and monitor several network segments by mirroring ports into the IDS port.

An IDS is an active device placed inline that blocks attack attempts by terminating network connections or user sessions according to the matching attack signatures or patterns. Since an IPS can also act as an IDS, during the IPS implementation initial stages, it is advised to set up the IPS in "learning mode" to profile traffic and avoid false positives that can impact some services availability.

The following are generic types of IDS/IPS.

- A **network intrusion detection system (NIDS)** is deployed to monitor network traffic.

- A **host intrusion detection system (HIDS)** is deployed to hosts (e.g., servers and desktops) to monitor traffic to and from those hosts.

- A **network intrusion protection system (NIPS)** is deployed inline to monitor all network traffic and block malicious traffic to prevent intrusions. Since these devices are placed inline, they can be a single point of failure. Therefore, it is highly recommended to implement the appropriate redundancy to avoid latency and decide to implement fail-open or fail-close if the device fails based on a comprehensive risk assessment.

- **Host intrusion prevention system (HIPS)** is deployed to monitor all traffic to and from a host and block if an intrusion is detected. Before deploying a HIPS, it must be ensured that the host device has the needed resources to avoid performance degradation.

IDS/IPS devices are the fundamental security control to prevent intrusions. However, it must be ensured that they have the proper set of rules to avoid false negatives or false positives that can affect the availability of the protected services.

The organization size and infrastructure complexity can also be considered to implement these controls in an all-in-one firewall.

Proxy and Content (URL) Filtering

Ideally, to reduce risk, organizations should not allow their employees to have unrestricted access to the Internet. However, considering that this scenario is not an option for most organizations, the next best option would be granting access only to the strictly needed websites. This is our recommendation. Users should only access websites for business needs.

Some, if not most, organizations allow their employees to access the Internet based on content categories, banning access based on the categories risk (e.g., hacking-related sites, some non-business categories or file sharing) or impact on performance or productivity (e.g., advertising, streaming, social media). This implementation has several risks since, although most websites are categorized, it is impossible to ensure that all sites effectively match the assigned category or, when the category matches, it is impossible to ensure that some of the content is not malicious like, for example, some websites that are commonly categorized as "information technologies" can contain malicious software or documents.

Additionally, some attacks often use recently created domains that are still to be categorized. For this reason, access to all uncategorized websites should also be blocked.

All downloaded content should be analyzed by antivirus software and the sandbox.

DLP: Data Loss Prevention

The purpose of a perimeter *network-based data loss (or leakage) prevention* (DLP) system is to detect and prevent unauthorized data exfiltration by examining the content of the web, email content, and attached files, as well as uploaded files looking for the predefined keyword, patterns and metadata fields such as data classification tags.

Most DLP tools work with defined policies. By policies, security professionals describe what type of information would be monitored in the network. These can be based on content properties (file size, metadata, domains of senders/recipients, number of recipients, etc.), file-type (works both with MIME types and extensions[15]), content classifiers (patterns such as credit card numbers, national ID numbers, social security numbers, etc.) or dictionaries (words, phrases, weighted words, predefined terms for various categories). Some DLP solutions find sensitive information in databases and file shares by fingerprinting technologies. They collect indexes from these sources, and when hashes of one or more records are matched (such as customer name next to his/her credit card number), they can create events to investigate. File fingerprinting also works with document templates, where the overall layout is the same, but the content can change (such as common forms, e.g., HR forms, pay slips, CVs, contracts, etc.). When combined with machine learning, where users train DLP for allowed and disallowed contents, it can produce much fewer false positives.

---

[15] Author's note: Never rely on extensions.

Indeed, false positives[16] and false negatives[17] are primary issues in DLP solutions. To decrease false positives, the number of matches in one content can be increased, but this would cause false negatives, where sensitive data to be sent successfully in smaller batches. Some DLP tools track such content over time.

One of the other methods to decrease the false positives is to validate data somehow. One example of a tracked pattern is a credit card number which is typically 16 digits. However, DLP technologies should never track any 16 digits, but those that comply with the Luhn algorithm to check the validity of the data. Furthermore, financial institutions may track certain BINs to decrease the possibility of false positives.

DLP technologies are now merging with NLP (natural language processing) and deep learning to help organizations better understand the semantics of the data to recognize the language and context of the communications. Better data sets give better analysis results and decrease the number of false positives.

Classification of sensitive data at the time of creation would certainly help DLP tools block such data. Tags or labels can be found in the metadata of supporting documents and files. DLP tools can also track that information.

In the first steps of implementing DLP, every organization is overwhelmed by the amount of captured data. By knowing your processes well and automation of internal processes that support DLP to implement exceptions, events are not created for BAU activities. Anomaly detection in the network and then evaluating for DLP also helps but should be done carefully.

Blocking on day one would impact your business and users. Instead, users and other stakeholders should be educated during the process on what is sensitive data and what is not, such as providing popups containing educational material when they try to send sensitive data.

Honeypot

A honeypot system is created to simulate a legitimate system to mislead attackers. These systems should be placed in an isolated network without connection to the remaining productive systems and should not host any real data.

---

[16] When events are created for content that is allowed to egress.

[17] When events are not created for the content that is already exfiltrated.

The system should be relatively hardened but with some exploitable vulnerabilities. This way, the attacker focuses on compromising the exploitable system and later moves other systems without realizing that that system is not a "real" system.

When the attacker compromises the honeypot, it should trigger an alert, and the intrusion is detected before any production system is attacked. From there, the attacker's actions can be closely monitored and blocked. With the analysis of this attack, you understand the modus operandi of this attacker.

Honeypots should not be used to explicitly provoke attacks.

WAF: Web Application Firewall

A *web application firewall* (WAF) is a network security device that filters, monitors, and blocks non-essential or malicious web traffic. They provide additional protection against attacks like SQL injection, cross-site scripting, cross-site forgery, security misconfigurations, or design flaws.

WAFs are considered a second layer of defense, where firewalls and IPS should be in front of them and are essentially reverse-proxy devices that intercept and check the traffic against defined security policies. Some WAFs use profiling to understand the application and provide better and efficient protection. Based on the policies, they either drop the traffic or present other information that would confuse the attacker. WAFs can use a positive or negative security model or a combination of the two. A positive security model contains a whitelist that filters traffic, dropping the rest. A negative security model contains a deny list that only blocks those specific traffic patterns, and the rest is allowed.

WAFs can be host-based, where it is located in the application's software. They are easy to configure; however, they consume the same local resources of the application. Hence some performance issues can be observed. Network-based WAFs can be used to overcome this problem, where special hardware is put in front of the application. However, they are more expensive than the host-based ones. Nowadays, cloud-based WAFs offer a more affordable solution, where all traffic is redirected to the cloud service providers through DNS changes. Traffic is analyzed in cloud platforms and then sent to the actual application. These are easy to deploy and scalable and have no hardware maintenance costs. However, some features may not be configurable in such platforms, and they may not be used where data privacy laws are stricter and may not permit cloud platforms.

To inspect encrypted traffic, WAFs must have a copy of the private key of the server certificates of the web servers they are protecting. Please see the "TLS Decryption" section for more information.

SSL VPN

Organizations can use SSL/VPN to allow their users to remote access corporate networks via an encrypted connection between the user computer (web browser or client software) on the internet and the SSL/VPN device. This device should enforce the use of TLS since SSL has several known vulnerabilities.

SSL/VPN can be used in two major ways.

- **Corporate remote access portal**: Corporate users use their web browsers to access a web portal and from there remote access internal corporate resources like internal websites, emulated sessions (SSH, Telnet, etc.), or remote desktop sessions that are published according to the user profile. The web portal should only allow a single SSL/TLS session per user. Data loss prevention mechanisms like remote printing or copy/paste should be implemented.

- **SSL/TLS as a tunnel to establish a VPN**: This way allows the remote host to access multiple network services by using SSL/TLS to establish a tunnel and encapsulate other protocols not exclusively web-based. VPN tunneling might require the user to install additional software in their computers like JavaScript or a VPN client. Since users can directly access internal corporate network resources (e.g., remote desktop), it is harder to implement some ingress and egress controls.

Considering the inherent risk of this connection, multi-factor authentication must be used.

DNS

A Domain Name System (DNS) is a naming system for computers, services, or other resources connected where a name is associated with an IP address or vice versa.

Organizations have internal DNS servers to translate internal resources names and external DNS servers to publish their domains and services names on the Internet (Figure 4-2).

The following are common DNS records.

- A **record** stores a hostname and its IPv4 address.

- A **Canonical Name record** (CNAME record) is commonly used to alias a hostname to another hostname.

- An **MX record** is a mail exchanger record that specifies a domain SMTP email server. This record is the corporate email gateway to route outgoing to the Internet and incoming emails from external servers.

- An **NS record** is a name server record that specifies a domain primary and backup name server.

- A **PTR record** is a reverse-lookup pointer record that contains the hostname that matches a certain IP address.

- A **TXT record** is a text record that allows organizations to publish information related to a host or other name, like readable information about a server, network, data center, DKIM, and DMARC, among others.

- An **SOA record** is a start of authority record that contains administrative information about the zone indicating the zone authoritative name server, domain administrator contact information, and other relevant information.

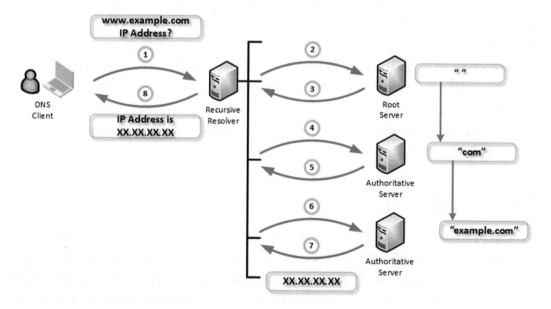

Figure 4-2. *Simplified DNS query process*

Internal DNS Servers

Internal DNS servers are used internally to resolve names and other information related to internal corporate assets. Usually, when they are requested to resolve names (or other information) from an external domain, they forward those requests to a predefined forwarder DNS server. An internal DNS server queries a DNS server outside the organization at a certain point.

It should be noted that DNS can be used as a covert channel, or DNS queries can indicate that internal hosts have been compromised, for example, by malware that is trying to access malicious websites. It is highly recommended to subscribe to or implement DNS security services such as DNS firewalls or DNS-layer security. All DNS queries are forwarded to this system and analyzed, and alert the SOC in case of malicious activity suspicions. DNS query logs can also be extremely useful to perform incident investigations.

External DNS Servers

Corporate external DNS servers are authoritative DNS servers accessible from the Internet with all the DNS records related to the organization domain. These servers return the IP address related to an asset from the organization domain (e.g., website, mail gateway, etc.).

Being exposed to the Internet, these servers are susceptible to several types of attacks like DNS poisoning, DNS amplification (which leads to DDoS), or DNS hijacking. Therefore it is highly recommended to constantly monitor these servers or place them in an external hosting provider. Some organizations provide these servers as a service with additional security features.

Message Security

Email, or in broader terms, messaging, is the core of companies' communication, so it is the number one threat vector used by cyberattackers to find security gaps. Spoofing, ransomware, phishing, zero-day attacks, and *business email compromise* (BEC) are some examples. Although end-user education is the top mechanism to prevent these attacks from being successful, additional security measures, such as message security, can be implemented.

Incoming emails can be sent by malicious users pretending to be sending emails from trusted sources (spoofing). To detect that, DMARC (Domain-based Message Authentication, Reporting, and Conformance) (Figure 4-3) protocol authorizes and authenticates email senders. If they have defined a DMARC DNS entry, then the Secure Email gateways (receiving email server) would check for the existence of corresponding records. If the email passes the authentication, it is delivered and trusted. If the email cannot pass the authentication, then based on the policy, it is delivered, rejected, or quarantined.

```
dig txt _dmarc.gmail.com

; <<>> DiG 9.10.6 <<>> txt _dmarc.gmail.com
;; global options: +cmd
;; Got answer:
;; ->>HEADER<<- opcode: QUERY, status: NOERROR, id: 31885
;; flags: qr rd ra; QUERY: 1, ANSWER: 1, AUTHORITY: 0, ADDITIONAL: 1

;; OPT PSEUDOSECTION:
; EDNS: version: 0, flags:; udp: 1460
;; QUESTION SECTION:
;_dmarc.gmail.com.              IN      TXT

;; ANSWER SECTION:
_dmarc.gmail.com.        600    IN      TXT      "v=DMARC1; p=none; sp=quarantine;
rua=mailto:mailauth-reports@google.com"

;; Query time: 95 msec
;; SERVER: 192.168.10.1#53(192.168.10.1)
;; MSG SIZE  rcvd: 129
```

Figure 4-3. *DMARC record for gmail.com*

DMARC also uses two email authentication mechanisms, Sender Policy Framework (SPF) (Figure 4-4) and DomainKeys Identified Mail (DKIM), for better sender identification, which is called *identifier alignment*. SPF publishes the IP addresses that send the email from that sender domain name (Figure 4-5). In the example shown in Figure 4-6 SPF (the record for _netblocks.google.com), when someone sends an email from gmail.com, SPF tells the IP addresses authorized to send mail.

```
dig txt gmail.com

; <<>> DiG 9.10.6 <<>> txt gmail.com
;; global options: +cmd
;; Got answer:
;; ->>HEADER<<- opcode: QUERY, status: NOERROR, id: 52404
;; flags: qr rd ra; QUERY: 1, ANSWER: 2, AUTHORITY: 0, ADDITIONAL: 1

;; OPT PSEUDOSECTION:
; EDNS: version: 0, flags:; udp: 1460
;; QUESTION SECTION:
;gmail.com.                        IN      TXT

;; ANSWER SECTION:
gmail.com.                141     IN      TXT      "v=spf1 redirect=_spf.google.com"
gmail.com.                141     IN      TXT      "globalsign-smime-dv=CDYX+XFHUw2wml6/
Gb8+59BsH31KzUr6c1l2BPvqKX8="

;; Query time: 8 msec
;; SERVER: 192.168.10.1#53(192.168.10.1)
;; MSG SIZE  rcvd: 159
```

Figure 4-4. *SPF record for gmail.com, pointing to _spf.google.com*

```
dig txt _spf.google.com

; <<>> DiG 9.10.6 <<>> txt _spf.google.com
;; global options: +cmd
;; Got answer:
;; ->>HEADER<<- opcode: QUERY, status: NOERROR, id: 10566
;; flags: qr rd ra; QUERY: 1, ANSWER: 1, AUTHORITY: 0, ADDITIONAL: 1

;; OPT PSEUDOSECTION:
; EDNS: version: 0, flags:; udp: 1460
;; QUESTION SECTION:
;_spf.google.com.                  IN      TXT

;; ANSWER SECTION:
_spf.google.com. 238      IN      TXT      "v=spf1 include:_netblocks.google.com
include:_netblocks2.google.com include:_netblocks3.google.com ~all"

;; Query time: 7 msec
;; SERVER: 192.168.10.1#53(192.168.10.1)
;; MSG SIZE  rcvd: 160
```

Figure 4-5. *SPF record for _spf.google.com, pointing to _netblocks.google.com*

```
dig txt _netblocks.google.com

; <<>> DiG 9.10.6 <<>> txt _netblocks.google.com
;; global options: +cmd
;; Got answer:
;; ->>HEADER<<- opcode: QUERY, status: NOERROR, id: 16491
;; flags: qr rd ra; QUERY: 1, ANSWER: 1, AUTHORITY: 0, ADDITIONAL: 1

;; OPT PSEUDOSECTION:
; EDNS: version: 0, flags:; udp: 1460
;; QUESTION SECTION:
;_netblocks.google.com.            IN      TXT

;; ANSWER SECTION:
_netblocks.google.com.    64       IN      TXT       "v=spf1 ip4:35.190.247.0/24 ip4:64.233.160.0/19
ip4:66.102.0.0/20 ip4:66.249.80.0/20 ip4:72.14.192.0/18 ip4:74.125.0.0/16 ip4:108.177.8.0/21
ip4:173.194.0.0/16 ip4:209.85.128.0/17 ip4:216.58.192.0/19 ip4:216.239.32.0/19 ~all"

;; Query time: 8 msec
;; SERVER: 192.168.10.1#53(192.168.10.1)
;; MSG SIZE  rcvd: 286
```

Figure 4-6. *SPF record for _netblocks.google.com*

DKIM provides a similar thing by providing a digital signature to the outgoing message to show that the sender in the sender domain is authorized to send emails. The recipient email gateway can verify the signature by looking up the sender's public key (the *p* in Figure 4-7) published in the DNS record.

```
nslookup -type=txt 20161025._domainkey.gmail.com

Server:  192.168.10.1
Address: 192.168.10.1#53

Non-authoritative answer:
20161025._domainkey.gmail.com     text = "k=rsa;
p=MIIBIjANBgkqhkiG9w0BAQEFAAOCAQ8AMIIBCgKCAQEAviPGBk4ZB64UfSqWyAicdR7lodhytae+EYRQVtKDhM+1mXjEqRtP/
pDT3sBhazkmA48n2k5NJUyMEoO8nc2r6sUA+/Dom5jRBZp6qDKJOwjJ5R/OpHamlRG+YRJQqR"
"tqEgSiJWG7h7efGYWmh4URhFM9k9+rmG/CwCgwx7Et+c8OMlngaLl04/
bPmfpjdEyLWyNimk761CX6KymzYiRDNz1MOJOJ7OzFaS4PFbVLn0m5mf0HVNtBpPwWuCNvaFVflUYxEyblbB6h/
oWOPGbzoSgtRA47SHV53SwZjIsVpbq4LxUW9IxAEwYzGcSgZ4n5Q8X8TndowsDUzoccPFGhdwIDAQAB"
```

Figure 4-7. *DKIM value for gmail.com, the selector is 20161025*

These protocols are there to verify the sender. However, we still need some control over the email content. There are technologies to reject or quarantine the emails based on the reputation of the domain that the email is coming from; however, this configuration needs to be well adjusted because reputation is based on many blacklist providers, which do not publish the same information and sometimes these providers are blacklisting domains based on false-positive information. So, tomorrow you may see that a very valid domain is blocked due to a blacklist.

Regardless of the reputation, a verified legitimate sender can still send malicious content, e.g., a virus, malware, a malicious code with autoexecute or autodownload abilities like a macro-enabled attachment that downloads a payload when opened. Thus, antivirus, anti-malware, and anti-spyware technologies must also be implemented to analyze content, attachments, and any links mentioned in the email body, just like antivirus software on a PC. Some vendors are using sandboxing technologies to analyze the attachments. Some use cloud-based threat intelligence platforms or hashes of the files to check the authenticity of the file and sender and if it contains any malicious code. Most vendors are now checking the reputations of the links provided in the email body, including scanning URLs in attachments and managed (shortened) URLs, which also minimizes the risk of clicking a malicious link in the content.

Such technologies also allow security professionals to track if end users have received malicious emails and even clicked the links, which can be useful during containment.

Directory Integration for External Applications

For most organizations, LDAP (the most popular ones are Active Directory, OpenLDAP, and Lotus Domino) plays a central role in identity, authentication, and access management. It serves as *the* place for user identities, and it provides access control to on-prem systems such as file shares, networks, and applications.[18]

Although this works well in LAN or WAN environments, as organizations are shifting to cloud-based applications, there must be a connection to the LDAP Service that checks the credentials. Directory integration provides this connection.

There are several methods to integrate such cloud-based applications with corporate LDAP.

One method exposes LDAP to the Internet, which poses a great risk to your entire organization. A second method would be to create the same LDAP structure in the cloud and synchronize it often. Although it may work for smaller organizations, it imposes a huge overhead on IT administrators in larger environments. A third option would be to use Directory-as-a-Service models, where an agent placed on the internal LDAP can

---

[18] Please see Single Sign On.

synchronize users to the cloud-based directory. This serves as the bridge between the on-prem LDAP and cloud infrastructure. The last approach is often chosen because it is simple, available, and security features (access controls on who can access cloud services or MFA) can be implemented.

Sandbox

Sandboxes are isolated environments that simulate the end-user operating environment to run programs and test incoming files. Untested, unverified, untrusted attachments, files, codes, programs are run first in sandboxes to see the impact on the host. In the isolated environment, every change or attempt is recorded to analyze the malware thoroughly.

Sandboxing technologies are heavily used in evaluating and mapping the behavior of malware (Figure 4-8). Researchers can evaluate how malware infects and compromises a target host by creating an environment that mimics or replicates the targeted desktops. This provides a crucial input to contain the malware and restore it to a normal operation in a real-life incident.

Sandboxes can be implemented in security devices and applications, such as web and email gateways, IPS, or even software testing. They run the content first in the sandbox, analyze the behavior and then release it to the user. This process provides an additional layer of protection against zero-day attacks, ransomware, and stealthy attacks like APTs (advanced persistent threats). In software testing, the code is first to run in the sandbox, which gives the developer flexibility to play with the code and see the impact.

Sandboxing should not be confused with containers. Traditional containers such as Docker, Linux Containers (LXC), and Rocket (rkt) are still sharing the host OS kernel, which can be compromised through the container application if necessary. Security measures are not implemented.

SHA256:	76f52cba288145242a77a8762282d8d0e6d8fb3160b5fefb7b92649e503c62a1
File type:	EXE
Copyright:	
Version:	
Shell or compiler:	COMPILER:Microsoft Visual C++ 6.0

Key behaviour 🐞

Behaviour:	Kill process
Detail info:	C:\WINDOWS\tasksche.exe
Behaviour:	Get TickCount value
Detail info:	TickCount = 404125, SleepMilliseconds = 2000.
	TickCount = 409375, SleepMilliseconds = 7000.
	TickCount = 417675, SleepMilliseconds = 15050.
	TickCount = 417725, SleepMilliseconds = 15100.
	TickCount = 429075, SleepMilliseconds = 26200.
	TickCount = 429125, SleepMilliseconds = 26250.
	TickCount = 437187, SleepMilliseconds = 34250.
	TickCount = 445450, SleepMilliseconds = 42450.
	TickCount = 462712, SleepMilliseconds = 59650.
	TickCount = 470825, SleepMilliseconds = 67700.
	TickCount = 473875, SleepMilliseconds = 70750.
	TickCount = 488037, SleepMilliseconds = 84850.
	TickCount = 502350, SleepMilliseconds = 99100.
	TickCount = 502450, SleepMilliseconds = 99200.
	TickCount = 505450, SleepMilliseconds = 102200.
Behaviour:	Find resource in self with type of PE
Detail info:	(FindResourceA) hModule = 0x00000000, ResName: , ResType: R
Behaviour:	Elevate privilege of process
Detail info:	NT AUTHORITY\SYSTEM
Behaviour:	Set special directory property
Detail info:	C:\Documents and Settings\Administrator\Local Settings\Temporary Internet Files
	C:\Documents and Settings\Administrator\Local Settings\History
	C:\Documents and Settings\Administrator\Local Settings\Temporary Internet Files\Content.IE5
	C:\Documents and Settings\Administrator\Cookies
	C:\Documents and Settings\Administrator\Local Settings\History\History.IE5
	C:\Documents and Settings\LocalService\Local Settings\Temporary Internet Files

Figure 4-8. *Behavior analysis of a WannaCry variant by Tencent HABO[19]*

---

[19] www.virustotal.com/ui/file_behaviours/76f52cba288145242a77a8762282d8d0e6d8fb3160b
5fefb7b92649e503c62a1_Tencent%20HABO/html

File Integrity

File integrity monitoring is a change-detection mechanism to validate the integrity of a file, folder, or registry setting and compares the current state with a defined baseline.

Most of the FIM solutions are capable of detecting changes, additions, and deletions of system and application executables, critical configuration and parameter files, and log and audit files in various systems including servers, workstations, network devices, and notify security professionals for further investigation if it is expected or not. If it was not expected, then it could be caused by a malicious insider or a cybersecurity attack.

There are many agent-based or agentless FIM solutions in the market, but overall, the technology compares the current file state with a known previous state. If the changed content does not need to be known, the easiest FIM method is to monitor the changes in the checksum of the file or the folder. If the changed content (diff) is needed, the actual contents are indexed by the solution, showing what has changed. It should be noted that the latter consumes more storage and time than the former.

FIM tools, unfortunately, generate too much noise. Even in the BAU activity of an application, temporary files are created and deleted on the fly. During OS updates, lots of changes are happening in the system files. So, organizations must find a way to implement FIM solutions to the ITSM or change management platforms. By this integration, the FIM solution would know the timeframe for an approved change and expect changes in the defined folders and create lesser noise and lesser false positives.

Encrypted Email

You use SMTP, POP, or IMAP when you send or receive an email. They are the protocols used to transmit email messages from a client to an email server and from one email server to another. They do not employ encryption natively, making the email exchange prone to eavesdropping, sniffing, and MitM attacks.

Nowadays, most email communication is encrypted in the transport layer (STARTTLS, for example, is the extension for SMTP to encrypt the channel, Figure 4-9); however, not all systems support TLS. In addition, end users would not know whether the recipient's email server supported TLS or not. They would only write the email and then click the Send button.

```
telnet aspmx.l.google.com 25
Trying TLS on aspmx.l.google.com[142.250.123.26:25] (10)
220 mx.google.com ESMTP u7si12575944jae.78 - gsmtp
EHLO test.mydomainthatiboughtforonlytesting.com
250-mx.google.com at your service, [40.76.159.115]
250-SIZE 157286400
250-8BITMIME
250-STARTTLS
250-ENHANCEDSTATUSCODES
250-PIPELINING
250-CHUNKING
250 SMTPUTF8
STARTTLS
220 2.0.0 Ready to start TLS
                  SSLVersion in use: TLSv1_3
                  Cipher in use: TLS_AES_256_GCM_SHA384
                  Perfect Forward Secrecy: yes
                  Certificate #1 of 4 (sent by MX):
                  Cert signed by: #2
                  Cert VALIDATED: ok
                  Cert Hostname VERIFIED (aspmx.l.google.com = mx.google.com |
DNS:smtp.google.com | DNS:aspmx.l.google.com | DNS:alt1.aspmx.l.google.com |
DNS:alt2.aspmx.l.google.com | DNS:alt3.aspmx.l.google.com | DNS:alt4.aspmx.l.google.com | DNS:gmail-
smtp-in.l.google.com | DNS:alt1.gmail-smtp-in.l.google.com | DNS:alt2.gmail-smtp-in.l.google.com |
DNS:alt3.gmail-smtp-in.l.google.com | DNS:alt4.gmail-smtp-in.l.google.com | DNS:gmr-smtp-
in.l.google.com | DNS:alt1.gmr-smtp-in.l.google.com | DNS:alt2.gmr-smtp-in.l.google.com |
DNS:alt3.gmr-smtp-in.l.google.com | DNS:alt4.gmr-smtp-in.l.google.com | DNS:mx1.smtp.goog |
DNS:mx2.smtp.goog | DNS:mx3.smtp.goog | DNS:mx4.smtp.goog | DNS:aspmx2.googlemail.com |
DNS:aspmx3.googlemail.com | DNS:aspmx4.googlemail.com | DNS:aspmx5.googlemail.com | DNS:gmr-
mx.google.com)

Not Valid Before: Aug 30 03:06:25 2021 GMT
Not Valid After: Nov 22 03:06:24 2021 GMT

                  subject= /CN=mx.google.com
                  issuer= /C=US/O=Google Trust Services LLC/CN=GTS CA 1C3
                  Certificate #2 of 4 (sent by MX):
                  Cert signed by: #3, #4
                  Cert VALIDATED: ok

Not Valid Before: Aug 13 00:00:42 2020 GMT
Not Valid After: Sep 30 00:00:42 2027 GMT

                  subject= /C=US/O=Google Trust Services LLC/CN=GTS CA 1C3
                  issuer= /C=US/O=Google Trust Services LLC/CN=GTS Root R1
                  Certificate #3 of 4 (added from CA Root Store):
                  Cert signed by: #3, #4
                  Cert VALIDATED: ok

Not Valid Before: Jun 22 00:00:00 2016 GMT
Not Valid After: Jun 22 00:00:00 2036 GMT

                  subject= /C=US/O=Google Trust Services LLC/CN=GTS Root R1
                  issuer= /C=US/O=Google Trust Services LLC/CN=GTS Root R1
                  Certificate #4 of 4 (sent by MX):
                  Cert is unsigned
                  Cert VALIDATED:

Not Valid Before: Jun 19 00:00:42 2020 GMT
Not Valid After: Jan 28 00:00:42 2028 GMT

                  subject= /C=US/O=Google Trust Services LLC/CN=GTS Root R1
                  issuer= /C=BE/O=GlobalSign nv-sa/OU=Root CA/CN=GlobalSign Root CA
EHLO test.mydomainthatiboughtforonlytesting.com
250-mx.google.com at your service, [40.76.159.115]
250-SIZE 157286400
250-8BITMIME
250-ENHANCEDSTATUSCODES
250-PIPELINING
250-CHUNKING
250 SMTPUTF8
MAIL FROM:<test@mydomainthatiboughtforonlytesting.com>
250 2.1.0 OK u7si12575944jae.78 - gsmtp
Sender is OK
QUIT
221 2.0.0 closing connection u7si12575944jae.78 - gsmtp
```

Figure 4-9. *A simple SMTP chat with gmail.com*

Therefore, there should be a transparent process for the users so that when they need to send a confidential email to an external recipient, they should not worry if the channel is encrypted. There are mainly two ways to ensure security when sending emails.

The first one is the secured web interfaces. In these systems, when the email gateway catches a message with one or more external recipients, and the classification is "confidential," it stores the message in the external web interface of the platform and only sends a link to the recipient. If the recipient has not registered yet to the platform, it also sends an email for registration. When the recipient registers to the system, logs himself/herself in (preferably with MFA), and sees the message in an external web interface, which is already HTTPS, it is protected against eavesdropping or sniffing.

Second is the key or certificate-based email exchange (i.e., S/MIME, PGP, or GNU Privacy Guard). Senders and recipients exchange keys or certificates before the email messaging and then encrypt the message with the correspondent's key or certificate so that only the private key owner can decrypt the message. This method is not as smooth and transparent as the former, and it requires supported email servers and email clients. For example, most webmail clients do not support S/MIME.

On-Premises Support Controls

Access Control

Every client (human or machine[20]) has an identity or unique user ID in the system that he/she/it is authenticated with. In addition, the group the user ID belongs to is also kept in the device. This user ID or group is used for allowing or disallowing content (file access or privileges) to the user. This is the essence of *access control.*

Most modern operating systems have *access control lists* (ACLs), which is the table containing user rights for each data object. Whenever a user attempts to read, write or access a file, the OS verifies if the user has the appropriate right in the ACL. If the rights are assigned by the owner of the object, the access control model is *discretionary*

---

[20] No, not the Skynet. Merely the application accounts or service accounts are meant here.

access control (DAC). If you assign groups or roles to the users and administrators assign privileges based on roles, then it is *role-based access control.* Most web applications use this type of approach for better visibility and saving time. Separate roles are created for different sections, where users can write on one section but only read other sections.

There is also a rule-based access control model, which uses rules for access for all users. These are typically used in firewalls. If further attributes are added to the model, it is called *attribute-based access control.*

Mandatory access control is based on the classification or sensitivity level assigned to the object. Data subjects can only access the object if they have sufficient clearance.

As in the examples, access controls are everywhere in the organization (files, folders, shares, applications, firewall rules, or physical access controls), making it a prime target of attackers. Typically, malicious actors spoof identities to bypass the ACLs or gain more privileges. OWASP considers *broken access control* the most serious web application security risk in their OWASP Top 10 2021.[21] MITRE (Table 4-5) has a good relationship matrix for this type of attack.[22]

Table 4-5. *MITRE CAPEC-151 Identity Spoofing Relationships*

Nature	Type	ID	Name
ParentOf	S	89	Pharming
ParentOf	S	98	Phishing
ParentOf	S	194	Fake the Source of Data
ParentOf	S	195	Principal Spoof
ParentOf	S	473	Signature Spoof
PeerOf	D	665	Exploitation of Thunderbolt Protection Flaws
CanFollow	D	16	Dictionary-based Password Attack
CanFollow	S	49	Password Brute Forcing
CanFollow	S	50	Password Recovery Exploitation

(continued)

---

[21] https://owasp.org/Top10/A01_2021-Broken_Access_Control/
[22] https://capec.mitre.org/data/definitions/151.html

Table 4-5. (*continued*)

Nature	Type	ID	Name
CanFollow	D	55	Rainbow Table Password Cracking
CanFollow	D	70	Try Common or Default Usernames and Passwords
CanFollow	M	94	Adversary in the Middle (AiTM)
CanFollow	D	509	Kerberoasting
CanFollow	S	555	Remote Services with Stolen Credentials
CanFollow	M	560	Use of Known Domain Credentials
CanFollow	D	561	Windows Admin Shares with Stolen Credentials
CanFollow	D	565	Password Spraying
CanFollow	D	568	Capture Credentials via Keylogger
CanFollow	S	600	Credential Stuffing
CanFollow	D	644	Use of Captured Hashes (Pass the Hash)
CanFollow	D	645	Use of Captured Tickets (Pass the Ticket)
CanFollow	S	652	Use of Known Kerberos Credentials
CanFollow	S	653	Use of Known Windows Credentials

Organizations need to centralize access control, review the ACLs or implement multi-factor authentication mechanisms to prevent unauthorized access. Access should be denied by default and only enabled to individuals with a business need with the least privileges.[23] Failed login attempts should be monitored, and the security operations center should be alerted. User accounts are needed to be locked after certain failed attempts. A good list of recommendations can be found in OWASP Proactive Control: Enforce Access Controls[24] and the OWASP Authorization cheat sheet[25] for better application development.

---

[23] www.cisecurity.org/controls/access-control-management/

[24] https://owasp.org/www-project-proactive-controls/v3/en/c7-enforce-access-controls

[25] https://cheatsheetseries.owasp.org/cheatsheets/Authorization_Cheat_Sheet.html

Secure VLAN Segmentation

VLAN segmentation, also known as zoning, implements physical and/or logical access controls to separate systems with different security and/or functionality needs. The simplest example for logical controls would be a firewall or a router configured to prevent traffic from passing between networks or VLANs. Having separate cabling for different purposes and/or different sensitivity levels would be an example of physical segmentation.

Segmentation is one of the key access controls in a corporate environment, which enables granularity. When properly implemented, VLAN segmentation provides better visibility on the network, improved mapping of the data flows, and better implementation of security. Security professionals can better tailor the needs for the defined VLANs or different types of traffic. For example, VOIP traffic can be isolated from the desktop workstation zones, both for security purposes (i.e., to prevent or hinder eavesdropping) and for efficient networking (i.e., to reduce congestion and avoid bottlenecks in the network) (Figure 4-10).

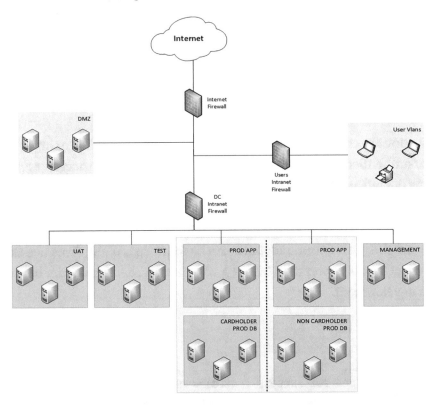

Figure 4-10. *Sample VLAN segmentations*

By applying segmentation controls, security professionals can minimize the risk of lateral movement by an attacker from a compromised system to another. For example, if a public-facing application or an internal endpoint is compromised, the attacker would have gained access to the entire organization if it was a flat network. However, if access control lists are applied, that server would have been in a DMZ and even compromised, it would be contained in its segment, or at least, the movement would not be as easy as flat networks.

In a corporate environment, the segmentation should be done by considering the two golden rules for any access control mechanism: *least privileged* and *need to know*. Users, applications, devices, or systems must be separated based on their accessing other networks. Moreover, segmentation should be done based on the criticality of the traffic, service nature (Table 4-6). When establishing segments, the following should be considered.

Table 4-6. *VLAN Segmentation Considerations*

Criticality	Perimeter VLANs are segregated according to the hosted system's criticality (e.g., highly critical, critical, non-critical).
Service Nature	Perimeter VLANs are segregated according to the hosted system's nature (e.g., cardholder data environment, front-end, middleware, database, fileserver, printer and scanner devices, ATMs, POS devices).
Type	Perimeter VLANs are segregated according to the hosted systems environment (e.g., DMZ, production, staging, quality, development, third-party access, extranet).

It can be used for quicker and more efficient compliance efforts, such as reducing the number of systems in scope for PCI DSS so that only those systems are required to undergo PCI DSS assessment, which would be a cost-effective, time-saving approach. It would also decrease the threat surface for the cardholder data environment. As a result, the risk to the organization would be reduced.

One key consideration for segmentation is not to have so many different segments, which leads to over-segmentation. This causes network connectivity issues, degrading performance, and non-sustainable access control lists.

Security Baselines

Security baselines (often called *benchmarks* or *configuration checks*) are minimally accepted recommendations used to harden OS, application, database, or service. They typically contain several settings, parameters, and security considerations for the defined system. Most of the requirements in a benchmark are scored to compare the overall security posture of the target system with others in the same region, business function, industry, or type of application. Most of the time, they complement vulnerability scanning. Thus many vulnerability management tools provide scanning for benchmarks.

Unfortunately, security hardening and business functioning are opposite sides of a seesaw. Where you want full security, there is always a compromise on the business end, which your users never want to see. So, for systems to be resilient to threats while still working efficiently and effectively, security baselines must be fine-tuned. They must apply to all server and workstation deployments to avoid gaps in the security posture.

Many industry-accepted, mature standards have impact levels for the considerations of security professionals. Low-impact or level-1 security baselines are generally base recommendations that can be implemented more quickly than those without any major performance impact. They intend to lower the attack surface while keeping the business functioning. High-impacts or level-2 baselines can be used where security is a must; however, if they are blindly implemented, there may be some adverse effect to the performance of the function.

Security professionals can create their own security baselines from scratch, use the following baselines, or a combination of where they can adjust the parameters that would fit their environment without any compromise on the intended security level.

The following are noticeable security baselines.

- CIS benchmarks[26]

- NIST SP 800-53b Control Baselines for Information Systems and Organizations[27]

- Microsoft Security Baselines[28]

- Security Technical Implementation Guides (STIGs)[29]

---

[26] www.cisecurity.org/cis-benchmarks/

[27] https://csrc.nist.gov/publications/detail/sp/800-53b/final

[28] https://aka.ms/baselines and https://techcommunity.microsoft.com/t5/microsoft-security-baselines/bg-p/Microsoft-Security-Baselines

[29] https://public.cyber.mil/stigs/

Redundancy

In its broadest terms, system redundancy means that if a system goes down, another takes its place. Critical systems should be highly available to rapidly recover from any interruption through hot, warm, or cold backups, active-passive, or active-active redundancy.

The lack of redundancy in mission-critical components is called a *single point of failure*. In security architecture design, it is important to implement redundancies, fault-tolerant systems, for information security devices.

Unfortunately, in most cases, redundancy implies the purchase of additional hardware or software, which increases costs. For a cost-effective approach, the following can be considered.

- Revenue or income-generating computing systems must have 99.99% availability, whereas, for others, 99% availability is accepted.

- Supporting security infrastructure should have a similar approach.

- RPO (*recovery point objectives*) and RTO (*recovery time objectives*) values should be planned and decided. Better (smaller) values mean higher operational costs (more storage, more hardware, etc.). Higher values mean lower operational costs, but you may risk losing important transactional data. The design should aim to reduce the cost *and* loss to a minimum. Less redundancy can be implemented in systems that are less susceptible to failures.

Load Balancing

Load balancing is distributing the computing loads over a cluster of (redundant) resources to maximize the system's efficiency. Current computing systems need to handle millions of requests per day, and sometimes it is not easy for a single system to respond to all requests in time. Thus, additional servers or systems should be added to the environment to process the requests and share the load. However, a front "gatekeeper" or a supervisor should distribute the load between servers based on several factors such as availability or the service/function requested. This supervisor should know if the back-end servers are live and ready to take requests or too busy to handle any requests. Moreover, this supervisor should understand requests and forward them to the correct server for that particular function. These devices are called *load balancers* (Figure 4-11).

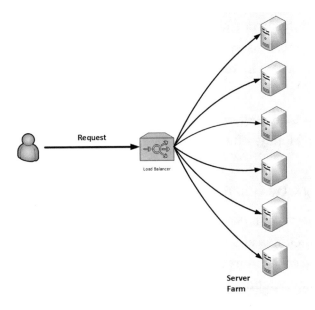

Figure 4-11. *Load balancing*

Load balancing is used for the following.

- **Scalability**: If you know you need more requests coming, you may increase the back-end servers.

- **Redundancy** (high availability (HA)): If one server is down, the load balancer knows that it should send the requests to others, which maintains the overall high availability of the application.

- **Maintainability**: Upgrades and updates need reboot time. When one server is rebooting, the others can still respond.

- **Security**: Modern load balancers also check for the request for signs of malicious content such as SQL injection, cross-site scripting attacks, or main DDoS attacks.

- **Acceleration**: Load balancers can offload or terminate TLS communication on themselves so that HTTP traffic (instead of HTTPS) is sent to the server without any TLS overhead. In addition, load balancers can store static content and respond from their cache.

Load balancers distribute the loads based on several techniques.

- **Round robin**: The basic load balancing technique where the request is forwarded one by one to every server in the cluster sequentially, without any prioritization.

- **Weighted round robin**: The same as the round robin, but back-end servers are weighted so that a high number of responses are sent to the most powerful server.

- **Randomized static**: Requests are forwarded to the servers randomly.

- **Least connection**: Requests are sent to the server with the least number of active sessions. The traffic is distributed based on the server load.

- **Weighted least connection**: Same as the least connection but back-end servers are weighted. If two servers have the same number of active sessions, the request is forwarded to the server with the higher weight.

- **Least response time method**: Requests are sent to the server having the least response time.

- **Least bandwidth method**: Requests are sent to the server with the least traffic measured in megabits per second (Mbps).

- **Hashing**: Requests are directed to the servers based on hashes of various information of the incoming packet, such as source/ destination IP address, port number, URL, or domain name, from the incoming packet. Some content-aware load balancers are using this method.

151

Load balancers distribute the load between servers (Layer 4, server load balancing, or SLB). Industry is now switching to application delivery controllers (Layer 7), where load is distributed between application nodes in an application and in a content-aware manner.

For example, in a user authentication request to authenticate, the conventional load balancer would send the whole request to the application server, which would process that information. In contrast, in ADC, the request would be directed to the authentication module of the application node, where it would be handled only by this module, making other nodes free for other requests.

Encryption

We have always used secretive ways to communicate with each other. Even older civilizations used cryptography (e.g., substitutions like a Caesar cipher or a Vigenère cipher) to hide the messages. Enigma coding machines were used during World War II to cipher radio messages. The purpose is always the same; you have the original message (*plaintext*), submit it to a *cryptographic algorithm* to encode it (or *encrypt*), and, as a result, you get a *ciphertext* that only people who know how to decode it (or *decrypt*) can retrieve the original message. All cryptosystems rely on algorithms, mathematical sets of calculations. It is crucial to protect the encryption key for publicly available cryptographic algorithms. Algorithms, however, can be made public (Kerckhoffs' principle) for better analysis of their weaknesses.

Confidentiality ensures that data remains private at rest, in transit, and in use. By encrypting data, you would ensure its confidentiality, as long as it is not decrypted along any of those phases. Even though data is encrypted, it is prone to cryptographic attacks such as analytic attacks, implementation attacks, and statistical attacks. The ciphertext is also susceptible to brute-force or rainbow tables attacks. If you have sufficient ciphertext and know the plaintext language, there are some methods to retrieve the plaintext by frequency analysis or birthday or replay attacks. This is the primary reason for the need to rotate the keys used for encryption.

Symmetric or asymmetric encryption algorithms are used based on the type of information you can require confidentiality.

Overall, organizations rely on these methods to protect their data. Portable devices are always prone to get lost or stolen, and if they contain sensitive information, they can harm the organization in various ways. Hence, full-disk encryption technologies are present to transparently encrypt the disk, mostly utilizing the Trusted Platform Module (TPM). Even if stolen, no one except the person knowing the PIN would have access to the disk, hence sensitive information.

Similarly, files in file shares can be encrypted. Many available solutions in the market can perform file and folder encryption. The same principle mentioned earlier can be applied to databases, where sensitive data is encrypted and stored in tables in the ciphertext. This would ensure that even DBAs, along with cyberattackers, cannot see the actual data. This assumes that the decryption key is stored elsewhere in a protected area. Transparent data encryption (TDE) technologies are also present to ensure on-the-fly encryption/decryption using the database encryption keys.

Encrypting your data at rest wherever it is stored does not provide encryption across communication channels. For that, the transport layer should be encrypted (i.e., TLS). HTTPS is the secure version of plaintext HTTP traffic, using TLS certificates. These certificates, ideally, are generated by a trusted certificate authority (CA). If the browser trusts the CA, secure communication between the client and server can be established.

Similarly, the secure version of Telnet, Secure Shell (SSH), provides end-to-end encryption using passwords, keys, or certificates to securely connect and administer the remote device.

VPNs should use secure channels by implementing TLS (as in the case of SSL VPNs) or IPsec as the traffic is transmitted through a public network, the Internet.

Wi-Fi networks also use encryption for communication. Wi-Fi Protected Access (WPA2 or WPA3) provides encryption to the network. Organizations can improve security using a certificate-based system to authenticate the connecting device, following the standard 802.11X.

Multi-tier and Multi-layer

Multi-tiering and multi-layering are some of the implementations of the concept of defense-in-depth.

Multi-layering

A multi-layer architecture allows the application of different security controls between each layer. If one layer is compromised, the remaining layer can still be protected.

One example of multi-layering is the implementation of transactional websites, where applications should have a presentation layer, a business logic or application layer, and a data layer.

- **Presentation layer**: The end-user graphical interface

- **Application layer**: The application processes requests from the presentation and applies the business logic rules

- **Data layer**: Typically, database servers with persistent data are accessed and manipulated by the application layer

Multi-tiering

A multi-tier deployment architecture deploys multiple subnets in the DMZ between the corporate networks and the Internet. Firewalls appropriately segment systems with strict filtering rules where devices residing in different tiers but the same layer should not communicate. For example, an organization can implement different tiers for their websites' front ends in the same layer, having a tier for their public websites with unauthenticated services, another tier for remote access front ends, and another tier for customers authenticated websites (e.g., Internet banking).

TLS Decryption

While minimal to low, encryption creates overhead on the server or the device. The overhead starts impacting the system's general performance when there is too much traffic. Overall, application servers should not be the ones terminating the TLS connection because it degrades the performance of the application component. Instead, ideally, the TLS communication should be terminated at the load balancer or WAF interfaces, which are designed for this process, and the connection between the network device and the server can be in cleartext. This would ensure that the application would process the request without the overhead, increasing response time. Of course, there are some shortcomings of this setup. Someone sniffing the network between the device and the application can collect highly sensitive information. In these cases, additional security features, such as network access control can come into the picture.

TLS decryption is also needed for inspection of the traffic. Secure communication often blinds the security and monitoring devices, which can be used maliciously for exfiltration of data or malware communication with a command and control (C&C) site. Thus, it is crucial to decrypt and inspect the TLS traffic as privacy laws allow. Using the root certificate on clients, acting as a certificate authority for HTTPS requests (unless it is using certificate pinning), it is possible to decrypt the traffic, perform the inspection required and permitted, and then re-encrypt the traffic before sending it to its original destination. There are, as mentioned, some privacy concerns over such inspection, so organizations can choose to implement exceptions for specific site categories such as banking, health, or government. It should be noted that, with the availability of TLSv1.3, Perfect Forward Secrecy (PFS) may require additional steps to decrypt the traffic.

Perimeter Static Routing

To avoid exposure to misconfigurations, automatic routing protocols should not be implemented between perimeter networks.

Ideally, routing between perimeter networks should be configured manually, and all traffic routed through and filtered by firewalls.

Heartbeat Interfaces

Heartbeat is a concept used when implementing high availability in security devices like firewalls. When implementing a cluster, regardless of the implementation type, active-passive or active-active, each cluster member device must know the other member(s) state. This is implemented with heartbeat interfaces.

For clusters of two devices, a heartbeat can be done with dedicated interfaces directly connected using patch cables without connecting other network devices like switches or hubs. These devices can be compromised or overloaded and cause heartbeat delays.

For clusters with more than two devices, switches can connect heartbeat interfaces in a distinct Layer 2 VLAN to avoid any impact from other traffic.

Disaster Recovery

Every organization has witnessed (or witnessed) a disaster in its life cycle. Whether it is a cyber incident or a natural disaster, IT systems are impacted by shutting down or some of the data lost. Disasters can happen anytime, so organizations need to be resilient enough to mitigate their effects from them. Proper plans and procedures should be designed, implemented, and tested before any actual disruption occurs in the organization.

To understand the mission-critical business systems and find their RTO and RPO, a *business impact analysis* (BIA) should be performed. BIA lists the threats to the business, the likelihood of the risks, the potential impact, and the human and technology resources needed to recover the business in case of a disruption. BIAs give an idea of the RPO and RTO values of the services provided so that a *business continuity plan* (BCP) is designed. It should be noted that the BCP should cover the organization's capabilities, so priorities should be defined.

BIAs are also important to identify the single point of failure. The disruptions mostly occur because of these systems. Nowadays, most mission-critical systems can work active-active (one in production, one in DR site), but budgetary limitations may cause organizations to purchase only one device. Then, cheaper backup alternatives (full backup, incremental backups, or differential backup) can be used.

Security professionals should not simply plan the BCP and wait for the disaster. The availability aspect of the systems should be by the design of the architecture. For example, when designing a new project, based on the budget provided, a redundant server, a secondary PSU connected to a different electrical network, or disks for RAID can be considered for fault-tolerant services.

Even though every system can have fault tolerance by itself or backups in place, it does not protect the building. Such facilities require electricity, HVAC, Internet connection and many others. Any failure in these areas degrade the performance or even cause service disruptions. Then, alternate processing sites should be considered. These sites include the following.

- **Cold sites** are standby facilities with electrical and HVAC equipment but no hardware or software and no data. They have the longest time to be active, between days to weeks.

- **Hot sites** are near-real-time sites with running hardware, software, and data, ready to become the main data center in one DNS update. They have the shortest time to activate, so they have the best RTO and RPO values, although costly to build and maintain.

- **Warm sites** have electrical and HVAC equipment, hardware, and software but no data. Time to activate is the time to restore the data to the storage units.

- **Mobile sites** are usually cold or warm sites, provide easy relocation, but performance is lower than other sites.

- **Service bureaus** are third-party companies that provide backup and recovery services and locations, servers, and storage units.

- **Cloud service providers** deliver "as a service" offerings. IaaS, or infrastructure as a service, provides cloud-hosted physical and virtual servers, storage, and networking. PaaS, or platform as a service, is a ready-to-use, cloud-hosted platform for developing, running, maintaining, and managing applications with zero OS maintenance. SaaS, or software as a service, is ready-to-use, cloud-hosted application software where you only provide data.

Larger organizations may choose to decrease backup and restore costs by having *mutual assistance agreements* (MAA) or reciprocal agreements with other companies having similar hardware and software. When disaster happens to one company, it can use the hardware/software equipment of the other company. Although confidentiality and competition are an issue here, state regulators may mandate companies to sign such agreements to prevent any disruption for the sake of public benefit.

Backup and restore plans, also known as business continuity plans, must be tested annually. This testing can be a read-through test, where the plan is only read to the audience, or through a more structured and scenario-based walk-through, also known as a tabletop exercise. Simulation testing can be performed with all the required personnel ready in the exercise. More ready organizations can choose to have a full interruption test, where they fully switch to a recovery site or only relocate personnel to have parallel testing.

Time Synchronization

Time is the quickest and simplest common reference point for all computing systems. Certificates, Kerberos tickets, events all rely on the accuracy and reliability of time. When two systems, one client and one server, are significantly different from each other, the certificate handshake is not completed, so a secure connection cannot be made. Moreover, inaccurate time means inaccurate time-outs for session management such as Kerberos tickets, which causes users to drop their sessions.

Time synchronization is also crucial in auditing and forensics. When SIEM tools correlate events to find a true incident, they rely on the accuracy of time.

In a centralized network, time can be provided by at least a one-time server, which also synchronizes time from a trusted external source time. These outside time sources can use NTP (Network Time Protocol), GPS (Global Positioning System), CDMA technology, or other time signals such as Irig-B, WWVB, JJY, and DCF77.

When it comes to NTP and time synchronization, there is a hierarchical system of time servers in a network, with stratum levels between 0 and 15. The levels indicate the device's distance to the reference clock.

Stratum 0 is a high-precision timekeeping device (e.g., an atomic clock, GPS, or another radio clock) with very little or no delay. Stratum 0 servers cannot be used on the network, so stratum 1 devices get the time from stratum 0, then stratum 1 provides time through stratum 2 servers or clients, and so on to the next stratum level. Considering that there would be delays between stratum levels, the higher the stratum number, the more inaccurate the time. Stratum 16 is considered unsynchronized.

When security professionals decide on time synchronization, they should use the best suited method for their needs and capabilities.

Although NTP from trusted sources works fine most of the time, it is not free of attacks, misuse, and abuse.[30]

---

[30] https://en.wikipedia.org/wiki/NTP_server_misuse_and_abuse

Log Concentrator

Log concentrators, also known as log collectors or aggregators, are the systems that backup the logs from the devices in near real time; even when the device generating the logs is compromised, logs are protected. They can also be used as a bandwidth saver, as some concentrators compress the required logs in a compressed file ready to be sent to SIEM (Figure 4-12). Most concentrators support encryption, so the shipped logs are sent over a secure channel, ensuring the integrity and confidentiality of the logs.

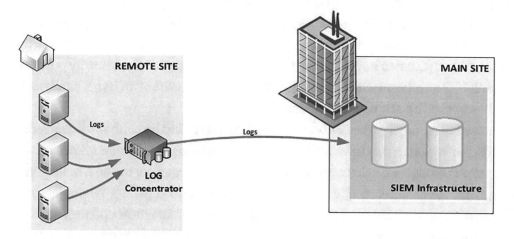

Figure 4-12. *Log concentrator*

Some log concentrators are "write-once" hardware designed to protect highly sensitive logs. Most of these systems reside in either logically or physically separated zones.

Routing and Management Networks

Management Networks

Management and other traffic not directly related to production (e.g., backups) should be segregated from the remaining VLANs to avoid any possible impact over business traffic and avoid being impacted in case of any compromise of the "business" networks. Device management traffic like iLO (integrated lights out) or iDRAC, network devices, security devices, virtualization platforms should be done through distinct VLANs.

Perimeter Routing Networks

Depending on the number of tiers and layers implemented in the DMZ and the need to connect some of them, there may be the need to implement a routing network that directly connects all perimeter firewalls to ensure connectivity inside the DMZ.

Centralized Management

In large organizations, where distant/overseas offices are present, management of network and security devices may become a challenging task to follow. IT and security professionals must spend lots of time configuring changes or applying patches to these devices. As it is prone to human error, this may result in gaps in the security posture. In addition, it may be an extremely difficult task to troubleshoot an issue, as all devices must be checked one by one to pinpoint the problem.

Instead of managing devices one by one, devices should be centrally managed. Security professionals can have full visibility, easier change implementations, and even automation through a single console. Most security devices now support management through APIs or proprietary communication protocols and consoles. When devices are onboarded to centralized management, security policies, signature updates, or patches can be distributed and managed from a central dashboard, increasing efficiency and effectiveness and reducing cost and risk. From the centralized management platform, devices can be easily monitored, and any issues regarding availability can be detected.

Physical Network Segmentation

VLAN hopping is an attack where the attacker can move between VLANs in the same switch. Although most switch vendors have effective protection mechanisms for this kind of attack, organizations should have physical network segmentation between each layer of their perimeter and implement distinct switches for each one of those layers. For example, one switch to support all networks directly connected to the Internet outside the perimeter, another switch to support all presentation layer networks, another switch to support all application layer networks, and another to support data layer networks.

Switch redundancy is also recommended.

Sinkhole

A sinkhole is a relatively simple to implement anomaly detection concept. It is very useful to detect misconfigurations and malicious activities.

Considering that internal networks should only route traffic to internal IP addresses and exclusively to the corporate address space, a device (e.g., router) can be configured as the corporate default router where all traffic to non-corporate IP addresses (public and private) or non-defined networks is redirected. Since that sinkhole should not receive any traffic in normal conditions, whenever it receives any network traffic, it can mean that there is a misconfiguration, the network is being manually or automatically probed, or a compromised device is trying to contact a command and control (C&C) external IP address.

A sinkhole must be integrated with SIEM, and the appropriate use cases must be defined to maximize the SOC response effectiveness.

The sinkhole concept has evolved to *network detection and response* (NDR), where enterprise network traffic is continuously analyzed, monitored, and compared with "learned normal network behavior" baseline. The NDR generates an alert whenever suspicious anomalous network traffic patterns are detected.

Public Key Infrastructure

Public key infrastructure (PKI) is the infrastructure to manage digital certificates and encryption with a public key that protects communications between the server and client. With PKI, server and client can be unknown to each other. It is not required for them to exchange keys or certificates before the actual handshake, as long as their certificates were issued by a certificate authority trusted by the client. PKI is mainly based on digital certificates that verify the identity of the devices or users.

PKI has three main components: digital certificates, certificate authority, and registration authority.

Digital certificates (conforming to X.509)[31] are electronic identification for users, devices, websites, and organizations.

---

[31] www.itu.int/rec/T-REC-X.509/en

A CA acts as a notary service for digital certificates. They issue and authenticate the digital identities of the users based on a hierarchical setup. For example, if a browser trusts one certificate authority, it also trusts every certificate issued by that CA until the expiration date of the CA root, intermediate certificates, or the actual certificate itself. For someone (or some organization) to obtain a certificate from a publicly trusted CA, the organization must provide a certificate request and identity information. After identity verification, CA issues a certificate (public key) to the organization to install the website. Anyone who trusts that CA would trust the digitally signed website certificate.

A *registration authority* (RA), on the other hand, is authorized by the CA to receive requests from users, collect and verify identity, and submit information to the CA.

It should be noted that the certificates should be checked to see if they are still valid using *certificate revocation lists* (CRL) or the Online Certificate Status Protocol (OCSP).

PKI can be used for the following purposes.

- Securing email communication (either the email or the transaction)

- Securing web communications (HTTPS)

- Securing other communication channels

- Digitally signing software code and applications (ensuring its integrity is kept along with any transmit)

- Encrypting and decrypting files, folders, disks

- Smartcard authentication

- Device authentication when connecting to the network

Public Key and Private Key

Meet Alice and Bob,[32] two fictional characters who explain any cryptographic system, and this book is no exception.

Alice and Bob wish to exchange information without other parties eavesdropping.

---

[32] Rivest, Ron L.; Shamir, Adi; Adleman, Len (February 1, 1978). "A Method for Obtaining Digital Signatures and Public-key Cryptosystems". Communications of the ACM. 21 (2): 120–126. CiteSeerX 10.1.1.607.2677. doi:10.1145/359340.359342. ISSN 0001-0782. S2CID 2873616.

Alice has a symmetric key, meaning that it can encrypt and decrypt data with the same key. Alice encrypts the plaintext and sends the ciphertext to Bob, and if Bob has the same secret key, he can decrypt and read the data. This process requires the secret key to be shared to all parties that read the ciphertext. This is called *symmetric encryption*. Although it is a fast process, the main drawback is that the distribution has to be secure because anyone sniffing the traffic when the key is being shared can see the key and use it. It also does not provide any non-repudiation because anyone can use the key and, if the key is compromised, everyone should change the keys. Examples are AES, 3DES, and International Data Encryption Algorithm (IDEA).

There are two parts of a key in asymmetric encryption: private and public. The public key can be distributed to anyone authorized to see the data. Only the private key can decrypt something encrypted with a public key. Examples are RSA, DSA, ECC, Diffie–Hellman key exchange.

So, Alice wishes to send data to Bob. She requests Bob's public key, then encrypts the data with the public key, then sends it to Bob. With a private key, Bob can decrypt the message and read it. It allows you to create a public key for the party reporting to you so that they may encrypt their incoming information, after which you can decrypt the information with a private key. In this way, the distribution is fairly easier than symmetric encryption.

In real-world implementations, public-key cryptography is very slow, so public keys are not very commonly used to encrypt actual messages. Instead, a hybrid approach is used.

1. Bob sends Alice his public key.

2. Alice generates a random symmetric key (usually called a *session key*), encrypts it with Bob's public key, and sends it to Bob.

3. Bob decrypts the session key with his private key.

4. Alice and Bob exchange messages using the session key.

5. The session key is discarded after communication.

PKI provides non-repudiation by signing by a private key (digital signatures), also ensuring the integrity of the data after signing.

6. Alice calculates the one-way hash of a document.

7. Alice encrypts the hash with her private key. The encrypted hash is now the document's signature.

8. Alice sends the document to Bob with the encrypted hash.

9. Bob uses the same one-way hash function to derive the hash, then he decrypts the encrypted hash with Alice's public key and compares the values. If they match, it is ensured that the document came from Alice, and the document's integrity was protected during transmission.

Security Monitoring and Enforcement

Privileged Access Management

Just as user access to systems is supervised, privileged access should also be monitored, tracked and managed, because *"with great power comes great responsibility,*[33]*"* and trust should not prevent controlling that power.

Indeed, at some point, we should trust IT administrators. They are the ones keeping the wheels turning. However, while administering the systems, some privacy concerns always arise due to potential privilege misuse. To prevent that and implement a true multi-layered defense, even system administrators should be monitored. Privileged access management (PAM) tools are used for this purpose.[34] They act as a safeguard to privileged identities. These identities are stored in a secure vault and used only when required, some even without displaying the password.

PAM is based on the least privilege principle, where users (or accounts) are only allowed to have the minimum access rights required to perform their BAU activities. In addition, PAM provides more granular visibility, control, and auditing over-privileged identities and activities.

---

[33] https://en.wikipedia.org/wiki/With_great_power_comes_great_responsibility
[34] www.gartner.com/doc/reprints?id=1-26UL300G&ct=210719&st=sb

In PAM, privileged accounts, such as superuser accounts, domain administrative accounts, local admin accounts, important SSH keys, emergency break glass accounts, application accounts, service accounts, or privileged business accounts, are onboarded to the tool. From that point, these accounts are managed by that tool. The passwords are changed in a defined time frame without any user interaction. Users can only log in to the PAM platform, and from there, they can remotely log in to the systems they are administering. This helps to track all administrative activities—most PAM tools can record entire sessions, including the commands typed by the user, through session management (Figure 4-13).

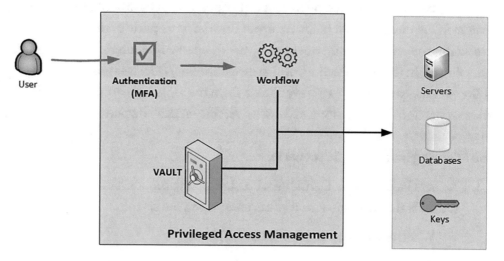

Figure 4-13. *Privileged access management*

PAM also supports automation, access approval requests, and workflows. For example, if you have a highly confidential server or database that you want to ensure the four-eye principle before login, you can set up a workflow where the system "manager" needs to approve the request before PAM allows access to the server. This would help audit the server and system admins' activities and provide a secure connection, which prevents MitM attacks.

PAM login process should implement multi-factor authentication to provide an additional security layer and prevent stolen user accounts from being used.

A key consideration is that there should not be any bypass method (admins having direct access to the systems), and admins should have no knowledge of the password used to connect. Organizations tend to have only one PAM tool to ensure that key passwords are kept in the least number of places possible, creating a single point of failure. In case of a disaster, access to critical platforms can be compromised.

Security Information and Event Management

Security information and event management (SIEM) tools are an essential system of an organization, typically managed by the security operations centers. SIEM collects all logs and events in the environment (sensory input from various parts of the body), analyzes and correlates them (like a brain does) and puts them in a meaningful understanding of what is going on in the organization, and acts accordingly (like treating a fever).

SIEM systems can aggregate relevant data from multiple log sources, such as servers, workstations, applications, network devices, security devices, and even threat intelligence feeds.

The following is an example scenario.

1. A user clicks an email, and the workstation downloads a malicious file from the Internet, and it starts encrypting the system.

   - When a user receives the email (MTA logs)

   - There is a log of the connection from the workstation to the malicious site, both for downloading the payload and C&C communication (firewall logs)

   - New, unusual processes, new registry, new scheduled tasks are created[35] (OS logs)

   - A file executing DLLs for bulk encryption (OS logs)

2. The malware tries several exploits and ports to move laterally.

   - Unusual system-to-system communication, maybe even a port scanning (network device logs)

   - Abnormal scripting activities (OS logs)

---

[35] www.sans.org/posters/hunt-evil/

All these events can be sent to SIEM for analysis, and the result would be a ransomware outbreak. If the security operations center has the necessary standard operating procedures (SOPs) on such malware outbreaks (or other threats), the outbreak could be contained with minimal impact.

SIEMs are also used for the case management of the organization. When events are collected, they are presented as cases to SOC analysts, requiring their manual review for that particular incident. Some events may lead to false-positive incidents, meaning that it is not a legitimate information security incident, but to verify that, SOC analysts need a good representation of the events, which is maintained by the case management modules of SIEM tools. These modules may also include additional data from the affected device, such as last vulnerability scan date, missing patches, information on resources, crash dumps, running services, local users, and groups, which are critical to identifying the incident (e.g., decrease the *mean time to detect*) and potential impact on the environment. Case management modules also provide granular access to the cases and audit trails, which then results in an efficient distribution of the analysts' workloads with better collaboration possibilities on the cases.

SIEMs provide key information to SOAR tools for an automated countermeasure to security incidents. Certain use cases with SOAR can be designed in a way that when an incident is confirmed, actions such as adding or modifying ACLs on the system to block malicious traffic, changing the privileges of user accounts, or even removing the accounts, setting up NAC measures to the device, or shutting down a service or even the device can be initiated by the SOAR.

Database Activity Monitoring

Database activity monitoring (DAM) tools track database activities such as the privileged user (primarily DBAs) monitoring, application activity monitoring, and unusual or undesirable activities, such as information or cybersecurity attacks, fraudulent activities. Some basic ones would only provide analysis of the accounts connected to the DBMS. But, newer technologies also allow security professionals to discover and classify data inside a database, then build rules to access those sensitive tables, conduct vulnerability management to discover missing patches on the DBMS, or security compliance benchmarking of the DBMS configuration.

DAMs can be implemented as stand-alone configurations and act as a network sniffer, software modules, or agents loaded on the database servers. Each one of these implementations has pros and cons, but the general idea is to catch every activity happening in a DBMS. Agent-based approaches can collect nearly every information required for efficient monitoring. Still, the agent should be installed in every DB, and usually, DBAs are very reluctant to install an agent to their systems. Plus, the DAM should support different DBMS platforms and versions. A sniffing approach requires no configuration changes to DB and creates zero overhead; however, it only works as long as they manage to capture every ingress and egress channel to and from the database, and they should have the capability to analyze secured traffic. In addition, network monitoring would not know the internal state of the DB. Remote connections to the databases are also used for monitoring purposes, but since they create some noticeable overhead, they may create performance issues.

DAMs collect, monitor, and audit all DB activities, including but not limited to SELECT, GRANT statements, to keep track of who or what accessed sensitive information. In addition, they can correlate multiple security-related events occurring in the DBMS and alert SOC analysts for a possible threat or a violation of rule-based or heuristic policies.

In large organizations, the workload to discover sensitive data in databases may be a hassle if there is no continuous communication between DBAs, business teams, and the security operations center. Thus, instead of keeping every activity in a DB (which consumes lots and lots of space), data classification can detect sensitive data. This classification can be based on table/column names, data schemas, searching for regular expressions, or even with a sample data set in that particular column. As a result, better activity monitoring can be done, which would have a better mean time to detect and mean time to respond to an incident. This information can also ensure compliance requirements such as encrypting sensitive data inside a database or auditing access.

Single Sign-on

Single sign-on (SSO) is a session and user authentication scheme that allows users to consolidate authentication and use only one or very few sets of login credentials. It keeps the number of sign-ons required from users to a minimum. It is an identity federation where the applications (Ad-aware, Kerberized, or SAML) retrieve the user authentication credentials such as Kerberos tickets and check with the authentication service to validate if the ticket is valid and the user is not asked for re-authentication.

SSO provides a better end-user experience. However, it also has benefits on security. With SSO, it is possible to keep track of user logins and avoid other login attempts. The user login attempts fail if the user has already logged in through SSO from a legitimate source. In addition, third-party applications do not know the actual user credentials, which as a result, minimizes the threat surface.

SSO is also criticized because it provides access to multiple applications, i.e., if the user credentials are compromised, then malicious threat actors may gain access to every application the user has rights to. To overcome this, the user credentials used for SSO should be supported by MFA, where OTPs or smart cards are used. Moreover, if SSO access is lost, the applications must switch to their generic authentication mechanisms; otherwise, users cannot log in.

Nowadays, federated logins from social platforms such as Facebook, Google, LinkedIn, Twitter are also possible through OAuth, but these may not be applicable for corporate environments.

Risk Register

A risk register is a tool in GRC (governance risk compliance) used for recording identified risks, their likelihood and impact, planned actions to reduce the risks, and a responsible person or department for managing these risks. In a security sense, it is the repository for information security-related risks, including but not limited to vulnerabilities observed in the organization assets, security findings from penetration tests, findings recorded in dynamic or static application security testing (DAST, SAST), audit findings, and others, so that security professionals can prioritize their remediation plans.

A risk register helps security teams effectively integrate their risks into the enterprise risk management program.

According to NIST IR 8286: Integrating Cybersecurity and Enterprise Risk Management (ERM),[36] a security risk register should contain the elements listed and described in Table 4-7.

---

[36] https://nvlpubs.nist.gov/nistpubs/ir/2020/NIST.IR.8286.pdf

Table 4-7. *Descriptions of Notional Cybersecurity Risk Register Template Elements from NISTIR 8286*

Register Element	Description
ID (risk identifier)	A sequential numeric identifier for referring to risk in the risk register
Priority	A relative indicator of the criticality of this entry in the risk register, either expressed in ordinal value (e.g., 1, 2, 3) or in reference to a given scale (e.g., high, moderate, low)
Risk description	A brief explanation of the cybersecurity risk scenario (potentially) impacting the organization and enterprise. Risk descriptions are often written in a cause-and-effect format, such as "if X occurs, then Y happens."
Risk Category	An organizing construct that enables multiple risk register entries to be consolidated (e.g., using SP 800-53 Control Families: Access Control (AC), Audit and Accountability [AU]). Consistent risk categorization helps compare risk registers during the risk aggregation step of ERM.
Current Assessment: Likelihood	An estimation of the probability of this scenario occurring before any risk response. This may also be considered the initial assessment on the first iteration of the risk cycle.
Current Assessment: Impact	Analysis of the potential benefits or consequences of this scenario if no additional response is provided. This may also be considered the initial assessment on the first iteration of the risk cycle.
Current Assessment – Exposure Rating	A calculation of the probability of risk exposure based on the likelihood estimate and the determined benefits or consequences of the risk. Other common frameworks use different terms for this combination, such as *level of risk* (e.g., ISO 31000, NIST SP 800-300 Rev. 1). This may also be considered the initial assessment on the first iteration of the risk cycle.
Risk Response Type	This is the risk response (sometimes referred to as the risk treatment) for handling the identified risk.

(continued)

Table 4-7. (*continued*)

Register Element	Description
Risk Response Description	A brief description of the risk response. For example, "Implement software management application XYZ to ensure that software platforms and applications are inventoried," or "Develop and implement a process to ensure the timely receipt of threat intelligence from [name of specific information-sharing forums and sources]."
Risk Owner	This is the designated party responsible and accountable for ensuring that the risk is maintained in accordance with enterprise requirements. The risk owner may work with a designated risk manager responsible for managing and monitoring the selected risk response.
Status	This is a field for tracking the current condition of the risk.

After identifying the risks, risk treatment activities are needed to be done. According to NISTIR 8286, the risk response types are described in Table 4-8.

Table 4-8. *Risk Response Types from NISTIR 8286*

Type	Description
Accept	Accept cybersecurity risk within risk tolerance levels. No additional risk response action is needed except for monitoring.
Transfer	For cybersecurity risks that fall outside of tolerance levels, reduce them to an acceptable level by sharing a portion of the consequences with another party (e.g., cybersecurity insurance). While some of the financial consequences may be transferable, there are often consequences that cannot be transferred, like losing customer trust.
Mitigate	Apply actions that reduce a given risk's threats, vulnerabilities, and impacts to an acceptable level. Responses could include those that help prevent a loss (i.e., reducing the probability of occurrence or the likelihood that a threat event materializes or succeeds) or that help limit such a loss by decreasing the amount of damage and liability.
Avoid	Apply responses to ensure that the risk does not occur. Avoiding risk may be the best option if there is no cost-effective method to reduce the cybersecurity risk to an acceptable level. The cost of the lost opportunity associated with such a decision should also be considered.

Once all required information is entered into a risk register, the security professionals can do the following.

- Identify all risks in the environment.

- Prioritize the actions.

- Start building risk treatment/response activities.

- Notify all related departments on the risks and action plans, let them involve in the process, report the residual risks.

- Reiterate the cycle for the next risk assessment.

Most GRC tools are capable of building risk registers and have built-in integration capabilities with most vulnerability management tools, security configuration compliance benchmarks, application security testing tools, SOARs, asset inventory, ticketing systems, and third-party risk assessment tools.

CHAPTER 5

Corporate Information Security Processes and Services

This chapter addresses all the processes and services in the organization's information security scope that should be implemented. Processes related to security awareness, training, and simulated attacks are addressed in the next chapter.

Security Governance

Security governance is how you support, manage, and shape your organization's efforts for security. It is different from security management. In "management", you implement, whereas in "governance", you oversee. Security governance is formed by the organization's business objectives and risk appetite, as well as industry best practices, legislation, and regulations mandated to the organization. It should not stop business processes to have an ideal security posture, since it should support business functions to be more secure and resilient to threat and vulnerabilities.

Security governance includes information security processes and technologies, competent people managing these, roles and responsibilities of everyone in the organization, organizational structure of the information security function, key risk indicator metrics, policies, and set of other documentation, which should be bound by a formal program.

An information security governance program should at least include the following.

- Policy management (exception management, self-assessment, annual review process of policies)

© Virgilio Viegas and Oben Kuyucu 2022
V. Viegas and O. Kuyucu, *IT Security Controls*, https://doi.org/10.1007/978-1-4842-7799-7_5

- Compliance management (compliance to the organization policies, national regulations, cybersecurity frameworks, etc.)

- Incorporation of information security to third-party risk management

- Ability to track and manage information risks through a risk register

- Providing targeted technical awareness and training

- Capability mapping (ability to map organizational capabilities to requirements and information security threats)

- Supporting risk management activities and residual risk management

The program should be owned and led by business management and supported by other roles in the organization. A good definition for the roles is mentioned in the RACI matrix in the 2018 *IGI State of The Industry Report*.[1]

- Accountable (the boss): Senior business management such as CEO or CISO

- Responsible (the doers): Mainly the information security function in the organization, plus the records and information management professionals, and people dealing with legal and compliance, business operations and management, risk management, data storage and archiving, and privacy in their areas of business

- Consulted (the advisors): Includes the preceding professionals and auditors

- Informed (the dependents): All employees

NIST 800-100[2] and ISO 27014:2020[3] underline the importance of consistent participation in these roles for an effective information security program. In addition, these frameworks suggest that organizations should integrate information security into the planning of corporate strategies to have a sustainable information security program.

---

[1] Information Governance Initiative. *IGI State of the Industry Report*: Volume III. Washington, DC: IGI. https://iginitiative.com/wp-content/uploads/The-State-of-IG-Report-Volume-III-highres.pdf. 2018.

[2] https://nvlpubs.nist.gov/nistpubs/Legacy/SP/nistspecialpublication800-100.pdf

[3] www.iso.org/standard/74046.html

There should also be an information security strategic plan for achieving the information security goals and objectives, which were defined in the program. Strategic plans are supported by tactical plans (mid-term schedules for goals) and operational plans (short-term detailed plans).

The main responsibility for establishing and maintaining security governance is the information security function in the organization, which should be oversight by an executive-level working group, committee, or equivalent body. This high-level working group should be responsible for the following.

- Overall enterprise-wide information security and ensuring information security is an integral part of all business processes

- Development of information security strategy

- Approving information security-related documentation, such as policies, procedures, standards, and system architecture

- Monitoring organization's information security projects and activities, their effectiveness against security threats and vulnerabilities, by setting up KRIs and KPIs

- Deciding risk-based information security improvement activities considering the current threat landscape, cost, and allocated budget

The information security function in the organization is responsible for the following.

- Executing and maintaining the information security strategy

- Coordinating and communicating the information security across the organization

- Define and manage the security services (including but not limited to network security, data security, endpoint security, incident response, and security event monitoring)

- Developing information security-related documentation, such as policies, procedures, standards, and system architecture

- Providing expert advice on all aspects of information security to business functions

- Running information security awareness programs and supporting information security-related training

- Monitoring effectiveness of security controls by establishing KRIs and KPIs

- Reporting overall status of all activities to the overseeing body

The rules to enforce in the information security program are mentioned in a *policy*, which is then supported by procedures, standards, guidelines, and instruction manuals.

Policies and Procedures

An information security policy refers to a set of directives documented to maintain the organization's information security. It also shows top management's commitment to information security, which is expected to be approved by the board. They are shaped by the organization's risk appetite and strategic planning, laws, regulations, and business processes.

The information security policy should be aligned with other policies, such as IT policies, HR policies, general safety or physical security policies, and business processes. If not aligned, information security is seen as a burden in the organization, making it unsustainable.

Policies have general formal statements, and they should be supported by other documentation such as standards, procedures, baselines, and guidelines. All these documents should be communicated, and employees and third-party providers should be made aware of these documents upon hire and annually.

There is no "one policy to rule them all" in policies and procedures for all organizations, so it must be shaped based on geography, industry, size, risk appetite, budget, and used technologies. Moreover, multiple departments in one organization may be involved in achieving such statements. They may have different naming conventions. The following are some key topics that can be included in an information security policy program.

- Information Security Governance

  - Information Security Awareness and Training

  - Risk Management/Assessment

  - Compliance/Auditing

- Acceptable Use of Technologies
- Clean Desk
- Ethics
- Remote Working

– Data Protection

- Data Classification and Labeling
- Information and Intellectual Property Handling
- Data Retention and Access
- Records Management and Archiving

– Data Privacy

– Endpoint Security

- Software installation
- Workstation Security
- Server Security
- Email Security
- Mobile Device Security (BYOD, COPE)
- Removable Media

– Application Security

- Secure Software Development
- Application Security Testing

– Network Security

- Wired and Wireless Communication
- Network Device Security
- Network Configuration
- Network Monitoring
- Cryptographic Security and Key Management

- Change and Patch Management
- Security Monitoring and Operations
  - Security Logging
  - Vulnerability Management
  - Penetration Testing
  - Threat Intelligence and Threat Hunting
- Incident Handling and Response
  - Cyber Crisis Management Plan
  - Response plan testing
  - Digital Forensics
- Recovery and Continuity
  - Business Continuity Planning
  - Disaster Recovery
- Identity and Access Management
  - Password Standards
  - Remote Access
- Cloud Security

Cybersecurity and Risk Assessment

Risk management is how you treat your risks in the organization. Through risk assessments, you identify and evaluate risks. Based on your risk appetite and budget, you prioritize and treat them to decrease the risk by either minimizing the impact of the risk or decreasing the probability.

The overall definition of the *risk* is any *threat* in which an event, action, or non-action adversely *impacts* the organization's ability to sustain its business or achieve its objectives. It is due to exploiting a *vulnerability*, which is a weakness or flaw in an asset or the lack of security controls.

The following is the general formula for risk.

$$RISK = (Threat \times Vulnerability) \times Impact$$

$$\underbrace{\qquad\qquad\qquad\qquad}_{}$$

Likelihood

Let's look at an example. In an environment that does not have a password policy, users have chosen weak passwords for their convenience to log in to the systems.

- **Vulnerability**: Passwords are vulnerable to brute-forcing via dictionary attacks.

- **Threat**: A malicious actor can exploit the vulnerability to break into the system.

- **Likelihood** is decided with the combination of threat and vulnerability. If the environment is prone to external attacks, the likelihood is more probable.

- **Impact**: When the malicious actor gains unauthorized access, the resources (primarily data) are prone to modification, deletion, or being stolen.

There are several ways to identify the endless possible threats, which are the causes of an unwanted incident that results in financial or material loss, damage, modification of assets or data, unauthorized access, denial of service, or disclosure of sensitive information. One way is *threat modeling*, which tries to identify, categorize and analyze the loss, the probability, and the possible solutions to reduce the threat. It is especially useful when designing an application. It is an exercise of what is being built (assets), what can go wrong (threat and threat agents), how do we mitigate them (controls), and validate if they are gone (testing).

There are also industry-accepted references or guides for threat modeling, such as a threat categorization model developed by Microsoft, known as STRIDE, which is described as follows.

- **Spoofing**: Can the attacker gain access by spoofed credentials, IP addresses, usernames, email addresses, MAC addresses, and so forth?

- **Tampering**: Can there be any tampering of data, whether it is in use, transit, or at rest?

- **Repudiation**: Can the attacker disguise themself from being audited or traced?

- **Information disclosure**: Can sensitive information be disclosed to unauthorized parties?

- **Denial of service**: Can the attacker harm the system so that the system is no longer responding to legitimate requests?

- **Elevation of privilege**: Can the attacker elevate his/her privileges to a higher level of credentials so that he/she can access more context or have rights to do more?

Another method is PASTA (Process for Attack Simulation and Threat Analysis).

- **Stage 1**: Define business, security, and compliance objectives (function of the application, number of users, data inputs and outputs, and BIA)

- **Stage 2**: Define the technical scope of assets and components (including application components, application boundaries, network topology, design diagrams, protocol and services, data interactions)

- **Stage 3**: Decompose the application (users, roles, responsibilities, data flows, ACLs)

- **Stage 4**: Threat analysis (threat intelligence, list of threat agents, threat scenarios, and likelihood)

- **Stage 5**: Vulnerability detection (Any vulnerability in the application based on OWASP Top 10 or MITRE CWE)

- **Stage 6**: Analyze and model attacks or attack enumeration (identification of attack surface, attack trees, and vectors, possible exploitation points)

- **Stage 7**: Risk/ impact analysis and development of countermeasures (business impact of threats, any gaps in the security controls, calculation of residual risk, and mitigation actions)

After identifying threats, vulnerabilities, and impacts, you can easily understand the risk. Through risk assessments, you can identify further or prioritize the actions.

There are quantitative and qualitative risk assessment methodologies. Quantitative analysis yield a risk analysis in monetary values. However, to calculate that, you must provide lots of quantitative information, such as the following.

- The asset value (AV) assigns monetary values to your assets.

- The exposure factor (EF) or loss potential is the percentage of the cost of the loss that happens.

- Single loss expectancy (SLE) (AV × EF) is the monetary value of the single loss.

- The annualized rate of occurrence (ARO) estimates how many times in one year risk can happen.

- The annualized loss expectancy (ALE) (ARO × SLE) is the cost of the total instances of this loss in one year.

- The cost of countermeasures includes licensing, installation costs, maintenance, support, annual repairs, the cost for testing, and evaluation.

The end of the quantitative analysis compares the cost and benefits review, including the ALE. If you see an acceptable decrease in the risk, you can implement the offered countermeasure. It should be noted that quantitative analyses are subjective, and organizations need to identify the monetary values for each threat, vulnerability, or loss.

On the other hand, qualitative risk analysis is based on opinions and scales of components of risk. So instead of monetary values, you assign scales, such as low, medium, high, critical to asset values, or frequent, likely, occasional, seldom, unlikely to likelihood. The common vulnerability scoring system (CVSS) (Figure 5-1) is a good example of qualitative risk analysis where vulnerabilities are scored against various metrics.

Base Metric Group		Temporal Metric Group	Environmental Metric Group	
Exploitability Metrics	Impact Metrics	Exploit Code Maturity	Modified Base Metrics	Confidentiality Requirement
Attack Vector	Confidentiality Impact	Remediation Level		Integrity Requirement
Attack Complexity	Integrity Impact	Report Confidence		Availability Requirement
Privileges Required	Availability Impact			
User Interaction	Scope			

Figure 5-1. CVSS metric groups[4]

So how do you treat or manage your risks?

The answer for the preceding password example is easy: having a better password policy with account lockout would decrease the likelihood of the risk. Brute-forcing is still possible, but, for instance, the account is disabled automatically after six wrong attempts, which makes the malicious actor's other attempts useless.

There may be some actions your organization cannot handle or afford. Then, you can accept the risk or transfer. Nowadays, many insurance companies are providing cyber-risk insurance policies, which may be helpful to transfer the risk.

Overall, the risk management actions are as follows.

- **Reduction** or **mitigation** (also known as *treating* the risk): By improving a security control and adding a new one, you decrease the risk's likelihood and/or impact.

  - Patching of servers would eliminate the vulnerability.

  - Adding more perimeter controls, such as IPS, WAF, would prevent some attacks from happening.

---

[4]www.first.org/cvss/v3.1/specification-document

- Implementing multi-factor authentication would provide some protection against credential thefts.

- **Acceptance** (also known as *tolerate*): Management decides that the risk is within the established risk acceptance criteria, so the organization accepts the risk.

- **Transfer**: By transferring the risk or insuring it, the potential cost is undertaken by another entity or individual.

- **Deter**: By implementing deterring actions to the risk, you discourage people aiming to cause the loss, which eventually reduces the likelihood of the risk. Security cameras, guards, WAFs, or MFA are examples.

- **Avoidance**: By selecting alternative technologies or options that have less risk than the first one, or simply canceling the initiative. Choosing IPS instead of IDS is an example.

- **Reject**: Pretend that the risk does not exist or simply ignore the risk. This is not a formal risk management activity nor recommended.

After the action, if there is still some remaining risk associated with the item, it is called *residual risk*. Organizations should aim to have minimal residual risks and preferably within the acceptable risk threshold.

There are numerous sources for risk management activities. There are even several frameworks and certification programs for professionals to consider because risk management is a risky activity.

- NIST Special Publication 800-37r2[5]

- ISO/IEC 27005: 2018 Information Security Risk Management[6]

- PCI DSS Risk Assessment Guidelines[7]

- ENISA Risk Management/Risk Assessment (RM/RA) Framework[8]

---

[5]https://nvlpubs.nist.gov/nistpubs/SpecialPublications/NIST.SP.800-37r2.pdf
[6]www.iso.org/standard/75281.html
[7]www.pcisecuritystandards.org/documents/PCI_DSS_Risk_Assmt_Guidelines_v1.pdf
[8]www.enisa.europa.eu/topics/threat-risk-management/risk-management/current-risk/business-process-integration/the-enisa-rm-ra-framework

- PMI Risk Management Professional (PMI-RMP)[9]

- ISACA Certified in Risk and Information Systems Control (CRISC)[10]

Penetration Testing

A penetration test is a simulated attack against computing systems that mimics an actual attack to identify and validate vulnerabilities, configuration issues, and business logic flaws. It includes several discovery and attack types, including port scanning, fuzz testing, vulnerability scanning, and social engineering. It is part of the vulnerability management activities and should be conducted annually to all public-facing applications by accredited third-party companies or organizationally independent internal resources.

Vulnerability scanning is not penetration testing. The main difference from those scans is penetration testing is the combination of automated tools (not necessarily vulnerability scanners but can be included) blended with manual testing, interpretation of the results, and verification of identified issues. The penetration tester may choose not to use those automated tools, but it increases the time spent on that project. Most vulnerability scans are safe tests, i.e., they do not exploit the vulnerability, or at least they are non-intrusive. Whereas in penetration tests, the tester can exploit the vulnerability to see how far they can go.

Most of the time, penetration testing is performed on the applications. However, penetration testers can use vulnerability scans of servers, endpoints, web applications, wireless networks, network devices, mobile devices, and other potential points of exposure. Hence, both applications, networks, and devices can be tested.

In a typical penetration testing, the team first plans the activity, including the information gathering and threat modeling. In this phase, the penetration tester understands the expectations from the organization, analyzes the business flows, collects data from various sources, and prepares the tools for the testing.

Testing follows the planning. The tester starts and stops the activity to the agreed scope at the agreed times to avoid missing other security-related incidents. The testing can be done in various ways, including a black box, where the tester does not know the system, other than the public ones, or a white box, where the tester has been given lots of

---

[9] www.pmi.org/certifications/risk-management-rmp

[10] www.isaca.org/credentialing/crisc

information, maybe even application credentials. Having white box certainly decreases the time spent on planning or discovery. Hence the tester can focus on finding more issues in limited-time engagements. Generally, organizations choose to have gray-box testing, which combines both, where the tester has been provided some information, such as IP addresses or application names. Preferably, the tests should not be performed on production systems but on pre-production systems where the setup is identical but with limited or anonymized data. It should be noted that some systems do not have a pre-production or testing environment, or the testing should be performed on production systems to see the real impact of an attack. In these cases, organizations must ensure that it does not affect the regular business flow.

During the penetration test execution, organizations should monitor their systems for any unintended changes. As mentioned, penetration tests can be intrusive. Likewise, the tester should notify the organization immediately if a certain service or application becomes unresponsive.

The last phase is the analysis and reporting, where the tester analyzes the results from various tools, validates if necessary, and then presents the report to the organization. Reporting should include an executive summary, the scope and time of the testing, the methodology used, any limitations encountered during the testing, and findings with descriptions, severity information, impacted devices, references, and possible solutions for remediation. The evidence (raw outputs of tools, screenshots, scan results, etc.) is sometimes added as appendixes. It should be noted that the processes for evidence retention and destruction must be documented and complied with.

Organizations must have the necessary means to track the findings discovered during a penetration test. After patching the vulnerabilities or changing the configurations, a retest is required to validate the remediation of the findings. This can be done by the same company or tester or by competent internal resources.

The qualifications of testers and companies should be checked before the engagement. They must possess a minimum level of expertise, ideally measured via certification bodies such as CREST, OSCP, GIAC, or accredited by the national accreditation bodies. Organizations can choose testers or companies certifications from the following common penetration testing certifications.

- Offensive Security Certified Professional (OSCP)[11] or Offensive Security Experienced Penetration Tester (OSEP)[12]

---

[11] www.offensive-security.com/pwk-oscp/

[12] www.offensive-security.com/pen300-osep

- Certified Ethical Hacker (CEH)[13]

- Licensed Penetration Tester Master (LPT)[14]

- Global Information Assurance Certification (GIAC) (e.g., GPEN,[15] GWAPT,[16] or GXPN[17])

- CREST Penetration Testing Certifications[18]

- NCSC IT Health Check Service (CHECK) certification[19]

- CompTIA PenTest+[20]

The penetration testers should be guided by a strict code of conduct or ethics. They may access highly sensitive information, so they should understand and follow professional and ethics responsibilities. This is also required to ensure the trustworthiness of the results.

Red Teaming

A red team is your contractual opponent. You try to defend your organization, assets, or information against red teams while the red team continuously attacks your systems and people. Although both aimed to find issues and eventually make the organization have a better security posture, the main differences between *penetration testing* and *red teaming* are the scope of the test and amount of people involved in each exercise. In penetration testing, one or two penetration testers generally try to find as many vulnerabilities as possible and exploit them. However, red teaming involves more people planning, attacking, and exploiting. The scope is also different; penetration tests are focused on a specific application or service, whereas red teaming can focus on the entire organization, including human factors, other physical elements, and external third-party resources.

---

[13] www.eccouncil.org/programs/certified-ethical-hacker-ceh/

[14] www.eccouncil.org/programs/licensed-penetration-tester-lpt-master/

[15] www.giac.org/certification/gpen

[16] www.giac.org/certification/gwapt

[17] www.giac.org/certification/gxpn

[18] https://crest-approved.org

[19] www.ncsc.gov.uk/information/check-penetration-testing

[20] www.comptia.org/certifications/pentest

Even though organizations found many vulnerabilities and issues during penetration testing and successfully remediated all, they may still be susceptible to red teaming exercises. Red teaming includes finding human vulnerabilities, so one red team member can use social engineering to have someone turn off one or more crucial security controls.

Red teaming exercises need to have a scope and goal defined and agreed upon by both parties. This is stated in the rules of engagement, where the boundaries of the attack are drawn, with defined exceptions, if any. Allowed and disallowed actions, approved targets, and restricted movements in the internal network should also be mentioned in the rules of engagement. For example, you would consider that the attack was successful in a healthcare facility if the red team finds PII data. Still, it should not go further, as it is a breach of personal data privacy laws and regulations. Similarly, if the red team gains access to core banking systems with write privileges in a financial institution, you would not want to see forged transactions in your production environment. Therefore these boundaries should be established in the rules of engagement.

It should also be noted that most red teaming exercises should be performed without the prior knowledge of the blue teams (the defenders) to assess their effectiveness in detecting the adversary actions.

Red teaming makes use of the kill chain in the organization. Like a cybercriminal, red team members act according to the following steps.

- **Reconnaissance**: Gather as much information as possible about the organization, potential targets, and threat surfaces.

- **Weaponization**: Create a weapon, such as an email attachment with a malicious payload, to create remote access to the organization.

- **Delivery**: Send the weapon to the target.

- **Initial exploitation and installation**: If payloads are successful, gain more grounds to have persistent access.

- **Internal Recon**: Gather more information about the internal network to increase the possibility for lateral movement.

- **Lateral movement**: Find possible ways to achieve the goal or objective.

- **Complete mission**: When the goal is achieved, debrief, and report the findings with the vulnerable path.

In the exercise debrief, red team and blue team findings are compared, and missing monitoring or security controls are identified, which can be used for immediate remediation activities or prioritization of future investments in the organization.

Code Review and Testing

Code review is the activity of checking the source code of an application by a competent individual or a team. The main goal is to detect the quality problems of the application, such as logic errors, vulnerabilities, potential defects like backdoors, buffer overflow or injections, or conformity to the coding standards.

The code reviewers should be different from the code author(s) and should also have experience in coding to understand the syntax of the language of the code. The reviewers are different and are not testers. As in most functional testing, the code is not analyzed at all.

There can be static testing in code reviews, where the source code is manually reviewed without executing the program, or dynamic testing, where the program is evaluated in its runtime environment by providing true or fuzzed data and observing the outputs. The latter is preferred where the organization does not have the program's source code.

Code reviews can also be done for learning or knowledge transfer. In peer reviews, two developers review each other's codes. The junior developer can learn several techniques, solution models, or quality expectations of the organization from the senior developer's code, and the senior developer can correct the mistakes or deficiencies of the others.

Code reviews should be a part of the SDLC (software development life cycle) or the DevOps processes (or SecDevOps). There are numerous ways to automate the code review process in software development. Organizations should use these techniques to remediate coding errors before deploying into production. Flawed code is always too difficult and expensive to remediate after release to production.

Code reviews have to be a standard to follow, which is a coding guideline that lists the libraries or coding techniques to use, naming conventions, and other procedures. Organizations must establish their standards or use industry-accepted frameworks on coding, such as Open Web Application Security Project (OWASP) guidelines.

OWASP is a community-driven platform to provide guidelines on improving software security. They publish and host many freely available and open resources such as the following.

- OWASP Top Ten,[21] which lists the top ten vulnerabilities in most of the applications and prevention techniques

- OWASP Code Review Guide[22]

- OWASP Security Testing Guides for web applications[23] and mobile apps[24]

- OWASP Security Knowledge Framework,[25] which provides a learning and training platform for developers

- ZAP (also known as OWASP Zed Attack Proxy),[26] a web application scanner to detect vulnerabilities

Code reviews can be done manually or by automated tools. Automated tools can be used for a very large number of lines of coding in a time-efficient manner; however, it should be noted that these tools can produce false positives and false negatives. This does not mean that manual coding is perfect; there are always some coding issues that can be overlooked. To minimize that, tool-assisted code reviewing can be used, where an individual analyzes the code. The tool helps the reviewer with recent changes, affected libraries, and provides review tracking.

Compliance Scans

Compliance scans, often called *security baseline checks*, scan systems against a given set of configuration checks (baseline). The security baselines are the minimum configurations that every system must meet.

---

[21] https://owasp.org/www-project-top-ten/

[22] https://owasp.org/www-project-code-review-guide/assets/ OWASP_Code_Review_Guide_v2.pdf

[23] https://owasp.org/www-project-web-security-testing-guide/

[24] https://owasp.org/www-project-mobile-security-testing-guide/

[25] https://owasp.org/www-project-security-knowledge-framework/

[26] https://owasp.org/www-project-zap/

Compliance scans complement vulnerability scans and are essential to confirm systems hardening. Systems should be hardened before going live, and the way to ensure that they have the minimum intended level of security is through compliance scans.

Most vulnerability scanning management tools can perform compliance scans. The difference between vulnerability scans and compliance scans is that systems are scanned for known vulnerabilities in vulnerability scans. In contrast, systems configurations are checked against the security baseline defined for those systems in compliance scans.

For example, in compliance scans, you can understand the following.

- Is the system's password policy is aligned with your standards (i.e., at least 14 characters, maximum age of 90 days, etc.)

- Are session timeouts defined to at most 15 minutes?

- Have remote communications been configured to be secure?

- Are unused Apache server modules disabled?

- Is the Oracle DB using the default public privileges?

- Has Microsoft Edge been configured to disallow downloads or add-ons from untrusted networks?

Compliance scans can be performed on operating systems, server software (web servers, virtualization, database servers, DNS, email, authentication servers), cloud providers, mobile devices, network devices, desktop software (web browsers, productivity software, online conferencing tools) and multi-function devices. As long as the system allows reading the configurations, a baseline can be created from scratch by the organization or from industry-accepted best practices.

Vulnerability Scans

Vulnerability scans help organizations to understand how exposed their assets are to vulnerabilities. Therefore, to have a comprehensive assessment of their assets, it is crucial to ensure that vulnerability scans cover all organization assets, supported by an effective asset management process that can also help detect dormant assets.

Agent-based scans require the installation of a vulnerability scan agent in all assets to produce more detailed assessment results.

Since it is impossible to install vulnerability scan agents in some devices (e.g., routers, IP phones, CCTV, etc.), organizations must also conduct network-based vulnerability scans to assess these devices.

To ensure the effectiveness of network-based vulnerability scans, the vulnerability scanners must reach all networks in all ports. This means that firewalls must be configured to allow traffic from the vulnerability scanner to all networks in all ports, making the vulnerability scanner a very attractive target since it can reach all the organization networks without any restrictions. Therefore, vulnerability scanners must be placed in an isolated network, ideally accessed only from a privileged access management (PAM) platform or through the vendor management console, and firewall rules should be scheduled to be active only during scan periods.

Another challenge of network-based vulnerability scans is that to produce more detailed results, scans must be authenticated. Vulnerability scanners must be integrated with PAM to ensure that these authentication credentials are not compromised or locally stored.

Network-based vulnerability scans should also assess the organization's external perimeter. These scans can be done from a scanner based on the Internet and any other access from the Internet.

Currently, it is also possible to adopt three distinct implementations.

- **On-premises**: Agents and network security scanners report to an on-premises control center where policies and vulnerability updates are distributed.

- **Cloud**: Agents and network security scanners report to a cloud-based control center where policies and vulnerability updates are distributed.

- **Hybrid**: Agents and network security scanners report to a cloud-based control center where policies and vulnerability updates are distributed. An additional on-premises control center synchronizes with the cloud control center. The on-premises can be used for reporting and integration with other on-premises platforms like asset management or risk register.

Information security professionals rely on standards like the Security Content Automation Protocol (SCAP) from NIST common classification and rating of vulnerabilities.

The following are the components of a Security Content Automation Protocol (SCAP).

- CVSS: Common Vulnerabilities Scoring System[27]

- CVE: Common Vulnerabilities and Exposures

- CCE: Common Configuration Enumeration

- CPE: Common Platform Enumeration

- XCCDF: Extensible Configuration Checklist Description Format

- OVAL: Open Vulnerability and Assessment language

CVSS: Common Vulnerability Scoring System

CVSS is a vulnerability scoring system that ranks vulnerabilities according to their severity which is calculated considering several factors from three metric groups: base, temporal and environmental. The base metrics can have a score from 0 to 10 (Table 5-1), which is then supported by the environmental and temporal metrics.

CVSS 3.0 has the following severity ranks based on base score range.

Table 5-1. *CVSS v3.0 Ratings*

Severity	Base Score Range
None	0.0
Low	0.2 –3.9
Medium	4.0 – 6.9
High	7.0 – 8.9
Critical	9.0 – 10.0

---

[27] https://nvd.nist.gov/vuln-metrics/cvss

CVE: Common Vulnerabilities and Exposures

NIST also has the National Vulnerability Database (NVD),[28] in which all vulnerabilities have a unique CVE identifier. The NVD defines vulnerability as follows.

> *A weakness in the computational logic (e.g., code) found in software and hardware components that, when exploited, results in a negative impact on confidentiality, integrity, or availability. Mitigation of the vulnerabilities in this context typically involves coding changes but could also include specification changes or even specification deprecations (e.g., removal of affected protocols or functionality in their entirety).*

The vulnerability CVE unique identifier is also associated with specific operating systems, databases, applications, and so forth.

Since the same vulnerability has the same CVE across the industry, it can be used across several platforms to search for details about that vulnerability.

The following are platforms with information about vulnerabilities.

- https://nvd.nist.gov/vuln/search

- http://cve.mitre.org

- www.cvedetails.com

- www.tenable.com/cve

CCE: Common Configuration Enumeration

CCE provides a unique identifier to security-related system configuration issues to facilitate and expedite the correlation of configuration information from several information sources and tools.

CPE: Common Platform Enumeration

Common Platform Enumeration (CPE) describes and identifies classes of applications, operating systems, and hardware devices from the organization's assets. Unlike CVE, CPE is not a unique identifier of products or systems. CPE identifies abstract product classes.

---

[28] https://nvd.nist.gov/

Vulnerability scanning platforms can relate vulnerabilities (CVE) and configurations (CCE) with CPE, which can help system administrators understand how many specific classes (CPE) are exposed or misconfigured. Then, it can trigger a configuration management tool to verify if the software is properly configured in compliance organization's policies and followed standards.

XCCDF: Extensible Configuration Checklist Description Format

Extensible Configuration Checklist Description Format (XCCDF) is a standardized language in XML format to specify security checklists, benchmarks, and configuration documentation, to replace the security hardening and analysis documentation written in a non-standardized way.

OVAL: Open Vulnerability and Assessment Language

Open Vulnerability and Assessment Language (OVAL) is an international information security standard for security testing procedures.

Vulnerability Scanning Procedures

Vulnerability scanning procedures must define the scanning frequency (daily, weekly, monthly, or quarterly) and the reporting frequency. Reports must reach the right people to conduct the appropriate mitigation actions.

The patch management process must also define mitigation SLAs according to the vulnerability severity (CVSS). A risk register must be maintained to keep track of the vulnerabilities that have exceeded the SLA thresholds.

Additionally, all new assets and applications must be subject to a vulnerability scan before connecting to the organization network or going live.

Firewalls and Network Devices Assurance

Since devices like firewalls, routers, and switches do not support vulnerability scanning agents, additional mechanisms must be implemented to detect vulnerabilities. They must also verify configuration and rule compliance with corporate policies that cannot be identified by network-based vulnerabilities scans.

The firewall and network devices assurance process has three main goals.

- Ensure that the firewall rule is compliant with corporate policies and standards

- Ensure configuration compliance with corporate standards and security baselines (e.g., CIS security baselines)

- Detect vulnerabilities that the vulnerability scans cannot detect

Periodic reviews should be implemented according to the exposure level and inherent risk, where review frequency of public-facing or Internet exposed and perimeter devices should be higher than internal devices. This process confirms that network segmentation is properly implemented. It also identifies unused, shadowed, and redundant rules; and recertifies rules, which is a regulatory requirement in some countries and mandated by some standards (e.g., PCI DSS requirement 1.1.7 states that organizations should review firewall and router rule sets at least every six months).

Security Operations Center

Like many other services, there are three possible implementation models for a security operations center (SOC) in-house or on-premises, outsourced and hybrid with an on-premises SOC with one or more managed security service providers.

The best implementation model for each organization depends on the organization's infrastructure size, the information security management system's maturity, and available resources, among many other possible factors.

In addition to the dedicated managed security services provider, the hybrid model can also include services from other cloud-based providers like endpoint detection and response (EDR) software or secure DNS vendors that can provide alert services.

The SOC must ensure that all security platforms, servers, and endpoints are on-boarded to SIEM and databases through a database activity monitoring platform since the SOC effectiveness depends on up-to-date and reliable internal and external information sources.

If the organization cannot have an internal SOC because it is too expensive, labor-intensive, or does not have the specific expertise, it can opt to outsource SOC operations to a *managed security services provider* (MSSP) that can provide constant real-time monitoring, response, and escalation services.

If the organization decides to implement an in-house SOC or hybrid, it must ensure adequate SOC personnel with appropriate roles.

Typically, the structure can be broken down into the following roles.

- Security analyst (tier one): Vulnerability monitoring, incident triage, and escalation

- Security analyst (tier two): Incident investigation, response and recovery procedures to remediate impact

- Threat hunter (tier three): Assesses the organization infrastructure based on the latest threat intelligence reports to identify malicious activities

- Manager (tier four): Oversees the SOC team, reports findings, defines action plans and use cases, escalates incidents to the organization's CISO

The SOC must be supported by the security engineering and architecture teams in the design, development, and maintenance of the security infrastructure.

Incident Response and Recovery

An information security incident is an event with a negative impact or potential impact on confidentiality, integrity, or availability of an organization's systems due to malicious activities.

NIST SP 800-61, *Computer Incident Security Incident Handling Guide*,[29] defines a "computer security incident as a violation or imminent threat violation of computer security policies, acceptable use policies or standard security practices."

Although security incident response and recovery fall under SOC responsibilities, the entire organization must support the process (e.g., IT, legal, HR departments) to minimize the incident impact and contain it in the quickest possible way.

The SOC might also need to liaise with and seek support from external parties, including software vendors, ISPs, MSSPs, law enforcement, and national or regulator *computer security incident response teams* (CSIRTs).

---

[29] https://csrc.nist.gov/publications/detail/sp/800-61/rev-2/final

According to NIST SP 800-61, the incident response process has four stages (see Figure 5-2).

- Preparation

- Detection & Analysis

- Containment, Eradication & Recovery

- Post-Incident Activity

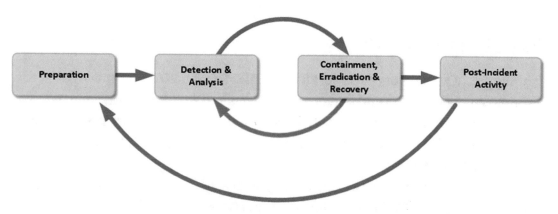

Figure 5-2. *Incident response life cycle*

Preparation

To ensure the SOC readiness to respond to information security incidents, organizations must

- establish appropriate capabilities

- develop and implement incident response policy, plan, and procedures (such as information sharing and internal and external escalation mechanisms)

- identify relevant stakeholders who should participate in the process according to incident type and impact

In the preparation stage, relevant information and means must be identified and provisioned to facilitate that the next two stages run as smoothly as possible. The following are some examples.

- Relevant stakeholders and stand-by teams contacts

- Incident reporting and escalation mechanisms (e.g., phone numbers, email addresses, online forms)

- Secure storage facilities

- Updated laptops and smartphones with the necessary analysis and forensic tools toolkit

- Digital forensics and backup devices for evidence collection and preservation

Detection and Analysis

Assuring that SOC monitors all devices like IPS, SIEM, DAM, EDR, and antivirus, ensuring prompt detection and a comprehensive understanding of the incident is essential. This means that all technical security controls (EDR, antivirus, IPS, firewalls, honeypot, proxy, etc.) and security events from other systems (e.g., failed login attempts) must be monitored by the SOC.

Additionally, incidents can be triggered by other sources like users (e.g., phishing reports, suspicious emails) or threat intelligence services.

SOCs can have attack vectors categories, but they can be used as follows.

- External/removable media

- Attrition (e.g., a DDoS brute-force attack against an authentication mechanism)

- Web

- Email

- Impersonation

- Improper usage

- Equipment loss or theft

- Other (an attack that does not fit in any of the other categories)

After an incident is created, the SOC starts the analysis process. It checks if it is a false positive or a real incident and classifies it according to its severity and attack vectors to be prioritized.

In case of a false positive, the rules that triggered the incident must be reviewed and added to a knowledge base to avoid future false positives.

Additionally, after ensuring that proper tools are in place, such as the capability to do remote memory dumps or disk imaging, a more detailed analysis needs the following.

- An accurate networks and systems profile

- A clear understanding of the normal behaviors (to detect potential anomalies)

- An effective log retention policy

- Event correlation

- Time is synchronized in all the organization assets

- A knowledge base built with information from previous cases

- Expertise from other teams

During the analysis process, all collected evidence must be preserved. NIST SP 800-86 *Guide to Integrating Forensic Techniques into Incident Response*[30] provides more guidance on forensic techniques and evidence collection and preservation.

Containment, Eradication, and Recovery

The containment, eradication, and recovery procedures are shaped based on the nature and impact of the attack and are highly dependent on proper preparation.

Containment provides time to develop a remediation plan and can go from simply disconnecting a desktop from the network to shutting down a system.

The containment strategy must be based on several criteria, including the following.

- Potential damage to and theft of resources

- Need for evidence preservation

- Service availability (e.g., network connectivity, services provided to external parties)

- Time and resources needed to implement the strategy

- Effectiveness of the strategy (e.g., partial containment, full containment)

- Duration of the solution

---

[30] https://nvlpubs.nist.gov/nistpubs/Legacy/SP/nistspecialpublication800-86.pdf

After containing the incident, it might be necessary to eradicate or eliminate all traces of the incident, like delete malware or disable breached user accounts, identify all exploited vulnerabilities and mitigate them.

During recovery, systems are restored and confirmed that they are functioning normally. The recovery process may also imply restoring clean backups, rebuilding systems from scratch, replacing compromised files with clean versions, installing patches, changing passwords, and strengthening network security.

Comprehensive and accurate documentation and up-to-date data flows and interdependencies are essential to reduce the recovery efforts with minimal trouble.

Post-Incident Activity

The post-incident activities consist of reviewing the incident and identifying improvement opportunities (also known as *lessons learned*) using and preserving the collected data.

The major goal of "lessons learned" is to identify what went wrong to avoid future similar incidents. This incident review must be done right after the incident to take advantage of the "near memory." The following are some of the questions that can be asked.

- Exactly what happened? Review incident timeline.

- What went wrong?

- What could be done to prevent the incident?

- How did the organization staff (including all staff, not only the responders) respond? For example, clicking a malicious email payload might indicate a lack of security awareness training.

- What kind of information was required? And when? Was it available?

- Were the analysis procedures effective?

- What could be done to improve the process?

- Could information sharing have helped to avoid or improve the response process?

- Which measures should be implemented to avoid similar incidents?

The collected data during the incident can build a risk scenario to be added to the risk assessment and use case to be configured in the SIEM correlating data and improving response times.

The data collected during the incident should be kept in accordance with the organization's retention policies and, where applicable, according to legal requirements.

Threat Hunting

Threat hunting, also known as cyber threat hunting, is the process conducted by SOC analysts of actively looking for undetected threats that might have secretly compromised an organization's network by looking beyond known alerts and known malicious threats.

Attackers like advanced persistent threats (APTs) can compromise the organization network and remain active and undetected for a long time collecting data and stealing login credentials to laterally move to other devices uncompromised until then.

The threat hunting process goes beyond the usual detection technologies, like security information and event management (SIEM) and EDR, by looking for hidden malware and patterns of suspicious activities. This can be done by combining several sources of information in addition to SIEM and EDR, and correlate that information based on known use cases, the SOC analyst's experience, artificial intelligence technologies, and threat intelligence, such as security advisories and alerts with *indicators of compromise* (IoCs) or indicators of attack (IoAs).

There are three distinct types of threat hunting.

- **Intel-based** hunting looks for IoCs provided by threat intelligence alerts and advisories IoCs to hunt for threats. These IoCs can be hash values, IP addresses, domain names, networks, or host artifacts provided by intelligence sharing platforms such as computer emergency response teams (CERT) that should be looked for by the SOC. For example, if one alert mentions a public IP address as an APT command and control, the SOC should look for it in all logs, such as proxy, to check if there were any attempts to access it. If confirmed, devices in the organization have been compromised.

- **Hypothesis hunting** is a proactive hunting model that uses a threat hunting library and playbooks aligned with the MITRE ATT&CK framework to detect APTs and malware in the organization's infrastructure. This approach uses known attackers IoAs and tactics, techniques, and procedures (TTP) to detect threats.

- **Custom hunting**: Based on the organization requirements and use cases considering the organization context factors like geopolitical issues or specific activity-related issues (e.g., finance, credit card, defense), it can include both intel and hypothesis models. When the threat hunting detects malware or confirms malicious activity, an incident must be created, and the mitigation process managed according to the security incident management process.

Threat Intelligence

Threat intelligence is the prior knowledge of what will happen to your organization, assets, or information so that you can prepare yourself to prevent or mitigate those attacks. Threat intelligence can provide useful information on the attacker's modus operandi, capabilities, sources, resources, and motives (also known as tactics, techniques, and procedures (TTP)). This information helps you build up efficient and focused defenses to protect the organization.

There are three categories of threat intelligence, strategic, tactical, and operational. Strategic threat intelligence helps the organization to understand the overall threat landscape. These are general information provided by security companies about the nation, the industry, or the organization. Tactical threat intelligence is more actionable. They may contain IoCs or the fingerprints of the malicious behavior so that organizations can act on security devices, such as proxy, email gateway, EDR, or IPS. Generally, these are malicious IP addresses, domain names, hashes of malicious payloads. Operational threat intelligence is the knowledge on potential cyberattacks or campaigns against the organization, with possible attack vectors.

Threat intelligent information mostly comes from the dark or deep web, where cybercriminals, threat actors, or hacktivists discuss their next attack, try to find support for their next moves, or try to sell stolen data. Organizations do not need to access those places to get that information; instead, they hire professional companies—generally, subscription-based software-as-a-service platforms provide threat intelligence feeds tailored to your organization or industry.

Establishing defenses before the actual incident is the main purpose of threat intelligence. However, it can also be used to decrease the incident response time. There are numerous threat intelligence platforms that analysts can send the hashes of files to check if they have been tagged in previous cyber incidents. In addition, threat intelligence can help to prioritize patching in larger organizations. For example, if the organization acquired an operational threat intelligence that their public website is attacked, the patching of those servers should be prioritized.

Threat intelligence data is also useful for risk management activities, particularly in deciding the likelihood of a certain threat. Moreover, most threat intelligence tools provide information on stolen customer data such as card details, names, and IDs, passwords. Organizations can use this information by either replacing the cards or forcing their end-users or consumers to change their passwords. Similarly, organizations can assess the risk that the third-party service providers introduce to their environment by cyber-risk scoring that the threat intelligence platforms offer nowadays.

In addition to commercial threat intelligence service providers, national CERTs also provide and expect other organizations to share threat intelligence information so that a national-level awareness and preparedness can be done.

Organizations can also use online threat intelligence tools to check their digital footprint on the Internet. There are many ready-to-use[31] and ready-to-install[32] tools for such purposes.

Security Engineering

Security engineering incorporates and integrates security controls with all other information systems from the organization.

---

[31] For a curated list, go to `https://github.com/jivoi/awesome-osint`.
[32] Please see Chapter 9.

Asset Management

The asset management process maintains oversight of the organization's IT assets inventory. This should be a continuous process to ensure that all devices are protected by security controls like antivirus, EDR, or vulnerability scan agents to provide reliable information on the organization's assets, security events, and vulnerabilities.

Currently, solutions (Figure 5-3) are available to integrate different asset repositories, like EDR, vulnerability scanners, Active Directory, and identify unmanaged assets or assets with missing agents.

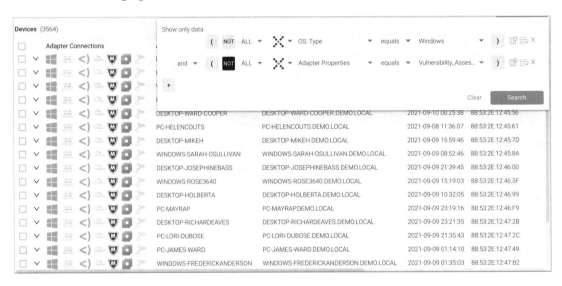

Figure 5-3. *Asset management and discovery platform*

Media Sanitation

Media Sanitation is another part of the asset management process. Organizations must implement an effective media sanitation policy to prevent data leakage to address all decommissioned and broken media.

NIST SP 800-53,[33] *Guidelines for Media Sanitization,* offers guidance on how organizations can sanitize media.

In their media sanitation policy, organizations must consider the asset classification and choose the right method according to the asset information sensitiveness.

---

[33] https://csrc.nist.gov/publications/detail/sp/800-88/rev-1/final

Media with highly confidential information should be degaussed or physically destroyed, and media with non-sensitive information can only be erased or overwritten. However, applying different sanitation methods might not be cost-effective and complex to manage. Therefore, some organizations opt to have only one highly effective sanitation method for the entire organization (e.g., physical destruction) or outsource this process.

Configuration and Patch Management

Network devices, security devices, and IT assets are dependent on configurations. It is fundamental to system hardening. Security professionals configure a device to be secure based on security baselines, organizational policies, or business needs for an application. All these configurations are needed to be done in configuration management.

In large organizations, where thousands of servers and devices are in place, it is nearly impossible to configure them manually, one by one. Hence, organizations are relying on automation by configuration management tools. These tools can detect the device's current configuration, say a firewall or many firewalls, and apply any security patch or even change the firewall configuration to add a new zone to all devices in one click, for example. These tools also cover applications. Whenever a new release is required, the configuration management tool uploads the required package to the servers, stops the application services, replaces the files, and restarts the services in all servers in the cluster. After services are up and running, it can send the provisioning scripts and collect outputs.

Thanks to these tools, it is easier to track which systems have the latest configuration changes, which systems require changes, or which systems do not have a prerequisite package. In addition, some of these tools support workflows, which enable security professionals to track the actual approval processes of the changes, change windows, impacted or pending devices, and assess the impact easily.

A centralized configuration management tool for large organizations also helps with overall security. The monthly patches are needed to be discovered and applied to all servers. Configuration managers can detect the missing patches, apply them in a defined time frame, and report any issues during the patching. Moreover, they are useful for setting up new virtual servers. When you need a new server, it can be deployed and installed in seconds via an OS template (an image), already hardened.

Security Architecture

According to NIST, *security architecture* is "a set of physical and logical security-relevant representations (i.e., views) of system architecture that conveys information about how the system is partitioned into security domains and makes use of security-relevant elements to enforce security policies within and between security domains based on how data and information must be protected."

Note   The security architecture reflects security domains, the placement of security-relevant elements within the security domains, the interconnections and trust relationships between the security-relevant elements, and the behavior and interaction between the security-relevant elements. The security architecture, similar to the system architecture, may be expressed at different levels of abstraction and with different scopes."[34]

In addition to security standards (device hardening, network devices, cryptographic, etc.) and security baselines, each organization must have a corporate security architecture to integrate all the technical security controls and clearly define the integration rules for every system.

The security architecture defines the corporate security standards (e.g., cryptographic, databases, authentication methods, file sharing, network segmentation, technologies, etc.) so project managers and system administrators know exactly where each component of their systems fit, the authorized technologies, and how to integrate it with the remaining systems.

This process should also include application security architecture (e.g., mobile application calls to third parties should be directly sent to the service provider or directed through the organization data center), including authentication methods (e.g., SAML, OAuth, etc.).

The security architecture design should address the organization's needs, requirements, and potentially related risks in an understandable design that includes in-depth security control specifications. Based on the organization's risk posture, business requirements, benchmarks, good practices, financial constraints, and legal and regulatory requirements, the security architect needs to define, among others, the following standards.

---

[34] NIST SP 800-37 Rev. 2 from NIST SP 800-160 Vol. 2

- How will external parties connect from the Internet? (HTTPS, IPSec, SFTP?)

- How will those parties authenticate? And which technologies should be used (directory services, authentication protocols, etc.)?

- How should the organization segment its perimeter and internal networks?

    - Critical, non-critical

    - Confidential, non-confidential

    - Cardholder, non-cardholder

    - Customer, partner, employee services

- How should this segmentation be implemented in communication devices?

    - Distinct devices per segment or perimeter zone?

- Which technology should be implemented for each layer? And how should it be hardened?

    - Front end

    - Middleware

    - Databases

    - Back office

    - Support Systems (DNS, Active Directory, file servers, internal portals, mail, etc.)

    - Legacy systems

- How should virtualization platforms be implemented?

- Which security controls should be implemented between each layer?

- How will communication be done between layers?

- Which security controls should be implemented in each asset? And are new assets on-boarded?

  - Hardening

  - Antivirus

  - Directory services integration

  - Policies

  - EDR

  - Vulnerability scanner agent

  - SIEM integration

  - DAM integration (for databases)

- How and where should a web application firewall be implemented?

- How and where should an intrusion protection system be implemented?

- How will all these systems be administered?

The security architecture should be a live process, frequently reviewed to define how new technologies should be on-boarded.

CHAPTER 6

People

Employees are our most valuable asset.

Here is your appreciation.

—Every CEO

A BBC TV quiz show airing between 2000 and 2012 called *The Weakest Link*,[1] originally hosted by Anne Robinson,[2] where contestants, taking turns, tried to create chains of correct answers in a row to increase the amount of money they would earn. One incorrect answer would break the chain, and the contestants would lose all the money in that chain. Cybersecurity is just like that. The strength of a cybersecurity posture is limited to the weakest link in the chain. Technology and processes are enablers to increase the overall strength of the organization's security. However, eventually, *people* are creating, developing, and using these. *People* present the greatest cybersecurity risk. One mistake or wrongdoing can break the chain, and then bad things happen.

People play the most important role in processes and technology when it comes to organizational security and protection. Organizations can only have the best protection possible when these three elements come together and work in harmony. Previous chapters covered the technology and processes aspect of cybersecurity. Now, it is people's turn.

Cybersecurity incidents happen when a person or a team fails to follow the processes developed to use the technologies. Yes, technologies can fail, and yes, processes, regardless of the implemented security controls, may not have been prepared with the best security posture; however, most incidents, if not all, were caused by people. An employee clicking a phishing email or plugging a malicious USB stick in a corporate desktop, intentionally or inadvertently leaking corporate information to a personal

---

[1] https://en.wikipedia.org/wiki/Weakest_Link

[2] https://en.wikipedia.org/wiki/Anne_Robinson

© Virgilio Viegas and Oben Kuyucu 2022
V. Viegas and O. Kuyucu, *IT Security Controls*, https://doi.org/10.1007/978-1-4842-7799-7_6

email, or losing a corporate laptop are only some examples of how the human factor can fail. According to Verizon DBIR 2021,[3] 85% of breaches involve the human element, and social engineering attacks as a pattern have continued to increase since 2017. COVID-19 forced many employees to work remotely, so there has also been a significant increase in these types of attacks since 2020.

Before digital transformation, only people with technical expertise could be responsible for maintaining the overall security posture of an enterprise. Mostly, there was always someone to handle patching, provide access, or instruct people what they should not do. Everyone always "hated" this person because there was always one "obstacle" (in fact, a required security control) created by this person that prevented colleagues from doing their jobs in time. This person always tried to prevent employees's "I should write my password to a sticky note, in case I forgot" attitude, which continuously created security gaps. Then, management realized that security should no longer be just a concern of the one IT security "guy" in their organization. So, information security management systems came into the picture, and suddenly employees became an integral part of the security chain. Security awareness and user education on cybersecurity became essential instead of optional.

Security Awareness

To ensure that all *relevant individuals* comply with information security policies, apply defined security controls and protect sensitive information in the organization from cyberattacks being compromised or disclosed to unauthorized actors, an effective security awareness program must be in place.

This program must be designed in a way that catches people's attention and convinces them security is worth the engagement.

Relevant individuals can be the following.

- Employees, including executives

- Third-party service providers, outsourced staff

- Customers, end users

- Basically, everyone that uses the system

---

[3] https://enterprise.verizon.com/content/verizonenterprise/us/en/index/resources/reports/2021-dbir-executive-brief.pdf

Rather than being too technical, a security awareness program must consist of understandable and down-to-earth content, which aims to a higher degree of the organization's security posture. It is also advised to establish a continuously improved security culture aligned with the organization's usual activities and risks and a security training program supported by technologies, processes, and incentives to ensure best practices are applied.

Overall, security awareness activities should have the following traits.

- It should be managed by a dedicated resource focused on building and maturing the role and initiatives of the program. This should be a senior-level management role, or equivalent, within the information security or risk teams.

- It should be sponsored by information security leaders or heads (e.g., CISO), authorized, and tracked by top management.

- It should be supported by a documented set of measurable objectives or metrics.

- It should improve the security-positive behavior of employees continuously. This can be achieved by gamification of training, making attendance compulsory, linking the results to personal/ departmental performance objectives.

- It should present achievable security controls to reduce the impact or probability of information security incidents. It should not be a burden or a cumbersome task for the employees, which may make the whole program unsustainable

- It should be modified based on the results of a formal information risk analysis

The content is also important.

- It should be prepared by an individual, departmental unit, working group, or committee that is skilled.

  • Hands-on experience with cybersecurity, cybersecurity programs, industry standards, regulatory requirements, and training techniques

  • A better understanding of enterprise's services, processes, and controls environments, so the content is aligned

- It should be kept up-to-date with existing and potential threats (threat landscape) to the enterprise systems and the sensitivity of the information, changes in the enterprise or the environment, current practices, and requirements aligned with national compliance regulations.

- It should be understandable by every job level in the enterprise, multilingual if needed. Very technical terms should be avoided. For better support on technical terms, users should be redirected to skilled IT security support agents.

- It should comprise the meaning of information security (e.g., CIA triad) and the importance of complying with information security policies and security controls/standards defined in these policies. It should also contain employee responsibilities for information security, including but not limited to reporting information security incidents.

Predefined metrics should track the effectiveness of security awareness. Some of those metrics are defined in Chapter 7. The following are additional ones.

- Measure the level of information security awareness of employees

  - The number of employees who completed the information security training

  - The number of employees who failed the training quiz in the first attempt

  - The number of employees who repeatedly clicked the link at the phishing simulation email

  - The number of employees who signed the information security policy

– Review the level of information security awareness regularly

  • The average percentage of the correct answers of the training quiz

– Measure the benefits of security awareness activities

  • A comparison of the number of security incidents due to human error per month – month-to-month and year-to-year

Security awareness is addressed in the frameworks described in Table 6-1.

Table 6-1. *Cybersecurity Standards and Frameworks That Address Security Awareness*

Framework	Description
COBIT	Security awareness and training policy (DS7)
ISO 27001/2	Information Security Awareness, Education & Training (A.7.2.2)
NIST 800-53	Security awareness and training (AT)
NIST 800-50	Building an Information Technology Security
NIST CSF	Awareness and Training (PR.AT)
PCI DSS	Requirement 12
CIS Controls	14 – Security Awareness and Skills Training

Table 6-2 presents sample security awareness plans.

Table 6-2. Sample Information Security Awareness Program Plans

	Q1			Q2			Q3			Q4		
Key Subjects	Changes in threat landscapes			Protection against social engineering			Acceptable use (telecommuting, email, and Internet use)			Data security, data privacy		
	Jan	Feb	Mar	Apr	May	Jun	Jul	Aug	Sep	Oct	Nov	Dec
Key Steps	Training Need Analysis	Phishing simulation	Delivery of Awareness Materials	Annual Information Security Awareness Training (CBT)	Phishing simulation		Notifications to all users on Acceptable use	Phishing simulation		Notifications to all users on Data protection policies, Data Privacy Laws	Phishing simulation	
Brief description and notes	Need analysis for targeted training	Fake email requesting to click a link that provides a ticket to the global event in the country in March	Posters (offices) banners (company portal), screensaver (PCs) about passwords, social engineering, the policy and incident reporting	-Must include the link to the policies- Must contain a quiz at the end-Users must sign the policy at the end	Fake email stating that the account has been compromised and the user has to change the password by giving all details about the credentials		-Must include a link to Acceptable Use Policy- Must include Incident Reporting processes- Users must sign the policy at the end	Fake email with a Zoom link		-Must include a link to Data Protection Policy-Must include for the Data Privacy annual Incident bonuses. Reporting processes- Users must signoff policy at the end	Fake email requesting user bank accounts	

Metric					
Number of people reported as phishing, opened the email, and clicked the link	-Who has or has not completed online Computer-Based Training – Completion link reports from Learning Management System- People have completed/ understand training and acknowledge they adhere to policies	Number of people reported as phishing, opened the email, and clicked the link	-Who has or has not completed online Computer-Based Training – Completion reports from Learning Management System- People have completed/ understand training and acknowledge they adhere to policies	Number of people reported as phishing, opened the email and clicked the link	-Who has or has not completed online Computer-Based Training – Completion reports from link Learning Management System- People have completed/ understand training and acknowledge they will adhere to policies

(continued)

215

Table 6-2. (*continued*)

	Q1	Q2	Q3	Q4
Senior Management/Administration	Training Need Analysis Phishing simulation	Annual Information Security Awareness Training Phishing simulation	Notifications are sent Phishing simulation	Notifications are sent Phishing simulation
Technical Departments – IT/ITSec/Project Management	forms are sent to all departments and collected	Phishing simulation – Report to Management	Phishing simulation – Report to Management Targeted training	Phishing simulation – Report to Management Notifications are sent Phishing simulation – Report to Management Annual phishing reporting to Management with lessons learned
Operations/Production			Notifications are sent	Targeted training Notifications are sent
HR		Prepares the targeted training materials and other deliverables	Targeted training notifications are sent Notifications are sent	Targeted training Notifications are sent
Finance/Accounting			Notifications are sent	Targeted training Notifications are sent
Marketing/Sales			Notifications are sent	Targeted training Notifications are sent

Figure 6-1 presents a sample security awareness content.

Security Essentials for Company XYZ

Treat each of your **passwords** like a personal item such as a toothbrush. 🖊 Don't let anybody else use it. Get a new one every three months. Don't put it in common places. Do not use the same passwords with your personal accounts.

Size matters when it comes to the strength of your password. Every password can be eventually hacked. What matters is how long it takes. When you have longer passwords with uppercase, lowercase letters, numbers, and special characters, you are making hackers' life a bit harder.

Be vigilant. Your first line of defense in cybersecurity is actually "You" 😊. Be cautious of anything suspicious.
Always check if a site is secure. 🔐 Do I know the sender of the email that has an attachment? Have I validated the link before I clicked? Do I really need to give all my details to this unknown caller who pretends to be a law enforcement officer?

Software and operating system updates: We know you are busy and have no time for an "update." It is easy to skip software updates; however, this can be a mistake that opens your door to hackers to steal your data, identity, money, and more.

Antivirus software: Winter is coming. Have you got your flu shot already? Better to protect your PC as well; antivirus software is the solution for computer viruses. 🦠

Mobile apps: Do apps need to see the messages on your phone? Do not install applications that you do not trust on your mobile device. Free apps may have different purposes. You should carefully read the permissions the apps ask for, then accept them. 📲

Backups: Will you still have access to your information if your computer breaks? Remember, you lost your contacts when your phone was broken. You were very upset about all the phone numbers that were lost. Take regular backups so that the same doesn't happen to your computer.

We know you are a social butterfly. But would you please not take pictures of our office, where your password and the highly confidential bidding document are clearly visible…??? #IamSecure 📸

Clean desk, clean screen. Going for a tea break? Make sure you lock your screen when leaving your desk. Five minutes will be more than enough for someone to infect your computer with a virus.

MFA: No, it is not the Ministry of Foreign Affairs. It is *multi-factor authentication*. Are you worried that your password is still not secure enough? It is always beneficial to take extra precautions. A password that only you know, a verification code from a device you own (such as an SMS), and a feature you own (fingerprint) will increase your security many times over.
Encrypt sensitive information. The minimum allowed encryption is AES-256 with recommended modes of operation for block ciphers of Galois/Counter Mode (GCM), Cipher Block Chaining (CBC), and Counter Mode (CTR)… Too technical? 😵 Why not ask for support from the Information Security team (infosec@companyxyz.co)?

Spotted an alien 👽, an elephant in the room, or an unknown person doing something to PCs? 🐘 Please report and notify the IT security team as soon as possible.
For more information, check out our information security policy, which can be found in the Company portal.

Your Information Security team
infosec@companyxyz.co

Figure 6-1. *Sample information security awareness content*

Security Training

Although it is said that employees, in general, may be the weakest link, the same can also be said for the cybersecurity workforce. If a cybersecurity professional is not qualified for a specific technology or a process, it may create a gap in the overall security posture. Hence, apart from employee awareness, targeted training of cybersecurity professionals is required. Security training provides employees with hands-on instructions and guidelines to perform their duties securely. It can be outsourced where the training is provided by a third party like a vendor/product-specific training, or in-house where practiced individuals can train new hires or less experienced teammates a peer-to-peer training.

Outsourced training programs are available through industry-accepted information security organizations such as SANS,[4] ISC2[5], ISSA,[6] ISACA,[7] and many others. These agencies also provide security certifications, where information security professionals can accolade their knowledge and experience into a credential. These certifications also offer competitive advantage career-wise, acting as "golden standards."

Most companies now seek individuals with globally recognized certifications (Appendix 2) as these programs ensure that the individual has the following.

- The necessary expertise (as most of the programs require a minimum of five years cumulative paid work experience in a variety of security areas)

- Continuously improving information security skills to stay updated on the latest threats and technology (as most of the certifications require a minimum of 120 hours of continuing professional education (CPE) in three years)

- Been endorsed by someone in the information security community (as most of the programs require endorsement from a certified individual)

- A commitment to behaving ethically (as most of the programs require the individual to follow the code of ethics of the certification)

---

[4] www.sans.org
[5] www.isc2.org
[6] www.issa.org
[7] www.isaca.org

Security training is crucial for individuals who want to advance in the information or cybersecurity fields. Experience is also important; the muscle memory for incident response would help you greatly in times of crisis. However, you cannot trust someone on, for example, malware containment that would not know the basics about Operating Systems, networking concepts, protocols, or network security. In addition, particular activities, such as risk management, should be done by competent and trained individuals. Otherwise, significant risks may not be addressed, which may create serious ramifications and impact the overall security posture of the enterprise.

Figure 6-2 presents some of the key jobs in cybersecurity.

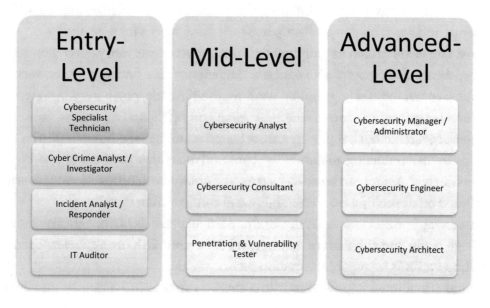

Figure 6-2. *Key jobs in cybersecurity*[8]

Role-based training is also useful to close skill gaps, leading to a more senior position. For example, to become a successful and helpful security assessor, the individual needs to understand networking, perimeter and endpoint management, protection, security and system architecture, change management, security assessments and testing, security operations, and identity management, and even secure software development. If the individual does not have capable knowledge or understanding in these areas, the assessment is only a tick-box exercise, which, in the end, would not have any value to the enterprise and the assessor.

---

[8]www.cyberseek.org/pathway.html

Security training should be aligned to improve knowledge, skills, and abilities. However, since there are a variety of jobs, different job descriptions, and different techniques, to have a common language in cybersecurity skill development, NICE (National Initiative for Cybersecurity Education) Cybersecurity Workforce Framework (NIST Special Publication 800-181 revision 1)[9] was created. NICE provides sets of building blocks for role-based training with competencies and knowledge, skills, and abilities, also known as KSAs. With the NICE Framework, organizations can create job profiles, education requirements, and training paths for security professionals based on cybersecurity roles required for the organization.

The NICE Framework's main building blocks are tasks, knowledge, and skills (TKS) statements, and it sets up a relationship between these blocks for a job profile.

A *task* can be described as "conduct and/or support authorized penetration testing on enterprise network assets." *Knowledge* is "knowing system and application security threats and vulnerabilities (e.g., buffer overflow, mobile code, cross-site scripting, Procedural Language/Structured Query Language [PL/SQL] and injections, race conditions, covert channel, replay, return-oriented attacks, malicious code)." The *skills* required are "in conducting vulnerability scans and recognizing vulnerabilities in security systems." *Ability* can be described as "the ability to identify systemic security issues based on the analysis of vulnerability and configuration data."

Please keep in mind that the KSAs for this particular task is not conclusive. More knowledge, skills, and abilities are required to fully accomplish the task. Please see Appendix 3 for KSAs in major information security fields.

NIST also maintains supplementary information on the NICE Framework, where a reference sheet can be found for TKS statements.[10]

Table 6-3 lists some security training in frameworks.

Table 6-3. *Security Training Frameworks*

COBIT	Security awareness and training policy (DS7)
ISO 27001/2	A.7.2.2 Information Security Awareness, Education & Training
NIST 800-16	Information Technology Security Training Requirements: a Role- and Performance-Based Model
CIS Controls	14 - Security Awareness and Skills Training (14.9)

[9] https://doi.org/10.6028/NIST.SP.800-181r1

[10] www.nist.gov/document/supplementnicespecialtyareasandworkroleksasandtasksxlsx

CHAPTER 7

Security Metrics

It has always been a struggle for information security professionals to measure "the effectiveness" of IT security controls. In the 1980s, "orange books" were released for security professionals as a standard to set basic requirements for assessing the effectiveness of security controls built into a computer system (Figure 7-1), which was a part of the Rainbow Series published by the U.S. National Computer Security Center. The most well-known orange book is the *Trusted Computer System Evaluation Criteria (TCSEC)* and its European counterpart, *Information Technology Security Evaluation Criteria (ITSEC)*. The Common Criteria for Information Technology Security Evaluation (in short, ISO/IEC 15408)[1] replaced those books. It created a framework for defining security levels for systems (hardware, software, or firmware) and determining acceptable testing methods and certifying system compliance to defined assurance levels.

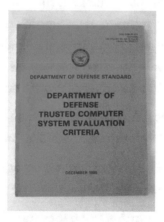

Figure 7-1. Department of Defense Trusted Computer System Evaluation Criteria

---

[1] www.iso.org/standard/50341.html

V. Viegas and O. Kuyucu, *IT Security Controls*, https://doi.org/10.1007/978-1-4842-7799-7_7

To ensure the effectiveness of their ISMS, organizations must create and monitor key performance indicators (KPIs) for each implemented control. Although information security KPIs intend to be extremely useful, they can also be confusing, misleading, time-consuming, or unusable. Each organization must avoid creating an excessive number of KPIs that are likely to only be reported but not properly followed up.

Although it might be considered a cliché, a SMART approach for defining security metrics works in most organizations.

- **Specific**: Target the area being measured, not a by-product or result.

- **Measurable**: The data collected is accurate and complete

- **Actionable**: It is easy to understand the data and to take action.

- **Relevant**: Measure what's important with the data.

- **Timely**: The data is available when you need it.

The recipe for success is to create a simple but comprehensive follow-up model with a dashboard with key performance indicators (KPIs) logically grouped according to each organization's specific structure, risk posture through key performance indexes (KPXs) and measured with adequate frequency.

Data quality is another factor that influences the monitoring process's effectiveness. Thus, the organization must also monitor each metric's data sources and quality and ensure that the existing controls logging policies are effectively configured. Additionally, misconfigured or not properly fine-tuned controls can lead to false rejection or false acceptance rates and create an incorrect perception of security and biased log data.

- A *false acceptance rate* (FAR) is the percentage of events considered as valid that should have been rejected (false negative).

- A *false rejection rate* (FRR) is the percentage of invalid events that should have been considered legitimate (false positive).

Each metric threshold and reporting frequency must be defined according to each organization's risk appetite. Most ISMS programs require the definition of thresholds for those metrics so that when a certain threshold has been reached, a flag must be raised to either improve the process or the security control. It is also expected to improve those thresholds for the next cycle to improve the organization's security posture. Security professionals should also refer to industry or region-specific average threshold values published by numerous research and analysis companies and online sources.

Another factor that must be considered when designing the monitoring KPIs is that not all systems have the same criticality or exposure. For example, Internet-facing systems are more exposed to external factors than internal systems, and the likelihood of those systems being attacked by external actors is higher than internal systems. Therefore, they need to be monitored with higher frequency and stricter thresholds.

The same approach should be taken, considering each system's criticality. Critical systems with a higher potential negative impact should be monitored more frequently with stricter thresholds.

The following sections review metrics that help build a dashboard to monitor your information security controls effectiveness.

Governance and Oversight

This section presents some selected metrics to measure the effectiveness of the information security program management.

Information security budget vs. information technology budget

This metric allows the information security manager to better understand the organization's information security posture by comparing the information security budget with the IT budget. The information security manager can also compare the information security budget (or percentage) against market benchmarks.[2] In a mature organization,[3] the IT security budget should be approximately 10% to 30% of the overall IT budget.

The number of times the board was briefed on information security matters during the last 12 months

Like the previous metric, this metric also allows the information security manager to understand the senior management posture in relation to information security. Senior management should be briefed at least once every quarter regarding the information security trends, current threat landscape, the organization's security posture, and employee awareness.

---

[2] www.csoonline.com/article/3432138/how-much-should-you-spend-on-security.html
[3] Kaspersky IT Security Economics 2020_Executive Summary.pdf

The number of information security–related exceptions granted in the last 12 months

The number of exceptions granted to the security policy allows you to better understand each department's security posture and potential constraints. If there are many exceptions, the policies and related procedures may need to be reviewed. Exceptions to corporate information security policies can be originated for several reasons.

- Obsolete systems that cannot be updated due to the following.

    - Dependencies from external systems or providers like service bureaus, settlement and clearing platforms, regulatory systems, etc.

    - Legacy and unsupported systems that cannot be updated or are too expensive to update

    - Unavailability of immediate upgrade windows due to service disruptions on mission critical systems

- Systems managed or owned by external parties

- Functional or application users that need specific properties

- Not supported encryption algorithms either by the counterpart or by technical limitations of the existing devices

- Application or database management system inability to implement encryption

- Legal or regulatory exceptions

The number of reported operational risk events in the scope

This metric allows you to monitor the risk events in scope trends and the adherence of the organization structure to the risk management system. For example, if you break down this metric by the department and consider the department's nature, you better understand each department's adherence and risk posture.

PCI DSS compliance ratio

As explained in previous chapters, PCI DSS has a relatively stricter scope when compared with ISO 27001 since it only applies to payment card data. For organizations that have ongoing certification or recertification processes, the ratio of compliance with PCI DSS is very useful to identify the areas where you need to apply greater effort and resources to achieve full compliance. Finally, when vetting vendors, the validity of each certification must always be confirmed.

ISO 27001 compliance ratio

Like PCI DSS, organizations can also obtain ISO27001 certification. However, the ISO 27001 scope is much wider because it can include the entire organization.

During the certification process, this metric can identify areas where you need to apply greater effort and resources to ISO 27001 achieve full compliance. You should always check the certification validity when vetting vendors.

Cybersecurity maturity level

The organization should measure the effectiveness and maturity level of the information security controls in the environment through cybersecurity assessments conducted by independent third parties. These maturity levels are based on industry-accepted levels such as CMMI (e.g., initial, managed, defined or planned, quantitatively managed, and optimizing). These assessments help the organizations prioritize their investments in less protected areas.

The total amount of losses to the organization due to cybersecurity incidents in one year

This metric estimates the average loss caused by a cybersecurity incident. This amount should also be compared with the estimated value of the residual risk for these types of incidents based on the available data sources (e.g., CSIRT, corporate associations, regulators, or managed security services providers).

Antivirus and Anti-Malware Metrics

The following security metrics measure the effectiveness of endpoint security controls.

The number of viruses detected by endpoint antivirus

This metric allows you to check the endpoint antivirus effectiveness, but it can also be used to understand the effectiveness of the remaining controls. For example, provided that endpoint antivirus tools/agents are properly updated, if the number of detected viruses increases, the perimeter controls are failing to block those viruses, and they are getting inside the organization. According to the virus type and propagation methods, it is possible to identify the potential faulty controls.

Email spam and malicious content blocked by corporate email antivirus

Organizations will always be flooded with spam and emails with malicious content. In some organizations, this type of content represents most of the received mails. If you have managed services where a third party provides email filtering, this metric allows you to monitor the effectiveness of that service.

If the organization manages the entire infrastructure, it is possible to use this metric to understand the trends, manage capacity, do a cost/benefit analysis and consider outsourcing this service.

The percentage of devices with antivirus, endpoint detection and response (EDR) agent, and vulnerability scanner agents installed (broken down by perimeter vs. internal, operating systems, desktop vs. server, and type of agent)

These are probably the most important metrics you can have to understand how protected your assets are. However, to ensure that this metric is accurate, you need to ensure that your inventory is properly maintained and accurate; otherwise, this metric can lead you to incorrect conclusions. The following are examples.

- If your inventory does not have all your assets, you may have a higher percentage of deployed agents than you effectively have. In extremis, you can have agents deployed in more assets than your inventory. Consolidation of your assets from different systems is recommended.

- Reported deployed offline agents. This can happen when you decommission assets and the agents are not removed from the repositories or a network issue that prevents agents from communicating with the centralized management.

The percentage of devices with updated antivirus (including average update time)

In addition to the previous metric that measures coverage, you also need to monitor if the agents (EDR, antivirus, vulnerability scanner) are updated; otherwise, their effectiveness can be compromised. To use this metric, you must define reasonable thresholds such as 24 or 48 hours to have the latest updates and pulled policies.

Other metrics that measure how long the organization is exposed to new viruses or lateral movements include the average time to push AV signature updates to all systems and the number of systems that exceed that average time, the length of time it takes to have all inventory updated, and the percentage of hosts performing full disk scanning on time.

Clean Pipes

Clean pipes are important as they release bandwidth to legitimate traffic and provide better visibility on the real threats that the organization receives. This section presents some metrics for clean pipes.

Spam and malicious content blocked by the ISP or filtering service provider

You can use this metric to evaluate the effectiveness of the service provider if you have this kind of filtering service subscribed.

Additionally, this metric can be correlated with the spam and malicious content blocked by corporate email antivirus metric so you can fine-tune the filtering policies on the filtering service provider side. Depending on the type of implementation, this metric and *email spam and malicious content blocked by corporate email antivirus* might be redundant.

Traffic blocked by ISP

This metric evaluates the effectiveness of the service provider and analyzes "noise" traffic trends. It should be analyzed in conjunction with DDoS mitigation reports, if available.

Network Security

Security metrics for a network ensure the perimeter security controls and internal network controls are implemented effectively.

WAF and IPS false positive alerts

By measuring the number of false positives, in your IPS and WAF, you can measure the negative impact of your security controls on the performance of your service and fine-tune them. However, if there are no explicit complaints about performance, it is hard to find those false positives. One possible way to do this is to review the WAF and IPS logs, use breach and attack simulators to analyze the effectiveness, and, aside from the clearly true positives, review the remaining potential false positives with the development and system administration teams.

Traffic detected in the black hole

The concept of a "black hole" passes by implementing a default gateway to the entire organization, to where all traffic to non-corporate networks is routed. Since it is not expected to receive any traffic in the black hole in a mature environment, any traffic received can measure the presence of unexpected or malicious agents in the organization network and misconfigurations.

Internet Access: Proxy and Content Filtering

The following controls help you identify user access attempts to unauthorized websites and detect traces of malicious agents in your network attempting to connect to command and control websites.

The number of attempts to access malicious/unauthorized websites

The attempt to access malicious websites usually is not a deliberate user action. It is often triggered by malicious content like email payloads executed by less informed users or infected USB drives. Using this metric gives you a perspective on how effective your endpoint controls are.

Depending on your organization's size and maturity level, it is better to implement a security operations center process to automatically raise an incident every time you detect an attempt to access a malicious website.

Malicious content download blocked by corporate content filters

Although slightly different from the previous metric, it serves the purpose of identifying attempts to download malicious content to your organization. Usually, these attempts do not result from users' deliberate actions.

Security Awareness and Training

Security Awareness and Training play an important role in the employees' understanding of information security. The information security function in the organization can make use of these metrics to assess the security awareness and training program.

The percentage of employees who have not completed the required security training

This measures the employees' adherence to security training.

Security awareness–training success ratio

At the end of most security awareness training, there should be some multiple-choice questions that measure the effectiveness of the security training and an overall perspective on the employees' security awareness level. It is also possible to set a minimum passing grade on the multiple-choice questions.

The number of employees who tried to access phishing websites

Web proxies can detect access attempts to phishing websites. This metric allows you to understand the effectiveness of phishing training over time.

The percentage of employees who tried to access phishing websites in the scope of a phishing simulation (repeated clickers)

One of the controls you should have is a periodic simulated phishing attack, where a phishing email is sent to all employees with a specific payload or link. This way, you understand how your organization's employees react to phishing attacks. Employees who executed the payload or clicked the links should be submitted to additional training.

The number of reported phishing emails

In addition to the previous metrics, measuring the number of reported phishing emails provides you additional information on your organization's employees' information security awareness maturity level.

The number of internally reported incidents

These are the trends in information security internally reported and on the employees' posture.

The number of conducted awareness training (e-learning or instructor-led) in the last 12 months

To comply with several security standards (e.g., ISO27001, PCI DSS), organizations must frequently provide security awareness training to their employees. In addition to attesting compliance with those standards, this metric also allows you to understand the organization's posture on information security. The participants must also review the quality of the delivered content.

The percentage of information security employees who had specific training (including workshops and conferences)

In addition to the general security awareness training, organizations must also ensure that their information security teams have regular targeted training, which can be monitored through this metric.

The percentage of information security roles staff with more than three years of experience

The maturity and expertise of the information security teams must also be monitored. By using this metric, you a perspective on the seniority of these teams

The percentage of certified information security staff (CISSP, CEH, GSEC, CISM, CISA, OSCP, CCSP, etc.)

Information security certifications can act as a benchmark and give a minimum assurance level on the human resources expertise level. Currently, several market regulators like central banks monitor organizations of qualified personnel by requesting organizations the number of employees with these certifications.

Firewall Management

Firewalls are one of the major first lines of defense for most organizations, and these metrics assess firewall management in the organization.

The number of unused firewall rules

The number of unused firewall rules allows you to have a clear perspective of the firewall rules management process. This metric should also be broken down by DMZ or perimeter and internal firewalls. Unused firewall rules mean a lack of cleanup processes, and systems are decommissioned without eliminating firewall correspondent firewall rules. In some cases, unused firewall rules can also mean that other rules are shadowing them.

The number of firewall reviews conducted in the last 12 months

Firewall review is the process that allows organizations to verify their rule sets compliance, the devices configurations, and vulnerabilities. Perimeter firewall reviews should be done more often than internal firewall reviews. Monitoring the number of conducted firewall reviews provides an understanding of the effectiveness of the firewall management process.

Percentage increase in the number of external attacks on the firewall

The variance in the number of attacks on your external interfaces gives you an outlook on the external attack trends. This should be compared to the periodic threat landscape reports. If you receive more attacks than expected, then you may have missed some threat surfaces or threat actors in your threat landscape.

The number or percentage of firewall rules added or changed within the last 90 days that were formally documented

Although this metric is not directly related to information security events, it is very useful to better understand the firewall management process and allocate the proper resources. Perimeter firewall rules sets are expected to have the least number of changes.

Enterprise Mobility Management

Mobile devices can present a serious threat to corporate networks when left unmanaged and pose a significant risk of data loss. These metrics can improve security and governance over mobile devices connecting to the corporate environment.

The number of security incidents with onboarded mobile devices

The occurrence of security incidents with mobile devices can be due to several reasons. However, considering the nature of these devices and the related risk, the number of incidents should be very low. All incidents must be analyzed in depth to avoid recurrences.

The number of mobile devices per user

Occasionally, employees can have one or two mobile devices. Having more devices may increase the threat surface, increasing the likelihood of sharing passwords and leaving devices unattended. In addition, it can be an indicator that the IT administrators use generic users to onboard such devices.

The number of unmanaged devices in the network

This is the total number of unmanaged devices being used in the company. Unmanaged devices can pose a security risk or increase the surface of the threat; hence, this number should be as minimal as possible.

The number of concurrent logins of a user from different devices

Although difficult to measure, this can be a good indicator that the device(s) or the user account(s) may be compromised.

Incident Management and Response

Being prepared for an incident and having complete visibility on the corporate network for the security events help organizations to respond and contain security incidents quickly, which then helps organizations minimize the risks that future incidents pose. In addition to security operations center performance metrics like time to react, mitigate, and recover. The following metrics assist organizations to have better incident management and response activities and their effectiveness.

The percentage of onboarded systems to SIEM

All systems should be onboarded to SIEM to collect security logs. This metric allows you to understand the SOC coverage and also to estimate the needed SOC resources to track the remaining systems

Amount of data being collected (events per second)

In addition to the previous metric, this metric allows you to estimate the needed human and technical resources for your SIEM and SOC.

The percentage of the number of events classified or turned into incidents in SIEM to the number of events in SIEM

If this metric is lower than the established threshold, the use cases that trigger an incident are not fine-tuned, or a lot of useless data is being collected that is not used for incident identification.

Silent log sources

After onboarding systems to SIEM, organizations must health-check those systems' connections by tracking the number of silent log sources. The SIEM onboard process must include a keep-alive mechanism.

The number of SOAR actions

Security Orchestration, Automation, and Response (SOAR) can be very useful to decrease workload and eliminate potential risks from manual workflows. The number of SOAR actions provides a better understanding of your automated tasks and faster mean time to resolution (MTTR).

The percentage of reported incidents to the local authorities

In highly regulated markets, organizations are legally obliged to report critical and/or high severity events to local authorities or regulators. Therefore organizations must closely track and monitor these events. These events can also affect organizations' security risk ratings.

The number of critical and high severity incidents

The number of incidents is a metric that you can use to understand the trends and allocate the proper resources to handle them. However, you need to have the appropriate incident reporting and response processes; otherwise, this metric is inaccurate and misleading.

The number of critical and high severity incidents with resolution time greater than three days

In addition to the previous metric, by measuring the resolution time, you can monitor the overall effectiveness of the security incident response process and confirm that you have the appropriate resources. In this metric, it is fundamental to have well-defined closure or resolution criteria. It can be decided when the threat is eliminated but systems are not recovered or with all systems recovered, or with post actions like password reset or without.

Total number of SOC raised incidents pending resolution (monthly backlog)

Similar to the previous metric, this metric also allows you to understand if you have the necessary resources to handle security incidents. Although organizations have the necessary resources to handle security incidents, sometimes their priorities are not focused on information security.

Vulnerability Management

Vulnerability Management metrics focus on detecting flaws and issues in the environment and can help organizations prioritize remediation activities.

Total number of critical, high, and medium severity vulnerabilities

By frequently monitoring the number of detected vulnerabilities in your systems, you understand how exposed your systems are. It is highly recommended to break down this metric by system

criticality classification and level of exposure. For example, this
metric can be broken down for DMZ, partner connections and
internal systems or, by card and non-card processing systems, or
applications

The number of assets/applications with critical and high vulnerabilities

Slightly different from the previous metric where there is no
information on the level of vulnerabilities concentration, this
metric allows you to understand how many assets/applications
are highly vulnerable.

Breaking down this metric by system/application criticality and
level of exposure is also highly recommended. Organizations
should also define thresholds for this metric according to their risk
posture. Critical and perimeter devices should have more strict
thresholds.

Average time to fix critical, high, and medium vulnerabilities

This includes the following.

- The mean time to mitigate a vulnerability according to its severity.

- The mean time to detect a new vulnerability according to the
vulnerability scan schedule.

Vulnerability age

Vulnerability age is the number of days since the vulnerability was
disclosed. High numbers mean that there is a problem to remediate
this vulnerability. It can also be used for remediation SLAs.

The number of critical vulnerabilities that fit certain criteria

This can be used for threat prioritization. Organizations should
focus on remediating these vulnerabilities as these are the ones
that would do most of the damage. Criteria could include the
following.

- High data loss: Successful exploitation results in massive data loss on
the host

- High lateral movement: After a compromise, the attacker has a high potential to compromise other machines in the network

- Worms: The vulnerability can be used in worms, which are malware that spreads itself without user interaction

- Denial of service: Successful exploitation results in denial of service

- Patch not available: Vendor has not provided an official fix

- Privilege escalation: Successful exploitation allows an attacker to gain elevated privileges

- Unauthenticated exploitation: Exploitation of this vulnerability does not require authentication

- Remote code execution: Successful exploitation allows an attacker to execute arbitrary commands or code on a targeted system or in a target process

- Availability of PoC or exploit code

- Patches not applied within 30/60/90 days of their release

The number of newly discovered assets

This shows that some systems are still not onboarded to the centralized asset management, and it can be a good indicator that a rogue system is residing in the network and asset inventory lacks quality.

Patches that can provide higher risk reductions

Most vulnerability management tools provide a percent you would reduce your risk by addressing the vulnerability in the environment. This can help to prioritize those patches.

The number of assets and/or applications with baseline or compliance scans failures

Baseline or compliance scans indicate if a particular asset has been hardened based on industry-accepted benchmarks. Overall, this metric can identify unhardened assets in the environment.

Penetration Testing, Code Review, and Security Assessments

Like vulnerability management metrics, penetration testing, code review, and security assessment metrics provide better insight for security professionals to focus the remediation activities on the riskiest application or system.

The number of websites and APIs running outdated TLS versions

Some organizations, according to their nature or size, have multiple websites. In this case, it's important to monitor the number of sites running outdated versions of TLS. The goal for this metric should be zero.

The percentage of web-facing applications with conducted security assessments or penetration tests

Internet-facing applications are the most exposed services of an organization in the cyber world. Therefore, these applications must be subject to security assessment before going live or after significant changes. Organizations must ensure that this metric is 100%.

The number of detected critical and high findings in web-facing applications from penetration tests

In addition to the previous metric, by monitoring the number of critical and high severity findings, you understand the security posture of the development teams or vendors related to each application and the quality of their deliverables. Applications with these types of findings should not go live before being fixed and retested.

The average time to fix critical and high severity penetration tests findings

This metric can be extremely useful for IT managers to allocate the necessary resources to fix critical and high severity findings.

Measuring outliers like findings that take too long to fix can also help identify applications with other types of constraints.

The percentage of web applications that are OWASP Top 10 compliant to total web applications

All web applications should be hardened, and most of the web application security assessment tools provide whether the web application is compliant or not. This metric can detect unhardened applications.

Change Management

To decrease risks, avoid mistakes, and increase productivity, organizations can use the following metrics related to change management. Deviations in these metrics can show an organization's maturity in overall information security management.

The number of emergency changes for systems in scope

The number of emergency changes of security devices can be originated by several reasons, like new vulnerabilities, fixes to malfunctioning features, or urgent configuration reviews. Security devices should have a stable configuration, and by monitoring emergency changes, you have an indicator of potential problems in your devices.

The number of rolled back changes for systems in scope

By monitoring the number of rolled-back changes in your security devices, you understand any problems in the change procedures or integrating with other devices (e.g., switches).

The percentage of change requests approved with information security review

Every relevant change needs to be reviewed by the information security function in the organization. This metric helps identify potential projects that information security professionals do not review.

Access Control

Access control metrics support the organization's user management process and sanitation of user repositories and avoid constraints like, for example, privilege creep, where users accumulate privileges over the years as they change roles or the use of shared accounts. Organizations should have the least number of user repositories to facilitate the management process and implement single sign-on and centralized management systems. The following metrics should take these factors into account and be done for each user repository.

The number of active external users that do not access the information systems for more than 30 days

External users' access to the organization systems should be implemented under the strict principle of "need to have." External users that don't access the systems for more than 30 days should be monitored and, preferably, their accounts locked until a new access request is done, in accordance with a defined user policy.

The number of active internal users that do not access the information systems for more than 30 days

Like the previous metric, this metric is applied to internal users. Although there can be some plausible cause for not accessing the systems for a long time (e.g., sick leave or training), the accounts should be automatically locked according to the corporate policy.

The number of terminated employees with active user accounts

This metric allows you to detect any potential problems in the employee checkout process. There should be no active accounts of terminated employees. Particular attention is needed to the applications that do not support a centralized authentication mechanism. Dormant user accounts may still be present in those applications. HR departments must accurately report the terminated employees, so this metric can be trustworthy.

The number of development users with access to production environments

Considering the nature of their work, development users should not have access to production systems. In case of exceptionally and temporally allowed, organizations must keep track of these accesses. If this metric is high for a long time, it might mean the organization has governance problems.

The number of access attempts by known generic user/ application accounts

This metric indicates the attempt of improper use of service accounts. In addition to this metric, systems should also report these events to the security information and event management platform to be tracked by the security operations center.

The number of privileged access management violations

It is an indication that IT administrators are not using a privileged access management (PAM) platform to log in to systems and perform administrative activities. You can measure this metric by observing the source IP of the remote connections to the system. If it is not from PAM, then it is a violation.

The number of applications that do not use centralized identity and access management solutions

Stand-alone applications that do not support or use centralized identity and access management (e.g., LDAP) may have dormant user accounts that may cause weakness to the environment.

Other Metrics

The following additional metrics can support the organizations to improve overall security posture, decrease the risks associated with those systems, and detect process flaws that would hinder any information security business-as-usual activity.

The number of audit findings related to information security

Audit findings indicate that your procedures or devices do not comply with the internal policies. Considering some policies use some standards as reference (e.g., ISO 27001, PCI DSS, or local regulatory standards), it may also mean that your organization is not complying with those standards. Organizations should have the least number of audit findings, and they should be addressed the fastest possible way.

The percentage of classified assets according to the corporate data classification policy

To have an effective data protection policy and implement the appropriate security controls, organizations must classify all their assets in accordance with that policy.

With this metric, organizations can have an outlook on the risk they are taking by not having all assets classified and consequently not applying their data protection policies accurately.

The lack of classification can influence all previous metrics and prioritize mitigation actions.

The percentage of databases monitored by a database activity monitor

Ideally, all databases should be onboarded to your database activity monitoring platform. To help you prioritize the onboarding process, you should break down this metric by the presence of sensitive data in the database.

The percentage of systems onboarded to privileged access management

Like the previous metric, all systems should be onboarded to the organization's PAM platform. To prioritize the deployment process, you should break down this metric by criticality.

Whitelisting of authorized applications/software/libraries implementation ratio

This metric allows you to understand the coverage level of an organization's whitelisting solution deployment. However, it's also very important to ensure the effectiveness of that software through the deployment of precise policies.

The percentage of domains with Sender Policy Framework (SPF) implemented (Yes/No if only one domain)

This metric can be used for organizations with several domains or only as a Yes/No control for organizations with only one domain.

SPF is an email authentication mechanism that all organizations should use to prevent sender email forgery and be publically detected if organizations are using it. By not having this mechanism implemented, organizations can negatively affect their risk rating score.

The percentage of domains with Domain-based Message Authentication, Reporting & Conformance (DMARC) implemented (Yes/No if only one domain)

Like the previous metric, DMARC is an authentication protocol designed to protect organization email addresses from spoofing. Since DMARC can also be publically detected, not implementing it can affect an organization's risk score.

The percentage of Regulatory control compliance

This metric can be extremely useful during certification processes to understand the level of compliance with certain regulatory frameworks or other international standards like PCI DSS and ISO 27001.

Summary

Organizations can implement many technologies and adapt to many processes, but some outputs from those technologies or processes need to be tracked to achieve an ideal security posture. Organizations must create and monitor these metrics for each implemented control.

When defining security metrics, organizations should choose **specific, measurable, actionable, relevant, and timely (SMART approach)** KPIs, for which the frequency is based on the overall risk appetite of the organization, as well as the criticality of the systems.

In this chapter, many useful metrics are presented in areas such as endpoint security, network security, vulnerability management, governance, and oversight. The thresholds for these metrics are defined by the organization itself and should be improved over time.

In the next chapter, there are three case studies that can help security professionals to understand the importance of tracking such metrics and prioritization of remediation activities.

CHAPTER 8

Case Studies

This chapter reviews three well-known attacks and identifies some of the referenced controls that could have been implemented to prevent or reduce the impact of these attacks. The case studies describe the incidents based on reports, interviews, or official investigations. Each attack differs in its nature, and the suggested controls were based on the reviewed information for each case, not meaning that other controls could have been applied.

The cases are chosen not because they were the most impacting ones (and indeed they are not),[1] but because they are real-life examples of how things can go wrong and how IT security controls could have been effectively implemented. It should also be noted that none of the authors were involved in any of these incidents or investigations. The recommendations in this chapter are merely the authors' interpretation of the incident.

Target Data Breach

Target Corporation is one of the largest retail companies in the United States. Cybercriminals targeted it in November and December 2013. The attackers gained access to Target's network and stole approximately 40 million records of financial (credit and debit card accounts) and 70 million personal information records.[2] The total cost of the breach was estimated at more than $200 million.[3]

On December 18, 2013, Brian Krebs, an independent Internet security news and investigative journalist, reported that the Target Corporation had been breached and 40 million credit card numbers had been stolen. Krebs later added that Target customers'

---

[1] www.csoonline.com/article/2130877/the-biggest-data-breaches-of-the-21st-century.html

[2] Mulligan, J. (2014, February 4). Written Testimony of John Mulligan. Target.Com. https://corporate.target.com/_media/TargetCorp/global/PDF/Target-SJC-020414.pdf

[3] www.reuters.com/article/us-target-cyber-settlement-idUSKBN18J2GH

© Virgilio Viegas and Oben Kuyucu 2022
V. Viegas and O. Kuyucu, *IT Security Controls*, https://doi.org/10.1007/978-1-4842-7799-7_8

credit and debit card information was sold between $20 and $100 apiece.[4] Target then confirmed the breach[5] but was not aware of the breach after contacting the US Department of Justice on December 12, 2013.[6]

Although it is not certain nor disclosed how the cybercriminals stole the data, one of the possible scenarios is that the hackers gained access through a third party and then looked for weaknesses in the environment. Existing vulnerabilities were used to compromise Target's systems and steal sensitive data. Among the explored vulnerabilities were some already known vulnerabilities and default or weak passwords.[7] In addition, credit and debit card details were compromised by RAM-scraping malware installed on POS devices that sent this information outside through staging points, such as FTP sites.[8]

The most likely scenario is shown in Figure 8-1.

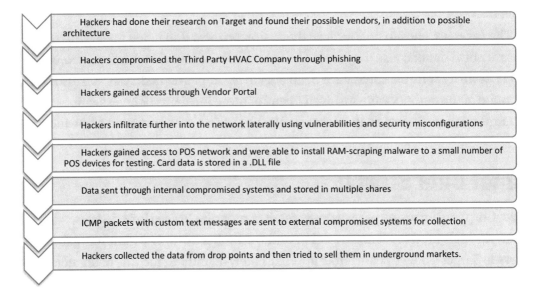

Figure 8-1. *Attack scenario*

---

[4] https://krebsonsecurity.com/2013/12/cards-stolen-in-target-breach-flood-underground-markets/

[5] https://corporate.target.com/press/releases/2013/12/target-confirms-unauthorized-access-to-payment-car

[6] US Senate Committee on Commerce, Science, and Transportation. "A "Kill Chain" Analysis of the 2013 Target Data Breach." www.commerce.senate.gov/services/files/24d3c229-4f2f-405d-b8db-a3a67f183883. March 2014.

[7] https://krebsonsecurity.com/2015/09/inside-target-corp-days-after-2013-breach/

[8] Ibid. 6, page 3.

The kill chain framework is applied to this scenario.

- **Reconnaissance**: The attackers tried to gather information through online sources, which at that time exposed the list of Target vendors, the link to the vendor portal, and main how-to documents for vendor provisioning. Furthermore, it is also possible that Microsoft customer solution case studies[9] displayed some of the tools used, the architecture, and some of the patching process.

- **Weaponization**: Attackers probably realized that the HVAC company had access to the Target vendor portal for electronic billing, contract submission, and project management purposes. So, they created a spear-phishing email possibly containing a password-stealing bot program designed for the employees of the HVAC company.

- **Delivery**: Possibly from the spear-phishing email, attackers either gained passwords to log in to the corporate network remotely or somehow exploited a vulnerability in the remote access tool to infiltrate the internal network. Then, the attackers could move laterally by exploiting multiple vulnerabilities and security issues throughout Target's environment. According to several sources[10,11] attackers compromised several critical systems, such as IT management software or even the domain controller, via outdated services or unpatched systems, such as Apache, IBM WebSphere, and PHP.

---

[9] http://download.microsoft.com/documents/customerevidence/8466_Target_Development_Technologies_Gro.doc and http://download.microsoft.com/download/3/A/D/3AD464EA-F2B4-4E62-B11F-14E37727557C/Target_Hyper-V_CS.PDF (obsolete)

[10] https://krebsonsecurity.com/2015/09/inside-target-corp-days-after-2013-breach/

[11] US Senate - Committee on Commerce, Science, and Transportation. (2014, March). A "Kill Chain" Analysis of the 2013 Target Data Breach. US Senate. www.commerce.senate.gov/services/files/24d3c229-4f2f-405d-b8db-a3a67f183883

- **Exploitation**: Once the attackers gained access to Target's network, they started testing their RAM-scraping malware on POS devices and cash registers. Every time a card was swiped, the data was stored in a DLL file. Although some of Target's security mechanisms detected the malware and reported it as malware.binary,[12] the Target security team did not respond as they should have. After successful tests, attackers could have sent the data to internal servers.

- **Installation**: Infected POS terminals sent card data and personal data to an internal compromised server via NETBIOS and SMB shares as a DLL file. To avoid detection, card numbers were encrypted.

- **Command and control**: Attackers maintained a persistent communication between themselves and the internal compromised server and sent the sensitive data to the Internet via FTP or through specially crafted ICMP packets with a data payload.

- **Action**: Attackers collected the stolen data from outside staging points and started to sell them in the black market.

Security Controls that could prevent this scenario (Table 8-1).

Table 8-1. *List of Security Controls That Could Have Prevented the Target Data Breach Attack*

Stage	Issue	Security Controls	
Recon	Exposure of confidential information to the Internet	AC-22 CIS-14.5	The content should have been reviewed if confidential vendor information (tools, architecture, patching process, etc.) had been removed from public sites.

(continued)

---

[12] www.bloomberg.com/news/articles/2014-03-13/target-missed-warnings-in-epic-hack-of-credit-card-data

Table 8-1. (*continued*)

Stage	Issue	Security Controls	
Weaponization and Delivery	Credentials compromised due to phishing attack	AT-2 AT-3 PR.AT-1 CIS-14.2	Employees should have been trained to recognize social engineering attacks, such as phishing.
-	Credentials compromised due to phishing attack	SI-3 DE.CM-1 DE.CM-4 CIS-9.7 CIS-10.1 CIS-10.5 CIS-10.7 CIS-13.2 CIS-13.3 CIS-13.7 CIS-13.8	Email servers should have included more defenses for malicious content. Malware should have been detected in both host and network layers.
-	Vulnerable Target vendor portal for third parties	PR.AC-3 PR.AC-4 PR.AC-7 DE.CM-6 IA-2(1) IA-2(2) AC-17 AC-19 CIS-6.3 CIS-13.5 CIS-15.6	The vendor portal logins should have been monitored. Legitimate user activity should have been profiled to detect abnormalities. Only authorized IP addresses should have accessed vendor portal access. Multi-factor authentication should have been enabled for all vendors.
-		PR.PT-3 CIS-13.10	Better application-layer filtering should have been used to prevent web application vulnerabilities from being exploited easily.

(*continued*)

Table 8-1. (*continued*)

Stage	Issue	Security Controls	
-	Attackers can move further into the network	PR.AC-5 DE.CM-1 SA-8 SI-4 CIS-12.2 CIS-13.2 CIS-13.3 CIS-13.4 CIS-13.6	Lateral movement of hackers should have been prevented by implementing better network segmentation and better network access rules. Lateral movement and the attacks should have been detected by better system monitoring and better analyzing the traffic flows.
-	Internal applications may have vulnerabilities, security misconfigurations, and even default user accounts that may help attackers to gain more access	PR.AC-1 PR.IP-1 AC-2 CM-11 IA-5 SA-22 CIS-2.2 CIS-2.3 CIS-4.7 CIS-5.3	Default user accounts, as well as generic user accounts, should have been disabled.
-		ID.RA-1 DE.CM-8 PR.IP-1 PR.PT-3 RA-5 SI-2 CIS-7.1 CIS-7.5 CIS-7.7	Better vulnerability management and better implementation of configuration baselines should have been done to detect and remediate vulnerabilities and security issues.

(*continued*)

Table 8-1. (*continued*)

Stage	Issue	Security Controls	
Exploitation	RAM-scraping malware was able to be installed on the systems without any security measures	CM-10 CM-11 DE.CM-7 CIS-2.5 CIS-2.6 CIS-2.7	File integrity monitoring and whitelisting applications on the POS devices would not have allowed the malware to be installed on the systems. Target's point of sale terminals could have been hardened more, not allowing unauthorized software installation and configuration.
-	Although warned by a security company, Target failed to investigate further and respond to the alerts	AT-3 SI-5 IR-1 IR-4 IR-6 IR-8 PR.AT-1 PR.AT-5 DE.DP-1 RS.CO-1 DE.DP-4 CIS-14.6 CIS-14.9 CIS-17.1 CIS-17.3 CIS-17.4	Although the BlackPOS malware contains features to evade detections, FireEye detected and reported to Target. Target security professionals should have responded better to those alerts.

(*continued*)

Table 8-1. (*continued*)

Stage	Issue	Security Controls	
Installation	DLL files containing card data and personal data are sent from POS devices to internal compromised servers	DE.AE-1 ID.AM-3 PR.AC-5 DE.CM-1 CA-9 SI-4 CIS-3.8 CIS-4.8 CIS-13.4 CIS-13.6	Internal traffic from POS devices to internal systems should have been better documented, tracked, and analyzed for unauthorized or abnormal flow. NETBIOS and SMB shares should have been disabled if they were not needed.
Command and Control	Files could be sent to three external staging points via FTP or crafted ICMP packets, working only between specific hours to avoid suspicion	DE.CM-7 PR.AC-5 SC-7(3) SC-7(4) CIS-9.3	All Internet traffic, including FTP traffic, should have been limited and better tracked through a proxy. Access should have been provided to only authorized sites. ICMP packets should have been disallowed.

As a result, between November 27 and December 15, 2013, attackers collected more than 11GB of data[13] that includes 40 million payment card data (card numbers, expiration dates, and CVVs) and 70 million personal data (name, mailing address, phone number or email address).[14] It is also reported[15] that some encrypted PINs might have also been compromised.

---

[13] https://krebsonsecurity.com/2014/01/a-closer-look-at-the-target-malware-part-ii/
[14] https://corporate.target.com/_media/TargetCorp/global/PDF/Target-SJC-020414.pdf
[15] Ibid.

DynDNS Distributed Denial-of-Service Attack

In October 2017, top-visited websites—including Amazon.com, BBC, CNN, Electronic Arts, Mashable, the *New York Times*, *People*, Shopify, Spotify, *The Wall Street Journal*, Yelp, and some government sites, such as that of The Government of Sweden[16]—became inaccessible for more than two hours due to the first wave of a series of distributed denial-of-service attacks (DDoS attacks) that targeted Dyn, Inc., a DNS provider company. The second and third waves also caused interruption in accessing those websites.

It was reported[17] that DynDNS servers were overwhelmed by a flood of several manipulated malicious requests from what is thought to be tens of millions of devices[18] (Figure 8-2) and became unresponsive in their authoritative requests, as well. It is believed that the requests were initiated from Internet-connected devices (IoT), such as webcams, printers, and routers, which became part of a botnet "army" after being infected by several types of malware, one of them called Mirai. It was reported that Mirai's source code was released before the attack,[19] making the attack possible for any interested actor, and eventually created many clusters for other attacks.[20]

[16] https://en.wikipedia.org/wiki/2016_Dyn_cyberattack

[17] www.dynstatus.com/incidents/nlr4yrr162t8

[18] www.wired.com/2016/10/internet-outage-ddos-dns-dyn/

[19] https://krebsonsecurity.com/2016/10/source-code-for-iot-botnet-mirai-released/

[20] https://blog.cloudflare.com/inside-mirai-the-infamous-iot-botnet-a-retrospective-analysis/

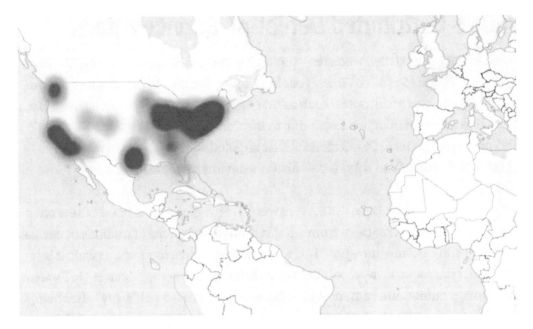

Figure 8-2. *Map of Internet outages in Europe and North America caused by the Dyn cyberattack (as of October 21, 2016, 1:45 p.m. Pacific Time)*[21]

Although the incident was resolved and services resumed the same day of the attack, it caused major concern in the cybersecurity community. This first well-coordinated and sophisticated attack caused major websites to be unreachable where millions of Internet-connected devices were used. Before this incident, a similar attack was reported, in which around 150,000 compromised IoT devices were used to create traffic and DNS servers to amplify the attacks reaching up to 1 Tbps.[22,23] It was one of the largest DDoS attacks in history at that time, when no one would think that Internet-connected baby-cams would be used to affect high-profile sites.

Security Controls that could prevent this scenario (Table 8-2).

[21] Wikimedia Commons. "File: Level3 Outage Map (US) - 21 October 2016.png. `https://commons.wikimedia.org/w/index.php?title=File:Level3_Outage_Map_(US)_-_21_October_2016.png&oldid=565260119`. May 27, 2021.

[22] `https://securityaffairs.co/wordpress/51640/cyber-crime/tbps-ddos-attack.html`

[23] `https://krebsonsecurity.com/2016/09/krebsonsecurity-hit-with-record-ddos/`

Table 8-2. *List of Security Controls That Could Have Prevented the DynDNS Attack*

Phase	Issue	Security Controls	Recommendations
Recon	Exposure of corporate and IoT devices to the Internet	ID.AM-1 ID.AM-3 ID.AM-4 DE.CM-7 PR.AC-4 PR.IP-1 AC-4 AC-20 CA-3 CA-7 CA-9 CM-3 CM-8 PE-20 PM-5 SA-9 SC-7 SI-4 CIS-1.x CIS-4.1 CIS-4.2 CIS-4.5	The infected IoT devices were found to be exposed from the Internet. Management interfaces of those devices (including DNS requests) should have been configured to accept only traffic from internal sources. It is not confirmed if any corporate device is used as a bot that facilitated the attack. Nevertheless, enterprises need to maintain their asset inventory, document the information flow, identify any unauthorized asset being installed in the network, and discover any open ports that are not needed for any authorized business need.

(continued)

Table 8-2. (*continued*)

Phase	Issue	Security Controls	Recommendations
Weaponization and Delivery	Mirai botnet was using a set of default credentials to infect the devices. Most of the IoT devices used the same root password, which makes them critically vulnerable.	PR.AC-1 IA-5 CIS-4.7 CIS-5.2	Finding such username/password combinations for IoT devices is quite trivial.[24] The manufacturers should not have used the same root password hardcoded to the devices' firmware.
Exploitation	DNS servers were used to amplify the attack.	DE.AE-5 DE.CM-1 SC-20 SC-21 SC-22 SI-4 CIS-4.9 CIS-13.6 CIS-13.11	Although not applicable to many DNS providers, DNS recursion should be disabled. In addition, Query filters in DNS policy can be implemented to drop inbound DNS query responses with no matching DNS query requests. Response rate limiting can be applied to DNS servers to reduce the effectiveness of the DNS amplification attack by reducing the number of requests per server.[25]

(*continued*)

---

[24] https://krebsonsecurity.com/wp-content/uploads/2016/10/IoTbadpass-Sheet1.pdf

[25] Security professionals should set an appropriate value for RRL, as it may increase the likelihood of a DNS cache poisoning attack to a legitimate requestor.

Table 8-2. (*continued*)

Phase	Issue	Security Controls	Recommendations
Exploitation	Thousands of bots are used to send manipulated packets.	DE.AE-2 DE.CM-1 PR.IP-9 PR.IP-10 PR.DS-4 PR.PT-4 PR.PT-5 RS.IM-2 IR-4 IR-6 IR-8 SC-5 SC-7 CIS-8.11 CIS-17-4 CIS-17.7	There are some methods to identify traffic originated by a non-human signal. Enterprises may detect such traffic with non-human characteristics to prevent or mitigate DDoS attacks. In addition, enterprises should be ready for a DDoS attack and develop and test their incident response and recovery capabilities. Enterprises can also choose to use mitigating actions for those attacks, such as anycast addressing, which can distribute the attack traffic across a network of other servers.

(*continued*)

Table 8-2. *(continued)*

Phase	Issue	Security Controls	Recommendations
Command and Control	Many IoT devices still use insecure configurations and default credentials, making them vulnerable to Mirai and its variants and becoming a bot for the botnet army by connecting to a C&C server.	ID.RA-1 DE.CM-8 PR.IP-1 PR.IP.2 PR.PT-3 RS.AN-5 CM-1 RA-5 SI-2 SI-5 CIS-4.1 CIS-7.1 CIS-7.5 CIS-7.7 CIS-16.1 CIS-16.2 CIS-16.10	IoT vendors need to design the devices based on functionality and considering the security aspect. Vendors should provide a sound vulnerability management program to minimize being infected by such malware.

NHS WannaCry Ransomware

On May 12, 2017, WannaCry, the first global ransomware attack, affected more than 230,000 computers in more than 150 countries.[26] The attack affected Spanish Telefonica, FedEx, Renault, Nissan Motor Manufacturing UK, the Ministry of Internal Affairs of the Russian Federation, and others.

WannaCry took advantage of a Windows Server Message Block (SMB) protocol vulnerability discovered approximately two months before. Microsoft had released patches to all Windows systems supported at that time and encrypted the infected systems' data. System owners were asked to pay a ransom in Bitcoin cryptocurrency to decrypt their data.

---

[26] NHS 'could have prevented' WannaCry ransomware attack - BBC News

WannaCry used the EternalBlue exploit to gain access to Windows computers, and the backdoor program DoublePulsar installed and executed itself.

The WannaCry kill-switch was discovered on the same day of the attack. It prevented already infected computers from being encrypted or further spreading, and helped to avoid a greater impact of the attack.

Although WannaCry had no specific target and did not match the "typical" kill chain framework, it significantly impacted England's National Health System (NHS). It affected many facilities, whose computers were infected or turned off to avoid infection further impact on NHS services.

This attack highlighted NHS vulnerabilities and exposed improvement needs of the NHS organizations' security controls and processes, including governance.

The NHS WannaCry impact can be explained for the following reasons.

- At the time of the attack, none of the impacted NHS organizations had applied the patch released by Microsoft two months earlier that patched the vulnerability exploited by WannaCry. The NHS Digital CareCERT bulletin also advised this patch on April 25, 2017.

- The organizations' firewalls protecting the connection to the network (N3) to interconnect the NHS organizations lacked the appropriate filtering rules to protect the organizations against the infection.

- Some critical medical equipment like MRI scanners and blood test devices were still using Microsoft Windows XP, which was already EOL'ed by Microsoft. Additionally, although some devices were not affected, the devices to operate or view the results (e.g., X-ray images) were not available. They were infected or quarantined because they were using unsupported software.

The NHS WannaCry incident lasted a week until May 19, 2017.

The attack disrupted the services of one-third of hospital trusts in England. Eighty out of 236 trusts were affected, 34 of them infected, and 46 reported service disruption, although not affected. WannaCry also infected 603 primary care and other NHS organizations.[27,28]

---

[27] www.england.nhs.uk/wp-content/uploads/2018/02/lessons-learned-review-wannacry-ransomware-cyber-attack-cio-review.pdf

[28] www.nao.org.uk/wp-content/uploads/2017/10/Investigation-WannaCry-cyber-attack-and-the-NHS.pdf

The impact on organizations providing accident and emergency services makes them unable to take patients. Some patients from five hospitals had to travel long distances for emergency treatment.

Almost seven thousand first medical appointments had to be rescheduled, including patients with urgent appointments for potential cancer.

Additionally, the impact on secondary care ended up affecting primary care since, for example, access to test results or patients' records was also affected.

Although social care organizations were not directly affected, WannaCry also negatively impacted social care performance. Organizations temporarily preemptively disconnected their connections to the NHS N3 network, and emails sent from the NHS were quarantined, forcing the activation of business continuity plans.

Some examples of security controls that could have prevented or reduced the impact of WannaCry on NHS (Table 8-3).

Table 8-3. *List of Security Controls That Could Have Prevented the NHS WannaCry Attack*

Control Identifier	Control (or Control Enhancement)	
AC-1	Access Control - Policy and Procedures	Access controls policies should have been in place to prevent access to information.
AC-3(11)	Access Enforcement | Restrict Access to Specific Information Types	Access controls (including firewall rules) to data repositories should have been in place to prevent WannaCry from spreading.
AC-4(15)	Information Flow Enforcement | Detection of Unsanctioned Information	Traffic between organizations over the N3 network should have been restricted and monitored.
AT-2	Literacy Training and Awareness	General security awareness training should have been effectively provided to all users. This might have reduced the likelihood of emails with the payload being open.

(continued)

Table 8-3. (*continued*)

Control Identifier	Control (or Control Enhancement)	
CA-2(1)	Assessment, Authorization, and Monitoring Control Assessments I Independent Assessors	Independent and specialized assessors should have conducted security controls.
CA-6	Authorization	All accesses, including firewall rules, should have been properly authorized.
CA-8	Penetration Testing	Penetration tests would have helped detect firewall rules identifying unnecessarily open ports and services in the affected devices.
CA-9	Internal System Connections	All connections should have been previously authorized and given on a need to have basis.
CM-1	Configuration Management: Policy and Procedures	Probably one of the most important controls that could have prevented or significantly reduced WannaCry impact. An effective configuration and patch management policy would have mitigated the vulnerability exploited by WannaCry much before the incident.
CM-2	Configuration Management: Baseline Configuration	Baseline security configurations would have disabled unnecessary services and reduced the WannaCry impact, especially on the affected devices.
CM-11	Configuration Management: User-Installed Software	User-installed (or executed) software should have been forbidden.
IR-1, IR-2, IR-3, IR-4, IR-5, IR-6, IR-7, IR-8	Incident Response Training	Incident response procedures, training, testing, handling, monitoring, reporting, assistance, and an incident response plan

(*continued*)

Table 8-3. (*continued*)

Control Identifier	Control (or Control Enhancement)	
MA-1, MA-2, MA-3	Maintenance	Maintenance policies and procedures, controlled maintenance and maintenance tools
RA-1, RA-3	Risk Assessment	Risk assessment policies and procedures seem to be proven ineffective. A more thorough risk assessment should have been conducted, which can help identify the risks and ineffectiveness of the patch management process.
RA-5	Vulnerability Monitoring and Scanning	Along with an effective patch management policy, the effective implementation of this control would have detected devices with SMB vulnerability and supported the patching process.
SA-1	System and Services Acquisition	Although it might seem of less importance for the WannaCry incident, effective systems and services acquisition would have assured that, for example, diagnostic devices were kept updated and patched.
SC-1, SC-2, SC-3, SC-4, SC-7	Systems and Communications Protection	Appropriate policies, separation of system and user functionality, separation of system and user functionality interfaces for non-privileged users, security function isolation, information in shared system resources, boundary protection
SI-2, SI-3,	System and Information Integrity	Flaw remediation, malicious code protection, security alerts, advisories, and directives, software, firmware, and information integrity

Overall, the WannaCry impact on the NHS could have been significantly reduced if all assets had been patched on time and communications between NHS organizations were less permissive, which would reduce the number of infected devices. It is also reported that, as a precautionary measure, NHS shutdown several systems, including medical devices, to stop the spread of malware, which then impacted the overall service availability of the NHS.

CHAPTER 9

Security Testing and Attack Simulation Tools

This chapter lists several security testing and attack simulation tools by type. These tools must be operated in a contained environment like an isolated network segment, or when used in other types of environments, they need to be executed with a well-defined, clear scope and duration explicitly authorized by the system's owners.

Although some of these tools are presented as part of a category, they can also perform tasks from other categories.

It should be noted that most of these tools are either freeware, open source, or freemium, where some of the functionality is free to use. Before using these tools, security professionals must read, understand, and agree with the licensing and terms of use. There may be commercial alternatives to these tools, which can provide better technical support rather than community support, which are not included here for competition reasons.

Penetration Testing Tools

- **Kali Linux**[1] (formerly BackTrack) is one of the most common penetration testing operating systems containing 300+ different tools for security testing.

- **Parrot Security**[2] is a Debian-based operating system that contains a suite of penetration testing tools for vulnerability scanning, forensics, and attack mitigation, as well as secure development.

---

[1] www.kali.org

[2] www.parrotsec.org

© Virgilio Viegas and Oben Kuyucu 2022
V. Viegas and O. Kuyucu, *IT Security Controls*, https://doi.org/10.1007/978-1-4842-7799-7_9

- **BlackArch**[3] is an Arch Linux penetration testing distribution based on Arch Linux that contains several cyber security tools.

- **Metasploit Project**[4] is a computer security project that provides information about security vulnerabilities and aids in penetration testing and IDS signature development. It is owned by Boston, Massachusetts-based security company Rapid7.

  Metasploit's best-known subproject is the open source Metasploit Framework, a tool for developing and executing exploit code against a remote target machine. Other important subprojects include the opcode database, shellcode archive, and related research.

  The Metasploit Project includes anti-forensic and evasion tools, some of which are built into the Metasploit Framework. Metasploit is pre-installed in the Kali Linux operating system.

- **Sandcat**[5] is a web browser with developer and pen-tester features. It was built over Chromium,[6] the open source project behind Google Chrome browser, and uses Lua scripting language, which is also used in other security tools like Wireshark, Snort, and nmap, and by the game industry and security. Sandcat includes the following features.

  - Live HTTP headers

  - Cookies and cache viewers

  - JavaScript Executor extension

  - CGI scanner extension

  - HTTP brute force

  - Script Runner extension

  - XHR editor

  - Various encoders/decoders

---

[3] https://blackarch.org

[4] www.metasploit.com

[5] www.syhunt.com/sandcat/

[6] www.chromium.org

- **Mimikatz** is a post-exploitation tool used by hackers and penetration testers to gather credentials on Windows computers by dumping these credentials from memory and using these credentials to access unauthorized information or perform lateral movement attacks.

- **Netcat** is a powerful tool that allows you to read, write, redirect, and encrypt network connections. Netcat handles a wide range of security testing and administration functionalities. Netcat integrates with Nmap and runs on Linux, Windows, and macOS.

Information Gathering and Intelligence

- **DIG** stands for Domain Information Groper and is a Linux command-line-based DNS lookup tool.

- **nslookup** (also known as name server lookup) queries DNS Servers for existing records (A, PTR, MX, TXT, etc.). The most common queries translate the hostname to an IP address or vice versa.

- **Whois** shows the information about a domain, the register of the domain, and the IP address of a domain name.

- **Shodan**[7] is a search engine designed to help find specific types of devices exposed on the Internet (IoT, webcams, routers, servers, etc.).

- **awesome-osint**[8] is an open source intelligence (OSINT) list of publicly available tools for a variety of purposes like specialty search engines, real-time search, social media search, and general social media tools, phone number research, domain and IP research, VPN services, OCR tools, social network analysis, privacy and encryption tools, DNS, among others.

- **Google Dork**[9] is a technique that uses Google (or other search engines as well) Tools to discover security vulnerabilities to exploit. It can also see which information of your organization has been indexed by the search engines.

---

[7] www.shodan.io/

[8] https://github.com/jivoi/awesome-osint

[9] An example: www.google.com/search?q=site%3Aapress.com+kuyucu+%2B+viegas

- **DNSdumpster** is a tool for discovering other hostnames related to a domain.

- **Netscan Pro** is a comprehensive set of information gathering and network troubleshooting tools. The set includes active discovery and diagnostic, passive discovery, DNS and local computer, and general Information tools.

- **Sigverif** is a file signature verification tool that detects unsigned drivers and verifies device drivers in devices with Windows operating system.

- **User2SID** and **SID2User** are two enumeration tools for Windows that make use of NULL sessions that allow retrieving the Security Identifier (SID) through a given username or the username through a given SID.

- **SNMPUtil** is a Windows-based Simple Network Management Protocol (SNMP) troubleshooting tool to verify SNMP configuration.

- **JXplorer** is an LDAP browser and editor generic to search, read and edit standard LDAP directories or directory services with an LDAP or DSML interface. JXplorer can run in any operating system that supports Java.

- **AlienVault**[10] is a toolset with several functionalities like threat detection, incident response, and compliance checks that can also act as a SIEM. Acquired by AT&T Communications and renamed as AT&T Cybersecurity. AlienVault Open Threat Exchange is still free to use as a cybersecurity information-sharing platform.

- **FOCA** (Fingerprinting Organizations with Collected Archives) is a scanning tool that finds metadata and hidden information in the documents it scans. The scanned documents can be hosted on web pages and found using Google, Bing, or DuckDuckGo or can also be downloaded and analyzed locally.

- FOCA can analyze several file types, including the most common Microsoft Office, Open Office, and PDF files.

---

[10] https://otx.alienvault.com

- **Spiderfoot** is an OSINT automated reconnaissance tool that gathers information on IP addresses, domain names, email addresses, and others by querying more than 100 public data sources.

Sniffers

- **TCPDump**[11] is a well-known command-line packet sniffer used by system administrators to diagnose network connections. It displays packets being transmitted and received from a computer.

- **Wireshark**[12] is also a well-known and powerful network interface sniffer and network protocol analyzer, supported in several operating systems (Linux, Windows, macOS, Solaris, FreeBSD, and others) and can read several capture files formats and also export output in several file formats (XML, CSV or plain text). Wireshark allows deep inspection of a variety of protocols, live capture, and reading of data from Ethernet, IEEE 802.11, PPP/HDLC, ATM, Bluetooth, USB, Token Ring, Frame Relay, FDDI, and others.

- **DSNIFF** is a toolkit with several tools for password sniffing and network traffic analysis.

  - dsniff, filesnarf, mailsnarf, msgsnarf, urlsnarf, and webspy are network sniffers designed to capture passwords, email, files, and other relevant information.

  - arpspoof, dnsspoof, and macof are network tools designed to enhance the interception of network traffic through techniques like arp and DNS spoofing.

  - sshmitm and webmitm are man-in-the-middle attack tools that proxy and sniff SSH and HTTPS traffic.

---

[11] www.tcpdump.org

[12] www.wireshark.org

Vulnerability Scanning

- **Core Impact** is mostly known as a vulnerability scanner. It is a comprehensive commercial penetration testing product widely used by several federal government institutions in the United States.

- **Nessus**[13] is one of the first and a well-known vulnerability assessment (or vulnerability scanner tool). Nessus has a free version with limited functionalities (Nessus Essentials) and two commercial versions, one for network-based scans and another (cloud-based) with agent-based scans. Nessus can also conduct compliance scans with the major security framework.

- **OpenVAS**[14] (Open Vulnerability Assessment System) is a vulnerability management platform and scanning tool capable of several types of vulnerability scans, like authenticated and unauthenticated large-scale scans.

- **Qualys VM** is a well-known cloud-based vulnerability management platform with a commercial and a free community edition.

Web Application Vulnerability Scanning

- **Fortify WebInspect**[15] is a web application vulnerability scanner with dynamic application security testing (DAST) feature which can find and prioritize vulnerabilities in web applications and check compliance with major compliance standards like PCI DSS, NIST 800-53, ISO 27000 family, OWASP, and HIPAA.

- **Nikto**, an open source vulnerability scanner, is especially suited for web servers. Nikto scans web servers for potentially unsafe files and programs, outdated versions, configuration issues, HTTP server options and tries to fingerprint the webserver software.

---

[13] www.tenable.com

[14] www.openvas.org

[15] www.microfocus.com/en-us/cyberres/application-security/webinspect

- **WebScarab** web application security testing tool deployed as a proxy that acts as a "man-in-the-middle" intercepting (and storing) the workstation web traffic and allowing its manipulation (requests and web server replies).

- **WebGoat**[16] is an OWASP initiative that intentionally created a Java-based insecure web application for teaching purposes.

- **LibWhisker** is a full-featured Perl module used by Nikto to support several features like crawling, NTLM authentication, hashing, and encoding.

- **StackGuard** is a compiler extension to implement automatic detection and prevention of buffer-overflow attacks using a "canary value."

- **HTTPRecon** (also known as HTTP fingerprinting) is a tool designed to help obtain the identification of given Httpd implementations.

- **ID Serve** is a tool designed to fingerprint HTTP and non-HTTP servers by obtaining information like make, model, and software version.

- **httPrint** is a tool to fingerprint web servers. It can also detect other web-enabled devices such as wireless access points, routers, switches, and modems.

- **Modlishka** is an HTTP reverse proxy that implements a distinct approach to handle browser-based HTTP traffic flows, allowing to transparently proxy multi-domain destination traffic (TLS and non-TLS) over a single domain, without the need to install additional certificates on the client. Modlishka simulates man-in-the-middle attacks and phishing penetration tests as a reverse proxy with 2FA "bypass" support.

- **Netsparker**,[17] **AppScan**,[18] **AppSpider**,[19] and **Acunetix**[20] are commercially available web application vulnerability scanning tools, with community editions or limited trials available.

---

[16] https://owasp.org/www-project-webgoat/

[17] www.netsparker.com

[18] www.hcltechsw.com/products/appscan/

[19] www.rapid7.com/products/appspider/

[20] www.acunetix.com

- **N-stalker**[21] is another commercial web application scanner. A free version is available with limited features that can be useful to be used in small infrastructure providers, non-profit organizations, and by individuals.

- **w3af**[22] is a vulnerability scanner and exploitation tool for web applications that can conduct penetration tests. w3af can be used with a graphical interface or command-line interface.

- **OWASP Zed Attack Proxy (ZAP)**[23] is another free and open source web application security scanner that can be used by "rookies" or professional penetration testers. Zed is a community-led open source software maintained by volunteers from all over the world.

- **Fiddler** is a web debugging proxy tool that logs all HTTP and HTTPS traffic between a computer and the Internet.

SQL Injection

- **SQL Map**[24] is an open source penetration testing tool that can be used for automated detection and exploitation of SQL injection flaws and take over database servers. Additionally, it can also do database fingerprinting to access the database server file system and execute commands on the operating system level.

- **SQLNinja**[25] exploits vulnerabilities of web applications using Microsoft SQL Server through SQL injection, aiming to gain remote access on the vulnerable database server. Penetration testers can use SQLNinja to automate the database server takeover process after discovering an SQL injection.

---

[21] www.nstalker.com/alliance/

[22] http://w3af.org

[23] https://owasp.org/www-project-zap/

[24] https://sqlmap.org/

[25] http://sqlninja.sourceforge.net/

- **Havij** (Carrot in Persian) is an automated SQL injection tool designed to help penetration testers to find and exploit SQL injection vulnerabilities on web pages. Havij is distributed by the Iranian security company ITSecTeam.

- **SQLBrute** is a tool written in Python to brute-force data out of databases using blind SQL injection vulnerabilities. SQLBrute supports time-based and error-based SQL injection attacks on Microsoft SQL Server and error-based on Oracle.

- **Pangolin** is an automated SQL injection tool. Pangolin supports MS Access, MS SQL, MySQL, Oracle, Informix, DB2, Sybase, PostgreSQL, and SQLite.

- **Absinthe**, initially released as a blind SQL injection tool, currently supports other SQL error-based injection features for MS SQL Server. Absinthe supports blind injection for Oracle, SQL Server, and PostgreSQL databases.

- **BOBCAT** is a tool designed to support auditors and pen-testers exploiting SQL injection weaknesses. BobCat can display database schema and linked servers and enable data retrieval from tables used by the exploited application user.

- **Marathon** is an SQL injection tool that performs time-based, blind SQL injection attack heavy queries. Marathon can be used on web applications using Microsoft SQL Server, Microsoft Access, MySQL, or Oracle databases.

- **SQLDict** is an SQL injection dictionary attack tool for SQL Server part of the Kali penetration test tools suite.

- **WebCruiser** is a web vulnerability scanner that can be used for attacks like cross-site scripting, local file inclusion, remote file inclusion, and SQL injection. WebCruiser supports Access, DB2, MySQL, MS SQL, and Oracle databases.

- **SQLiX**[26] is an OWASP project SQL injection tool coded in Perl able to crawl, detect SQL injection vectors, fingerprint back-end databases, grab function calls and execute system commands on MS SQL database servers. SQLiX has a distinct approach from other SQL injection tools, and it can find normal and blind SQL injection vectors without reverse-engineering the original SQL request.

- **DVWA** (Damn Vulnerable Web Application)[27] is a vulnerable web application created to help security professionals test their skills and tools in a legal environment, help developers understand and improve the processes of securing web applications, and be used as a lab by teachers and students in classroom environments.

Network Tools

- **Nmap**[28] is a very well-known powerful tool for port scanning and service discovery. Nmap has several scan techniques, including firewall and IPS evasions, and allows operating system fingerprinting of the scanned devices.

- Nmap is portable and runs in several operating systems, including Windows, macOS, and Linux. It can be used in conjunction with exploitation frameworks like Metasploit and supports scripting.

- **HPing**[29] is a scanning tool that works on Windows and several Linux flavors, and it acts as a packet builder and analyzer. HPing can perform most Nmap scans.

---

[26] https://wiki.owasp.org/index.php/Category:OWASP_SQLiX_Project

[27] https://dvwa.co.uk

[28] www.nmap.org

[29] http://www.hping.org

- **Colasoft Packet Builder**[30] is a network packet builder to create tailored network packets. It can also test network protection against attacks.

- **Angry IP Scanner** (also known as IPScan) is an easy to use and quick tool that detects which hosts are active in a network. Angry IP Scanner can be easily detected, however. It can run on Linux, Windows, and macOS X.

- **Superscan** is a port scanning tool that allows the detection of open TCP and UDP ports on the scanned devices and identifies the services running on the open ports. Superscan can also run whois queries, ping, ICMP traceroute, and Windows enumeration like NetBIOS information, user and group accounts, shares, and trusted domains.

- **LOKI** is a covert channel tool that implements ICMP tunneling, which is a technique to bypass firewalls by obfuscating the actual traffic over ICMP.

- **Super Network Tunnel** is a covert channel tool that obfuscates the actual traffic through HTTP tunneling.

- **Secure Pipes** is another obfuscation tool that implements and manages SSH tunnels and can also be used as a SOCKS proxy.

- **Ostinato**[31] is an open source packet creator and traffic generator that allows tailoring specific scenarios to test networks.

- **Bitvise** is another obfuscation tool to implement SSH tunnels.

- **Send-Safe Honeypot Hunter** is a Windows-based tool that checks if HTTPS and SOCKS proxies addresses are honeypots.

- **Queso** is a port scanning tool.

- **Cheops** is a port scanning tool.

- **Argus**[32] is an open source network activity auditing tool that can track and report the status and performance of network transactions in network traffic.

---

[30] www.colasoft.com/packet_builder/

[31] https://ostinato.org

[32] https://openargus.org

- **PacketFence**[33] is a free and open source network access control (NAC) solution that includes a captive portal for registration and remediation, centralized wired, wireless, and VPN management, industry-leading BYOD capabilities, 802.1X, and role-based access control.

- **p0f**[34] is a passive TCP/IP sniffer fingerprinting tool that attempts to identify a device operating system by analyzing traffic between that device and the device where it's running.

- **Nagios**[35] is a tool to monitor networks, systems, and infrastructure and create alerts when defined thresholds exceed.

- **OSSEC**[36] is an open source host intrusion detection system that can be customized for specific needs through a wide variety of configuration options and custom alerts.

- **BetterCAP** is a multipurpose tool for attack and reconnaissance of Wi-Fi, Bluetooth Low Energy devices, wireless HID hijacking, and IPv4 and IPv6 networks. It can do the following.

  - Scan Wi-Fi networks, deauthentication attacks, clientless PMKID association attacks, WPA/WPA2 client handshakes capture

  - Scan, read and write Bluetooth Low Energy devices and enumerate their characteristics

  - Scan and perform mousejacking attacks on 2.4Ghz wireless devices

  - Probe and recon IP network hosts

  - Perform MITM attacks through ARP, DNS, DHCPv6, and NDP spoofing

  - Sniffing for credentials

  - Port scanning

---

[33] www.packetfence.org
[34] https://lcamtuf.coredump.cx/p0f3/
[35] www.nagios.org
[36] www.ossec.net

- **MITMf** (Man-in-the-Middle framework) is a toolset to perform MITM attacks with SMB, HTTP, and DNS server and SSLStrip proxy included. MITMf can perform active packet filtering and manipulation, which allows the manipulation of any type of traffic or protocol. It captures FTP, IRC, POP, IMAP, Telnet, SMTP, SNMP, NTLMv1/v2 (HTTP, SMB, LDAP etc.) and Kerberos credentials by using Net-Creds.

Breach and Attack Simulation

- **CALDERA**[37] is a framework based on the MITRE ATT&CK framework that allows you to automate adversary emulation, assist red team exercises, and support incident response.

- Caldera has two components—a core system and plugins—that expand the core framework capabilities with additional functionalities.

- **Atomic Red Team**[38] is a library of basic security tests that allows security teams to test their security controls.

System Information Tools

- **Sysinternals** has several resources and utilities to manage, diagnose, troubleshoot, and monitor Windows devices.

- **Process Explorer** is similar to Windows Task Manager with enhanced features.

- **Process Monitor** is a monitoring tool that shows real-time file system, Registry, process activity, and thread activity.

---

[37] https://github.com/mitre/caldera
[38] https://atomicredteam.io/

- **SysMon** provides information about processes, connected networks, and file changes.

- **TCPView** is a comprehensive list of all TCP and UDP endpoints on a certain system.

- **Lynis**[39] is a tool used for security audits, compliance tests with major standards (e.g., NIST and CIS benchmarks), and system hardening that can also detect vulnerabilities and conduct penetration tests. Lynis can run in most Unix-based systems.

- **HAL Device Manager** (short for Hardware Abstraction Layer or Hardware Annotation Library, similar to the infamous **H**euristically programmed **AL**gorithmic computer from Arthur C. Clarke's *Space Odyssey* series, now known as **HardInfo**) is a tool that provides detailed information about the hardware of the system. **lshw** also provides very similar information.

- **BPF performance tools** are a set of comprehensive Linux tools for performance measuring of applications and systems (Figure 9-1).

---

[39] https://cisofy.com/lynis/

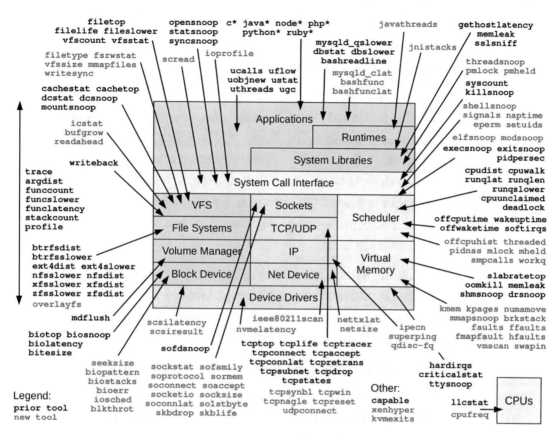

Figure 9-1. *BPF performance tools[40]*

Password Cracking

- **Cain and Abel** (frequently referred to just as Cain) is a password recovery tool for Microsoft Windows systems, using methods like network packet sniffing, cracking password hashes using dictionary attacks, brute-force, or cryptanalysis attacks.

- **ScoopLM** captures LM/NTLM authentication information (LanManager and Windows NT challenge/response) on the network. ScoopLM supports both NTLMv2 on NetBT (Win 9X/NT) and Microsoft-DS (445 SMB-NTLMSSP).

---

[40] https://github.com/brendangregg/bpf-perf-tools-book

- **KerbCrack** is a toolset (kerbsniff and kerbcrack) that is a Kerberos sniffer and password cracker for Windows systems. Kerbsniff can capture Windows 2000/XP Kerberos logins data.

- **John the Ripper** is a free password cracking software tool. Although it was originally developed for the Unix systems, currently, it supports other operating systems. John the Ripper is widely used for password testing and breaking. It combines several password cracking techniques and detects password hash types. It can be used with several encrypted password file formats like various Unix versions (based on DES, MD5, or Blowfish), Kerberos AFS, and Windows NT/2000/XP/2003 LM hash.

- **LC5 L0phtCrack** is a password audit and recovery tool to check password strength and recover lost Microsoft Windows passwords using attack techniques like dictionary, brute-force, and hybrid attacks and rainbow tables.

- **GetAdmin** is a tool for getting administrator rights on legacy Windows NT 4.0 systems.

- **HK.exe** can exploit a Local procedure call flaw on Windows NT to escalate non-admin user privileges.

- **Hydra** is a network logon password cracker that uses several types of attacks like dictionary attacks, brute-force attacks, among others, and supports several protocols. Hydra allows the attacker to remotely gain access to a system.

- **Hashcat** is a password hash cracking tool for MD5, SHA1, and several other hash algorithms. Hashcat can run on Linux, OS X, and Windows systems.

- **Mklink** is a Windows tool that creates symbolic links to directories and files. It also creates hard file links or directory junctions that are shown as NTFS files or directories. Symbolic links can be used for elevation of privileges or arbitrary write/delete.

- **CeWL**[41] (Custom Word List generator tool) crawls a certain URL and returns a list of words which can then be used by other password cracking tools.

- **Ophcrack**[42] recovers Windows passwords using rainbow tables.

Session Hijacking

- **Ettercap** is a free comprehensive suite for man-in-the-middle attacks that run on Unix, Linux, macOS X, BSD OS, Solaris, and Microsoft Windows with features like live connections sniffing, content filtering, password capturing, among others. It supports active and passive eavesdropping of many protocols and includes features for network and host analysis.

- **Hunt** is a tool to exploit well-known weaknesses in TCP/IP protocol. Hunt can hijack connections, detect ongoing connections, normal active session hijacking, ARP spoofing, synchronize the true client session with the server after the hijacking, and reset connections.

- **Paros** (most known as a proxy) is a Java-built web proxy to assess web application vulnerabilities. It can view and edit HTTP/HTTPS messages on the fly and change items such as cookies or form fields.

- **Burp Suite**[43] is a very well-known penetration testing and vulnerability discovery tool to evaluate web applications security. It has a commercial and a community edition.

- **Juggernaut** is a network sniffer that can also hijack TCP sessions. Juggernaut runs on Linux. Juggernaut can monitor all local network traffic or be activated by specific traffic like a login prompt and capture the following login traffic, including passwords.

---

[41] https://digi.ninja/projects/cewl.php
[42] https://ophcrack.sourceforge.io/
[43] https://portswigger.net/burp

- Juggernaut can also keep a connection database and monitor all TCP-based connections, and eventually hijack a session.

- **Hamster Sidejack** is a tool that acts as a proxy that replaces cookies with session cookies stolen from someone else and hijacks those sessions. A ferret program is needed to sniff cookies.

- **sslstrip** is a man-in-the-middle attack tool for SSL stripping. It can be used just to transparently hijack HTTP traffic on a network or to detect HTTPS links and redirects and replace them with similar-looking HTTP or HTTPS links.

- **Firesheep** is a Firefox extension that intercepts unencrypted session cookies from websites like Facebook or Twitter and displays the victims' identities in the Firefox sidebar. Clicking the victim's name takes over the victim's session.

- **PolarProxy** is an SSL/TLS proxy used by incident responders and malware researchers to look for malware by intercepting and decrypting TLS encrypted traffic, which is saved in a PCAP file to be analyzed with Wireshark or an intrusion detection system (IDS).

Steganography

- **Image** embeds text and files into image files, with optional encryption.

- **Snow**[44] is a text-based tool that conceals information in whitespaces.

- **MP3Stego** is a stenographic tool that hides information in MP3 files.

- **S-Tools** is a tool that hides files in BMP, GIF, and WAV files just by dragging and dropping files. S-tools supports IDEA, DES, Triple DES, and MDC encryption algorithms and can protect files with passwords.

---

[44] http://www.darkside.com.au/snow/

- **WBStego** is a steganography tool that hides information in bitmaps, ASCII, HTML, and Adobe Acrobat. WBStego supports Blowfish, Twofish, CAST, and Rijndael (AES) encryption algorithms and password protection.

- **OpenStego** can attach any file in an image file with encryption and password protection. OpenStego supports BMP, GIF, JPEG, JPG, PNG, and WBMP file formats.

- **XIAO** is a tool that allows users to hide files within the image (BMP) or audio (WAV) files that support RC2, RC4, DES, Triple DES, and Triple DES 112 encryption algorithm and MD@, MD4, MD5, and SHA Hashing algorithms, and password-protected files.

Windows Log Tools

- **ElSave** is a command-line tool to clear the event logs locally or remotely, but it only works with administrative privileges.

- **Winzapper** is a tool to selectively delete event logs on Microsoft Windows NT 4.0 and Windows 2000 Security Log. While this Winzapper is running, security events are logged. (Please note that there is a trojan horse with the same name with no relation to this tool.)

- **Evidence Eliminator** is a Windows-based tool that deletes hidden information (SWAP files, application logs, temporary files, registry backups, recycle bin, clipboard data, etc.) from the hard drive that standard procedures might not be able to delete. Evidence Eliminator overwrites previously allocated disk space to make it harder to recover deleted information.

- **Auditpol** (Windows native) is an audit policy program command-line tool included in Windows 10/8/7 and Windows Server, located in the System32 folder. Auditpol manages and audits policy subcategory settings. Hackers use Auditpol to disable auditing on compromised devices.

Wireless Network Tools

- **Netstumbler** (Network Stumbler) is a tool for Windows that facilitates detection of wireless LANs using the 802.11b, 802.11a, and 802.11g WLAN standards. The program is commonly used for the following.

  - Wardriving

  - Verifying network configurations

  - Finding locations with poor coverage in a WLAN

  - Detecting causes of wireless interference

  - Detecting unauthorized ("rogue") access points

  - Aiming directional antennas for long-haul WLAN links

- **Kismet** is a wireless network and device detector, sniffer, wardriving tool, and wireless intrusion detection. Kismet works with Wi-Fi interfaces, Bluetooth interfaces, some SDR (software-defined radio) hardware, and other specialized capture hardware.

- **Netsurveyor** is a Windows-based tool that provides many of the same features as Netstumbler and Kismet. It supports almost all wireless adapters without any significant additional configuration and acts as a tool for troubleshooting and during the installation of wireless networks.

- **Aireplay-ng** generates deauthentication packets for wireless sniffing purposes. One of its main purposes is to generate traffic to be used by **aircrack-ng** to crack WEP and WPA-PSK keys. Aireplay-ng features several attacks that can deauthenticate wireless clients to capture WPA handshake data, fake authentications, interactive packet replay, and handcrafted ARP request injection.

- **AirCrack-ng** is a suite of tools to assess Wi-Fi network security. It focuses on different areas of Wi-Fi security such as monitoring, packet capture, and export of data to text files for further processing by third-party tools.

- **CommView for Wi-Fi** is a wireless network monitor and analyzer for 802.11 a/b/g/n networks that captures packets to display important information such as the list of Access Points and workstations, per-node and per-channel statistics, signal strength, a list of packets and network connections, protocol distribution charts, etc.

- **WiFish Finder** is a tool to assess if Wi-Fi devices active in the air are vulnerable to Wi-Fishing attacks through passive traffic sniffing and active probing techniques.

- **WiFiFoFum** is a wardriving tool to locate, display, and map discovered Wi-Fi networks. This tool scans 802.11 Wi-Fi networks and provides the scanned networks SSID, MAC, RSSI, channel, and security. When using GPS, this can also log the discovered network's location.

- **Airsnarf** is a tool to create a rogue wireless access point to steal usernames and passwords from public wireless hotspots that demonstrates an inherent vulnerability of public 802.11b hotspots-snarfing usernames and passwords.

- **Wepcrack** can break 802.11 WEP secret keys.

- **Kismac** is a wireless network discovery tool for macOS X with features similar to Kismet.

- **WeFi** is a Wi-Fi hotspot finder to connect to open Wi-Fi hotspots.

- **SMAC** and **TMAC** are both MAC spoofing tools.

- **Wi-Fi Inspector** is a tool designed to see all the devices connected to a network regardless of the device nature (consoles, TVs, PCs, tablets, phones, etc.), providing important device information like IP address, manufacturer, device name, and MAC address.

- **BBProxy** is a security assessment tool that is written in Java and runs on Blackberry devices. It allows the device to be used as a proxy between the Internet and an internal network.

Bluetooth Attacks

- **Blooover II** is a J2ME phone auditing tool that checks if phones are vulnerable. This tool supports BlueBug, HeloMoto, and BlueSnarf attacks and sends malformed objects via OBEX.

- **BlueScanner** is a tool to detect Bluetooth devices that are within the range of the system where it is running from. Since BlueScan is non-intrusive, it does not establish a connection with the found devices; it is not detected.

- **BTBrowser** tool finds and enumerates nearby Bluetooth devices.

- **BLEAH** (**Bl**uetooth **L**ow **E**nergy **A**ttack tool) attacks Low Energy devices through sniffing and man-in-the-middle attacks on nearby devices.

Website Mirroring

- **HTTPTrack** is a tool to download a www site to a local directory, build the original site directories, get HTML, images, and other files, and adjust the original site's relative link structure.

- **Black Widow** is a site ripper and sniffer that can pull full copies of a website to a local machine for later examination.

- **Archive.org** (Wayback) provides access to archived copies of previous versions of websites.

Intrusion Detection

- **WebsiteCDS** is a tool that scans an entire web folder to look for changes in the code. If changes are detected, it sends an email alert. This mechanism can detect website tampering.

- **Snort**[45] is a free, open source packet sniffer and IDS.

---

[45] `www.snort.org`

- **Suricata** open source threat detection engine that can act as an IDS, intrusion prevention (IPS), and network security monitoring (NSM) tool.

Mobile Devices

- **zANTI** is an Android application toolkit to assess a network exposure level that simulates an attacker to identify possible vulnerabilities.

- **TunesGo** is an Android tool with an Android root module that recognizes and analyzes the connected Android device and roots it automatically.

- **LOIC (Low Orbit Ion Cannon)** is an application that performs network stress testing and (distributed) denial-of-service attack attacks.

- **DroidSheep** is a simple Android tool for web session hijacking (sidejacking), that captures session cookies over the wireless network and hijacks a web session profile of another person who is connected to the same network.

- **Other Android rooting tools** include SuperOneClick, Superboot, OneClickRoot, Kingo, unrevoked, RescueRoot, and UnlockrootPro.

- **iOS jailbreak tools** include Userland, iBoot, Bootrom, evasi0n7, GeekSn0w, Pangu, Redsn0w, Absinthe, and Cynthia.

Social Engineering

- **Maltego** is an open source tool for intelligence gathering and forensics. It allows the identification of key relationships between the gathered information and discover previously unknown relationships like, for example, which email addresses are linked to social profiles, mutual friends, companies, and websites.

- **Social Engineering Toolkit (SEF)**[46] has tools that can automate things such as extracting email addresses out of websites and general preparation for social engineering and was designed to perform attacks against the human element.

- **Censys**[47] is an inventory of Internet assets that helps you understand each asset's attack surface, ownership, history, and cloud configuration.

IoT (Internet of Things)

- **RIOT OS**[48] is an open source operating system that supports most low-power IoT devices with (32-bit, 16-bit, 8-bit) microcontroller architectures.

- **ARM mbed OS** is a free IoT operating system for Internet-connected devices based on 32-bit ARM Cortex-M microcontrollers with connectivity, security, storage, device management, and machine learning features.

- **Nucleos RTOS** is a real-time operating system (RTOS) that supports 32 and 64-bit embedded platforms. It was designed for medical, industrial, consumer, aerospace real-time embedded systems, and IoT.

- **IoT Inspector** is a cloud-based vulnerability scanner platform that scans and analyzes IoT devices uploaded firmware.

- **IoTsploit** is a cloud-based IoT vulnerability scanner and firmware analyzer.

- **Firmalyzer** is an IoT and embedded device vulnerability scanner.

---

[46] www.social-engineer.org/framework/se-tools/computer-based/social-engineer-toolkit-set/

[47] https://censys.io

[48] www.riot-os.org

- **JTAGulator** is an open source hardware hacking tool that identifies on-chip debug (OCD) connections from test points or component pads on a target device and can extract program code or data, modify memory contents, or affect device operation in real-time. Depending on the complexity of the target device, manually locating is available.

- **KillerBee** is a security evaluation tool for IEEE 802.15.4/ZigBee systems.

- **Attify Zigbee Framework** is a GUI wrapper tool to support the usage of KillerBee for IoT/radio security professionals.

- **Foren6** is a non-intrusive (passive) 6LoWPAN (IPv6 over Low Power Wireless Personal Area Networks) network analysis and sniffer tool.

User Awareness: eLearning

- **Cofense Phishme**,[49] **KnowBe4**,[50] and **Keepnet**[51] are some of the commercial simulated phishing attack services that, in addition to the phishing reporting Outlook add-on can assess the organization's employee security posture against phishing attacks.

- **LUCY Security**[52] security awareness and several types of simulated attacks, including phishing.

- **Infosec IQ**[53] is a phishing simulation and security awareness training platform.

- **Gophish**[54] is an open source phishing framework that conducts simulated phishing attacks and tests an organization's exposure to those attacks.

---

[49] https://cofense.com/product-services/phishme/

[50] www.knowbe4.com

[51] www.keepnetlabs.com

[52] https://lucysecurity.com

[53] www.infosecinstitute.com/form/iq-demo

[54] https://getgophish.com

- **Sptoolkit** (Simple Phishing Toolkit) is an open source phishing toolkit that is designed to conduct simulated phishing attacks.

- **Immersive Labs**[55] is an online security training courses provider that offers a wide variety of training courses designed by the audience or by use case.

- **OpenSesame**[56] is an online security training courses provider.

Forensics and Incident Response

- **True Image**[57] is a mirroring, imaging, and cloning tool that allows the creation of exact disk images.

- **Autopsy** [58] is a GUI-based open source digital forensic tool to analyze hard drives and smartphones.

- **Encrypted Disk Detector**[59] is a non-intrusive tool that checks encrypted physical drives. It supports TrueCrypt, PGP, BitLocker, and Safeboot encrypted volumes.

- **MAGNET RAM Capture**[60] is a free imaging tool that captures the physical memory content of a computer allowing the investigator to analyze artifacts in memory.

- **CrowdResponse**[61] and **CrowdInspect**[62] are Windows applications that collect system information for incident response.

- **Defraser**[63] is a forensic tool to detect and repair full and partial multimedia files in the data streams.

---

[55] https://immersivelabs.online

[56] www.opensesame.com

[57] www.acronis.com/en-us/products/true-image/

[58] www.sleuthkit.org/autopsy/

[59] www.magnetforensics.com/resources/encrypted-disk-detector/

[60] www.magnetforensics.com/resources/magnet-ram-capture/

[61] www.crowdstrike.com/resources/community-tools/crowdresponse/

[62] www.crowdstrike.com/resources/community-tools/crowdinspect-tool/

[63] https://sourceforge.net/projects/defraser/

- **Exiftool**[64] can read, write and edit meta information for a number of file types, like EXIF, GPS, IPTC, XMP, JFIF, GeoTIFF, Photoshop IRB, FlashPix, etc.

- **SIFT** (SANS Investigative Forensics Tool)[65] is a toolbox of free and open source incident response and forensic tools created for digital forensic investigations.

- **DumpZilla**[66] is a forensic tool created to extract information from Firefox, Iceweasel, and Seamonkey browsers.

- **PALADIN**[67] is a well-known Live-CD toolbox with over 100 forensics tools distributed in 33 categories to support forensic investigators.

- **Volatility**[68] is an open source memory forensics tool designed to support incident response and malware analysis. Volatility runs on Microsoft Windows, macOS X, and Linux.

- **Oxygen-Forensic Detective**[69] extracts, decodes, and analyzes data from several types of digital sources, including mobile devices and IoT devices, device backups, Universal Integrated Circuit Card (UICC), media cards, drones, and cloud services. Among others, it can also extract system files and credentials from Windows, macOS, and Linux systems.

- **Xplico**[70] Network Forensic Analysis Tool (NFAT) is designed to extract applications data from internet traffic such as HTTP, SIP, IRC, POP, IMAP, or SMTP traffic.

---

[64] https://exiftool.org

[65] www.sans.org/tools/sift-workstation

[66] www.dumpzilla.org

[67] https://sumuri.com/software/paladin/

[68] www.volatilityfoundation.org

[69] www.oxygen-forensic.com/en/products/oxygen-forensic-detective

[70] http://www.xplico.org

HoneyPots

- **Kippo**[71] is an SSH honeypot developed in Python that can store shell interaction of the attacker and log brute-force attacks.

- **Glastopf**[72] is a Python developed web application honeypot, among other features, it emulates vulnerabilities by type and detects unknown attacks.

- **HoneyThing**[73] is a honeypot for IoT systems.

Summary

There are lots of freeware, open source, and freemium tools available for cybersecurity professionals to use to discover security controls flaws, detect misconfigurations and vulnerabilities. With these tools, organizations can understand their environments better by seeing them through the eyes of an external party and prioritizing their mitigating actions.

It should be noted that there are commercial alternatives to these tools, which can provide better support for large organizations.

It should also be noted that security professionals must use these tools with caution, as they may harm the organization or potentially disclose sensitive information. The licensing and terms of use should be read, understood, and agreed upon before use.

---

[71] https://github.com/desaster/kippo

[72] https://github.com/mushorg/glastopf

[73] https://github.com/omererdem/honeything

APPENDIX 1

IT Security Technical Controls, Processes, and Services Matrix

This appendix is a support tool that allows readers to map the existing security controls in their organizations and produce a comprehensive gap analysis. This high-level matrix identifies each technical security control, processes to be implemented, and services to be subscribed.

CLIENTS

UNMANAGED CLIENTS & MOBILE DEVICES (BYOD)	SHORT DESCRIPTION
MDM: Mobile Device Management	An MDM solution is implemented to control mobile devices (including BYOD) access to corporate resources. MDM enables remote device management, enforces configurations, supports troubleshooting, and can push/remove apps or manage data.
MAM: Mobile Application Management	A MAM solution is implemented for mobile devices provisioning and controlling access to corporate and commercially available mobile apps.
NAC: Network Access Control	An NAC solution is implemented to ensure only allowed/authorized corporate devices are connected to corporate networks. It detects the addition of unauthorized devices into the network and creates alerts/notifications to SOC.

(continued)

© Virgilio Viegas and Oben Kuyucu 2022
V. Viegas and O. Kuyucu, *IT Security Controls*, https://doi.org/10.1007/978-1-4842-7799-7

UNMANAGED CLIENTS & MOBILE DEVICES (BYOD)	SHORT DESCRIPTION
MFA: Multi-Factor Authentication	Remote access to corporate resources is done using multi-factor authentication (e.g., password+token).
RASP for Mobile Apps	Runtime application self-protection for mobile applications is a security mechanism to identify abnormal behavior in the application and mobile device by measuring and analyzing runtime and device information.
SECURE CONNECTIONS	
IPSEC, SSH, and TLS	Access to corporate services (i.e., an organization's public website) through untrusted channels are properly encrypted using TLS or IPSec (e.g., access to the company's Internet public websites must be encrypted, remote connections to internal services must be encrypted). Using strong cryptography and security protocols to safeguard sensitive data during transmission over open, public networks, including the following: • Only trusted keys and certificates are accepted. • The protocol in use only supports secure versions or configurations. • The encryption strength is appropriate for the encryption methodology in use. **The use of EV certificates in public websites is highly recommended.**
Clean Pipes	A solution is maintained and managed by the ISP to protect Internet connections from well-known bandwidth consumption denial of service attacks.
Anti-DDoS	These are on-premises solutions to mitigate/prevent DDoS attacks.

(*continued*)

MANAGED DEVICES

Directory Service Integration	All workstations, Windows, and Linux, are integrated with a Directory service (the most popular are Active Directory, OpenLDAP, and Lotus Domino) using secure channels, such as Kerberos authentication protocol.
Centralized Endpoint Management	Centralized system management is a product for managing and administering distributed systems of computers running Windows operating systems, macOS, Linux or Unix, and other operating systems. These systems provide remote control, patch management, software distribution, operating system deployment, and network access protection.
TPM: Trusted Platform Module	TPM provides hardware-based security functions and should be implemented in all corporate laptops to ensure system integrity and avoid unauthorized hardware installation.TPM usually supports full disk encryption with Microsoft BitLocker.
VPN Client	Managed devices allowed to connect remotely have a VPN client installed.
NAC: Network Access Control	Managed devices are properly authorized to connect to corporate networks through the implementation of NAC.
Data Classification	Data classification software would help employees to classify data based on organization policies. Most of them can edit metadata or a document, making them available for productivity platforms or even by encapsulating the data.
UAM: User Activity Monitoring	User activity monitoring (UAM, also known as UEBA or NDR) solution is implemented to monitor and track end-user behavior on devices, networks, and other company-owned IT resources. User activity monitoring tools help detect and stop insider threats, whether unintentional or malicious.

(continued)

ENDPOINT PROTECTION

Phishing Reporting Tool	Phishing reporting tools allow end users to report potential phishing emails. This sends a notification to the security operations center or the centralized sandbox of the secure email gateway to check.
Host IPS or EDR	Host intrusion protection and endpoint detection and response solutions monitor and analyze suspicious activities and potentially block malicious content.
Desktop Firewall	Desktop firewalls, also known as personal firewalls, control network traffic from and to a computer, allowing or dropping the packets based on security rules.
Antivirus	Antivirus software can scan, detect, prevent and delete malware from computer systems, most of them based on signatures or heuristic behavior. All managed devices must have active and updated antivirus software managed centrally.
Anti-Spyware	Anti-spyware software can scan, detect, prevent and delete unwanted spyware, track or spy on user behavior such as internet activity, login credentials, and sensitive personal information. Managed devices have active and updated anti-spyware software managed centrally.
Full Disk Encryption	Disks are encrypted using hardware or software to prevent unauthorized access to the data storage. Unlike file and folder encryption, every bit of the disk (except MBR) is encrypted, making it extremely difficult to decrypt without a key. It is advised that logical access is managed independently of operating system authentication mechanisms, and decryption keys are not linked to user accounts.
Application Control and Application Whitelisting	Application control mechanisms are used on computer systems to ensure that only authorized/approved applications can be installed or executed. Users are unable to run or install unauthorized applications on managed workstations.

INFRASTRUCTURE

ON-PREMISES
PERIMETER SECURITY

Firewall	All incoming and outgoing network traffic is monitored and controlled by firewalls based on determined and frequently reviewed security rules.
IDS and IPS	Perimeter networks are monitored and protected by intrusion detection/protection systems.
Proxy and Content (URL) Filtering	Content filtering, commonly referred to as a proxy, is implemented to restrict and control the internet content users can access.
DLP: Data Loss Prevention	DLP is a platform that detects and prevents potential data breaches/data exfiltration transmissions according to corporate policies.
Honeypot	A honeypot (bait) system is a mechanism to detect unauthorized attempts or attacks to the information systems by continuous monitoring of the systems. Honeypots may have "baits" in the system or deception technologies to attract more attackers
WAF: Web Application Firewall	WAF is a network device that filters, monitors, and blocks traffic to web applications providing additional protection against attacks like SQL injection, cross-site scripting, security misconfigurations, or design flaws.
SSL VPN	SSL VPN platforms can provide easy yet secure remote access to corporate resources through SSL or TLS protocol.
DNS	Distinct internal and external DNS servers are implemented.External DNS is protected against DDoS attacks.Domain Name System Security Extensions (DNSSEC) should also be implemented.
Message Security	A message security platform scans email content, including antivirus, anti-phishing, and anti-spoofing.
Directory Integration for External Applications	Integrates applications with directory services to centrally manage and authenticate users.
Sandbox	This isolated environment simulates the end-user operating environment to run programs and test incoming files.Sandboxes provide an additional layer of protection against zero-day attacks, ransomware, and stealthy attacks like APTs (advanced persistent threats).

(continued)

ON-PREMISES
PERIMETER SECURITY

Encrypted Email	Encrypted email is a technology that allows sending and receiving emails securely with external parties. Either the email channel is encrypted, or an automated email is sent to the recipient containing a secure link to the email content.
TLS Decryption	TLS decryption is implemented for outbound user access, where legally allowed.
Perimeter Static Routing	Perimeter static routing is implemented in perimeter networks
Physical Network Segmentation	All perimeter networks are physically segregated. Distinct communication devices are implemented for each perimeter zone (e.g., Internet connections and DMZs are supported by distinct switches).

ON-PREMISES SUPPORT
CONTROLS

Access Control	Define and manage who can write, view, or use resources in all corporate devices, applications, and databases.	
Secure VLAN Segmentation	Criticality	Perimeter VLANs are segregated according to the hosted systems criticality(e.g., highly critical, critical, or non-critical).
	Service Nature (e.g., FE, MW, DB, etc.)	Perimeter VLANs are segregated according to the hosted system's nature (e.g., cardholder data environment, front-end, middleware, database, fileserver, etc.).
	Type (Prod, Quality, Dev, etc.)	Perimeter VLANs are segregated according to the hosted systems environment (e.g., production, staging, quality, development, etc.).
Security Baselines	Security baselines are a set of recommendations used for OS, application, or service hardening. They must be based on industry-accepted, mature standards and applied in all server deployments.	
Redundancy	Critical systems should be highly available.	

(continued)

ON-PREMISES SUPPORT CONTROLS

Load Balancing	Load balancing is distributing the computing loads over a cluster of resources to maximize the system's efficiency.
Encryption	All internal production traffic is encrypted (production data in transit). TLS/SSL is implemented in all internal portals.Emulation access (e.g., 5250, 3270) is encrypted. Data at rest (e.g., files, databases) is encrypted.
Multitier and Multilayer	Multiple layers of protection are implemented with devices from distinct manufacturers (e.g., several firewall layers from distinct manufacturers).
Distinct Heartbeat Interfaces	Network security devices have dedicated heartbeat interfaces.

EXTRANET & INTERNAL SERVERS

File Integrity Monitoring	File integrity monitoring is a mechanism that validates the integrity of a file, folder, or registry setting. It can check critical application files/folders as well as OS-level files.
Disaster Recovery	Critical platforms have disaster recovery plans set and tested at least annually.
Time Synchronization	All corporate devices must have the same time. The organization should synchronize time from trusted sources (e.g., GPS). A time synchronization policy should be enforced on all devices (e.g., workstations, servers, ATMs, CCTV, etc.)
Log Concentrator	Relevant server events are reported to a log concentrator.
Routing and Management Networks	Routing and management networks are implemented in the perimeter.
Centralized Management	All IT devices (security devices) are centrally managed.
Sinkhole	All internal non-corporate traffic should be routed to a specific router (sinkhole) and reported to the SIEM platform for investigation.
PKI: Public Key Infrastructure	A PKI is implemented.Internal certificates are issued to workstations, servers, and internal websites.

(continued)

SECURITY MONITORING
& ENFORCEMENT

PAM: Privileged Access Management	A PAM solution secures, controls, and monitors privileged accounts. All administrative access is from PAM, and violations are reported.
SIEM: Security Information and Event Management	SIEM collects and analyzes data from IT security systems and other relevant devices.
DAM: Database Activity Monitoring	Database activity monitoring is implemented to monitor and analyze database activity
SSO: Single Sign-On	SSO is an authentication method that allows users to authenticate over multiple applications and websites using the same credentials.
Risk Register	A security risk register collects, analyzes, and aggregates security risks.

PUBLIC CLOUD (IaaS and PaaS)

UEBA: User and Entity Behavior Analysis	UEBA monitors user behavior in cloud services and reports any abnormal activity
Firewall	A firewall is in place to protect all connections to a cloud service.
CASB: Cloud Access Security Broker	CASB is a security policy enforcement solution that enforces and ensures the proper security measures are implemented between the cloud solution and the customer organization.
PAM: Privileged Access Management	A PAM solution secures, controls, and monitors privileged accounts is implemented. All administrative access is from PAM, and violations are reported.
MFA: Multi-factor Authentication	Remote access to corporate resources can only be done using multi-factor authentication (e.g., password+token).
IDS/IPS: Intrusion Detection/ Protection Systems	Perimeter networks are monitored and protected by IDS/IPS.
Cloud DLP	Cloud data loss prevention enforces corporate DLP policies across data stored in the cloud.

(continued)

PUBLIC CLOUD (IaaS and PaaS)

Encryption	Cloud content is encrypted according to corporate policies.
File Integrity	File integrity monitoring for critical servers is implemented.
Honeypot	A honeypot (bait) system is in place.
Active Directory Integration	Cloud authentication and authorization services are integrated with the corporate Active Directory.

SOFTWARE AS A SERVICE (SaaS)

UEBA: User and Entity Behavior Analysis	UEBA monitors user behavior in SaaS services and reports any abnormal activity.
SECaaS	An external entity provides SECaaS security.
CASB: Cloud Access Security Broker	CASB is a security policy enforcement solution that enforces and ensures the proper security measures are implemented between the cloud solution and the customer organization.
MFA: Multi-factor Authentication	Remote access to corporate resources can only be done using multi-factor authentication (e.g., password+token).
Encryption	Cloud content is encrypted according to corporate policies.
Active Directory Integration	Cloud authentication and authorization services are integrated with the corporate Active Directory.

INFORMATION SECURITY PROCESSES AND SERVICES

GOVERNANCE

Security Governance	An information security governance program should include the following. • Compliance management (compliance to the organization policies, national regulations, cybersecurity frameworks, etc.) • Policy management (includes exception management, self-assessment, and annual review process of policies) • Incorporation of information security to third-party risk management • Ability to track and manage information risks through a risk register • Targeted technical awareness and training • Capability mapping (ability to map organizational capabilities to requirements and information security threats) • Support risk management activities and residual risk management
Policies and Procedures	Information security policies and procedures should include the following. • Compliance with organization policies, national regulations • Support technical security standards • Documentation of security configuration baselines • Job descriptions and roles and responsibilities

SECURITY OPERATIONS CENTER

Incident Response and Recovery	A formalized security incident procedure should include the following. • Presence of a cyber crisis management plan • Ability to correlate events • Defined SOC cases and thresholds • Standard operating procedures for specific scenarios • SOC event knowledgebase • Incorporation of lessons learned into procedures • SOC asset onboarding processes • Annual review of the SOC health

(continued)

SECURITY OPERATIONS CENTER	
Threat Hunting	Proactively search, detect, and isolate organizational systems, networks, and infrastructure for advanced threats that might be evading the existing security controls
Threat Intelligence	• Subscription to multiple threat intelligence services that can provide cybersecurity threat intelligence regarding the organization, the sector, the country. • Presence of threat awareness program that includes a cross-organization information-sharing capability for threat intelligence • Incorporate threat indicators (i.e., IoCs) into existing IT security controls (e.g., EDR, IPS, etc.)
CYBER SECURITY & RISK ASSESSMENT	
Penetration Testing	Conduct penetration testing of public-facing applications annually by qualified independent internal resources or an accredited third party.
Red Teaming	Conduct red-team exercises to simulate attempts by adversaries to compromise organizational systems in accordance with applicable rules of engagement.
Code Review and Testing	Perform a manual code review of applications using the industry-accepted, mature processes, procedures, and/or techniques, such as OWASP (Open Web Application Security Project) guidelines.
Compliance Scans	Devices are scanned to confirm compliance with standards and security baselines.
Vulnerability Scans	Devices are frequently scanned for vulnerabilities.
Firewall Assurance	A firewall assurance process reviews firewall (and network devices) rules and configuration compliance and identifies vulnerabilities.

(continued)

SECURITY AWARENESS	
Security Training	Users should be educated using security awareness and a targeted training program.
Simulated Phishing	User awareness and overall employee security posture can be measured by sending simulated phishing attacks.
SECURITY ENGINEERING	
Asset Management	This is an active and continuous process to identify IT assets and identify related security risks.
Configuration and Patch Management	This is an established configuration management process for all security devices.
Security Architecture	In addition to security standards and baselines, a corporate security architecture defines implementation and integration rules for all security controls and systems.

APPENDIX 2

Information Security Certifications

This appendix lists industry-accepted, globally recognized, vendor-neutral information/cybersecurity certifications.

Certification Organization	Credential abbreviation	Certification Title	Subject
SECO-Institute	S-ISF	Information Security Foundation	Management
	S-ISP	Information Security Practitioner	Management
	S-ISME	Information Management Security Expert	Management
	S-CISO	Certified Information Security Officer	Management
	S-ITSF	IT Security Foundation	General Cybersecurity
	S-ITSP	IT Security Practitioner	General Cybersecurity
	S-ITSE	IT Security Expert	General Cybersecurity
	S-CITSO	Certified IT Security Officer	General Cybersecurity
	S-DPF	Data Protection Foundation	Privacy
	S-DPP	Data Protection Practitioner	Privacy
	S-CDPO	Certified Data Protection Officer	Privacy
	S-EHF	Ethical Hacking Foundation	Penetration Testing
	S-EHP	Ethical Hacking Practitioner	Penetration Testing
	S-SPF	Secure Programming Foundation	Software Development
	S-DWF	Dark Web Foundation	Threat Intelligence

(continued)

V. Viegas and O. Kuyucu, *IT Security Controls*, https://doi.org/10.1007/978-1-4842-7799-7

Certification Organization	Credential abbreviation	Certification Title	Subject
(ISC)2	CISSP	Certified Information Systems Security Professional	Management
	CISSP-ISSAP	Information Systems Security Architecture Professional	Security Architecture
	CISSP-ISSEP	Information Systems Security Engineering Professional	IT-Administration
	CISSP-ISSMP	Information Systems Security Management Professional	Management
	SSCP	Systems Security Certified Practitioner	IT Administration
	CCSP	Certified Cloud Security Professional	Cloud Security
	CAP	Certified Authorization Professional	Auditing
	CSSLP	Certified Secure Software Lifecycle Professional	Software Development
	HCISPP	HealthCare Information Security and Privacy Practitioner	Healthcare
CompTIA	Security+	CompTIA Security+ [12]	IT Administration
	CySA+	CompTIA Cybersecurity Analyst	Security Analysis
	PenTest+	CompTIA Pentest+	Penetration Testing
	CASP+	CompTIA Advanced Security Practitioner	General Cybersecurity

(*continued*)

Certification Organization	Credential abbreviation	Certification Title	Subject
ISACA	CISA	Certified Information Systems Auditor	Auditing
	CISM	Certified Information Security Manager	Management
	CRISC	Certified In Risk and Information Systems Control	Risk Management
	CGEIT	Certified in the Governance of Enterprise IT	Management
	CSX-F	Cybersecurity Fundamentals	General Cybersecurity
	CSX-T	Cybersecurity Technical Foundations	General Cybersecurity
	CSX-P	Cybersecurity Practitioner Certification	General Cybersecurity
	CSX-A	Cybersecurity Audit Certification	Auditing
SANS GIAC	GSE	Security Expert	General Cybersecurity
	GSEC	Security Essentials	General Cybersecurity
	GCIA	Certified Intrusion Analyst	Security Analysis
	GISF	GIAC Information Security Fundamentals	General Cybersecurity
	GCED	Certified Enterprise Defender	Cyber Defense
	GCWN	Certified Windows Security Administrator	IT-Administration
	GPPA	Certified Perimeter Protection Analyst	firewalls
	GMON	Continuous Monitoring Certification	Threat Intelligence
	GCCC	Critical Controls Certification	Cyber Defense
	GDSA	Defensible Security Architecture	Security Architecture
	GCUX	Certified UNIX Security Administrator	IT-Administration
	GCDA	Certified Detection Analyst	Threat Intelligence
	GDAT	Defending Advanced Threats	Cyber Defense
	GCIH	Certified Incident Handler	Incident Response
	GPEN	Penetration Tester	Penetration Testing

(continued)

Certification Organization	Credential abbreviation	Certification Title	Subject
	GWAPT	Web Application Penetration Tester	Penetration Testing
	GXPN	Exploit Researcher and Advanced Penetration Tester	Penetration Testing
	GMOB	Mobile Device Security Analyst	Security Analysis
	GAWN	Assessing and Auditing Wireless Networks	Wireless Security
	GPYC	Python Coder	Software Development
	GCFA	Certified Forensic Analyst	Forensics
	GCFE	Certified Forensic Examiner	Forensics
	GREM	Reverse Engineering Malware	Malware Analysis
	GNFA	Network Forensic Analyst	Forensics
	GCTI	Cyber Threat Intelligence	Threat Intelligence
	GASF	Advanced Smartphone Forensics	Forensics
	GSLC	Security Leadership	Management
	GSNA	Systems and Network Auditor	Auditing
	GISP	Information Security Professional	General Cybersecurity
	GLEG	Law of Data Security & Investigations	Forensics
	GCPM	Certified Project Manager	Management
	GSTRT	Strategic Planning, Policy, and Leadership	Management
	GSSP-JAVA	Secure Software Programmer-Java	Software Development
	GSSP-.NET	Secure Software Programmer- .NET	Software Development
	GWEB	Certified Web Application Defender	Software Development
	GICSP	Global Industrial Cybersecurity Professional	Critical Infrastructure Security

(continued)

Certification Organization	Credential abbreviation	Certification Title	Subject
	GRID	Response and Industrial Defense	Critical Infrastructure Security
	GCIP	Critical Infrastructure Protection	Critical Infrastructure Security
	GEVA	Enterprise Vulnerability Assessor	Threat Intelligence
	GOSI	Open Source Intelligence	Threat Intelligence
	GBFA	Battlefield Forensics and Acquisition	Forensics
	GCSA	Cloud Security Automation	Cloud Security
EC-Council	CSCU	EC-Council Certified Secure Computer User	Security Awareness
	CND	EC-Council Certified Network Defender	IT-Administration
	CEH	EC-Council Certified Ethical Hacker	Penetration Testing
	CEH-Master (Practical)	EC-Council Certified Ethical Hacker Master (Practical)	Penetration Testing
	ECSA	EC-Council Certified Security Analyst	Penetration Testing
	ECSA-Master (Practical)	EC-Council Certified Security Analyst (Practical)	Penetration Testing
	LPT-Master (Practical)	EC-Council Licensed Penetration Tester (Master)	Penetration Testing
	EIISM	EC-Council Information Security Manager	Management
	CCISO	EC-Council Certified Chief Information Security Officer	Management
	ECIH	EC-Council Certified Incident Handler	Incident Response
	CHFI	EC-Council Computer Hacking Forensic Investigator	Forensics

(continued)

307

Certification Organization	Credential abbreviation	Certification Title	Subject
	EDRP	EC-Council Disaster Recovery Professional	Disaster Recovery
	ECES	EC-Council Certified Encryption Specialist	Encryption
	CASE Java	EC-Council Certified Application Security Engineer Java	Software Development
	CASE .Net	EC-Council Certified Application Security Engineer .Net	Software Development
	CTIA	EC-Council Certified Threat Intelligence Analyst	Threat Intelligence
	CSA	EC-Council Certified SOC Analyst	Security Analysis
	ECSS	EC-Council Certified Security Specialist	General Cybersecurity
Offensive Security	OSCP	Offensive Security Certified Professional	Penetration Testing
	OSWP	Offensive Security Wireless Professional	Penetration Testing
	OSEP	Offensive Security Experienced Penetration Tester	Penetration Testing
	OSED	Offensive Security Exploit Developer	Penetration Testing
	OSWE	Offensive Security Web Expert	Penetration Testing
	OSCE	Offensive Security Certified Expert	Penetration Testing
	OSEE	Offensive Security Exploitation Expert	Penetration Testing
EITCI	EITCA/IS	EITCA Information Technologies Security Academy	General Cybersecurity
CSA	CCSK	CSA Certificate of Cloud Security Knowledge	Cloud Security
Cloud Credential Council	PCSM	CCC Professional Cloud Security Manager Certification	Cloud Security
IAPP	CIPP	Certified Information Privacy Professional	Privacy
	CIPM	Certified Information Privacy Manager	Privacy
	CIPT	Certified Information Privacy Technologist	Privacy

(continued)

Certification Organization	Credential abbreviation	Certification Title	Subject
CREST	CPSA	CREST Practitioner Security Analyst	Penetration Testing
	CRT	CREST Registered Penetration Tester	Penetration Testing
	CCT App	CREST Certified Web Application Tester	Penetration Testing
	CCT Inf	CREST Certified Infrastructure Tester	Penetration Testing
	CCSAS	CREST Certified Simulated Attack Specialist	Attack Simulation
	CCSAM	CREST Certified Simulated Attack Manager	Attack Simulation
	CCWS	CREST Certified Wireless Specialist	Wireless security
	CPTIA	CREST Practitioner Threat Intelligence Analyst	Threat Intelligence
	CRTIA	CREST Registered Threat Intelligence Analyst	Threat Intelligence
	CCTIM	CREST Certified Threat Intelligence Manager	Threat Intelligence
	CPIA	CREST Practitioner Intrusion Analyst	Security Analysis
	CRIA	CREST Registered Intrusion Analyst	Security Analysis
	CCNIA	CREST Certified Network Intrusion Analyst	Security Analysis
	CCHIA	CREST Certified Host Intrusion Analyst	Security Analysis
	CCMRE	CREST Certified Malware Reverse Engineer	Malware Analysis
	CCIM	CREST Certified Incident Manager	Incident Response
	CRTSA	CREST Registered Technical Security Architect	Security Architecture

(continued)

Certification Organization	Credential abbreviation	Certification Title	Subject
IACRB	CCFE	Certified Computer Forensics Examiner	Forensics
	CCTHP	Certified Cyber Threat Hunting Professional	Threat Hunting
	CDRP	Certified Data Recovery Professional	Disaster Recovery
	CEPT	Certified Expert Penetration Tester	Penetration Testing
	CEREA	Certified Expert Reverse Engineering Analyst	Malware Analysis
	CMWAPT	Certified Mobile and Web Application Penetration Tester	Penetration Testing
	CMFE	Certified Mobile Forensics Examiner	Forensics
	CPT	Certified Penetration Tester	Penetration Testing
	CRTOP	Certified Red Team Operations Professional	Red Team
	CREA	Certified Reverse Engineering Analyst	Malware Analysis
	CSSA	Certified SCADA Security Architect	Critical Infrastructure Security
	CSAP	Certified Security Awareness Practitioner	Security Awareness
SABSA	SABSA-SCF	SABSA Chartered Security Architect: Foundation Certificate	Security Architecture
	SABSA-SCP	SABSA Chartered Security Architect: Practitioner Certificate	Security Architecture
	SABSA-SCM	SABSA Chartered Security Architect: Master Certificate	Security Architecture
The Open Group	OG0-041	Open FAIR Foundation	Risk Management
	TOGAF9-F	TOGAF 9 Foundation	Security Architecture
	TOGAF9-C	TOGAF 9 Certified	Security Architecture

APPENDIX 3

Knowledge, Skills and Abilities (KSAs)

This appendix lists some KSAs for major information security areas.

Acquisition Management

KSA ID	Description
K0126	Knowledge of secure acquisitions (e.g., relevant contracting officer's technical representative [COTR] duties, secure procurement, supply chain risk management)
K0148	Knowledge of import/export control regulations and responsible agencies to reduce supply chain risk
K0154	Knowledge of supply chain risk management standards, processes, and practices
K0163	Knowledge of critical information technology (IT) procurement requirements
K0164	Knowledge of functionality, quality, and security requirements and how these will apply to specific items of supply (i.e., elements and processes)
K0169	Knowledge of information technology (IT) supply chain security and risk management policies, requirements, and procedures
K0257	Knowledge of information technology (IT) acquisition/procurement requirements
K0264	Knowledge of program protection planning to include information technology (IT) supply chain security/risk management policies, anti-tampering techniques, and requirements
K0266	Knowledge of how to evaluate the trustworthiness of the supplier and/or product
K0270	Knowledge of the acquisition/procurement lifecycle process

(continued)

© Virgilio Viegas and Oben Kuyucu 2022
V. Viegas and O. Kuyucu, *IT Security Controls*, https://doi.org/10.1007/978-1-4842-7799-7

Acquisition Management

KSA ID	Description
K0523	Knowledge of products and nomenclature of major vendors (e.g., security suites—Trend Micro, Symantec, McAfee, Outpost, Panda, Kaspersky) and how differences affect exploitation/vulnerabilities
S0086	Skill in evaluating the trustworthiness of the supplier and/or product
A0009	Ability to apply supply chain risk management standards
A0031	Ability to conduct and implement market research to understand government and industry capabilities and appropriate pricing
A0039	Ability to oversee the development and update of the lifecycle cost estimate
A0045	Ability to evaluate/ensure the trustworthiness of the supplier and/or product
A0056	Ability to ensure security practices are followed throughout the acquisition process
A0064	Ability to interpret and translate customer requirements into operational capabilities

Continuity Planning and Disaster Recovery

K0210	Knowledge of data backup and restoration concepts
K0021	Knowledge of data backup, types of backups (e.g., full, incremental), and recovery concepts and tools
K0365	Knowledge of basic backup and recovery procedures, including different types of backups (e.g., full, incremental)
K0026	Knowledge of disaster recovery continuity of operations plans
S0032	Skill in developing, testing, and implementing network infrastructure contingency and recovery plans
S0150	Skill in implementing and testing network infrastructure contingency and recovery plans

Cyber Defense Analysis and Support

K0098	Knowledge of the cyber defense service provider reporting structure and processes within your organization

(continued)

312

Acquisition Management

KSA ID	Description
K0107	Knowledge of and experience in insider threat investigations, reporting, investigative tools, and laws/regulations
K0157	Knowledge of cyber defense policies, procedures, and regulations
K0190	Knowledge of encryption methodologies
K0408	Knowledge of cyber actions (i.e., cyber defense, information gathering, environment preparation, cyberattack) principles, capabilities, limitations, and effects
S0063	Skill in collecting data from a variety of cyber defense resources
S0096	Skill in reading and interpreting signatures (e.g., snort)
S0124	Skill in troubleshooting and diagnosing cyber defense infrastructure anomalies and working through resolution
S0170	Skill in configuring and utilizing computer protection components (e.g., hardware firewalls, servers, routers, as appropriate)

Cyber Intelligence

K0409	Knowledge of cyber intelligence/information collection capabilities and repositories
K0525	Knowledge of required intelligence planning products associated with cyber operational planning
K0550	Knowledge of target, including related current events, communication profile, actors, and history (language, culture) and/or frame of reference
K0553	Knowledge of tasking processes for organic and subordinate collection assets
K0554	Knowledge of tasking, collection, processing, exploitation, and dissemination
K0562	Knowledge of the capabilities and limitations of new and emerging collection capabilities, accesses, and/or processes
K0568	Knowledge of the definition of collection management and collection management authority
K0404	Knowledge of current collection requirements
K0571	Knowledge of the feedback cycle in collection processes

(continued)

Acquisition Management

KSA ID	Description
K0578	Knowledge of the intelligence requirements development and request for information processes
K0580	Knowledge of the organization's established format for collection plan
K0595	Knowledge of the relationships of operational objectives, intelligence requirements, and intelligence production tasks
K0596	Knowledge of the request for information process
K0602	Knowledge of the various collection disciplines and capabilities
K0458	Knowledge of intelligence disciplines

Cyber Intelligence Analysis

KSA ID	Description
K0110	Knowledge of common adversary tactics, techniques, and procedures in assigned area of responsibility (i.e., historical country-specific tactics, techniques, and procedures; emerging capabilities)
K0115	Knowledge of emerging computer-based technology that has potential for exploitation by adversaries
K0312	Knowledge of intelligence principles, policies, and procedures, including legal authorities and restrictions
K0315	Knowledge of the principal methods, procedures, and techniques of gathering information and producing, reporting, and sharing information
K0352	Knowledge of all forms of intelligence support needs, topics, and focus areas
K0354	Knowledge of all relevant reporting and dissemination procedures
K0355	Knowledge of all-source reporting and dissemination procedures
K0358	Knowledge of analytical standards and the purpose of intelligence confidence levels
K0359	Knowledge of approved intelligence dissemination processes
K0386	Knowledge of collection management tools
K0391	Knowledge of collection systems, capabilities, and processes
K0387	Knowledge of collection planning process and collection plan

(continued)

Acquisition Management

KSA ID	Description
K0389	Knowledge of collection sources, including conventional and non-conventional sources
K0390	Knowledge of collection strategies
K0394	Knowledge of common reporting databases and tools
K0401	Knowledge of criteria for evaluating collection products
K0441	Knowledge of how collection requirements and information needs are translated, tracked, and prioritized across the extended enterprise
K0456	Knowledge of intelligence capabilities and limitations
K0457	Knowledge of intelligence confidence levels
K0459	Knowledge of intelligence employment requirements (i.e., logistical, communications support, maneuverability, legal restrictions)
K0460	Knowledge of intelligence preparation of the environment and similar processes
K0461	Knowledge of intelligence production processes
K0462	Knowledge of intelligence reporting principles, policies, procedures, and vehicles, including report formats, report-ability criteria (requirements and priorities), dissemination practices, and legal authorities and restrictions
K0463	Knowledge of intelligence requirements tasking systems
K0464	Knowledge of intelligence support to planning, execution, and assessment
K0484	Knowledge of midpoint collection (process, objectives, organization, targets, etc.)
K0492	Knowledge of non-traditional collection methodologies.
K0514	Knowledge of organizational structures and associated intelligence capabilities
K0544	Knowledge of target intelligence gathering and operational preparation techniques and life cycles
K0577	Knowledge of the intelligence frameworks, processes, and related systems

Cyber Operational Planning

KSA ID	Description
K0028	Knowledge of the organization's evaluation and validation requirements

(continued)

Acquisition Management

KSA ID	Description
K0234	Knowledge of full-spectrum cyber capabilities
K0316	Knowledge of business or military operation plans, concept operation plans, orders, policies, and standing rules of engagement
K0367	Knowledge of basic cyber operations activity concepts (e.g., footprinting, scanning, and enumeration, penetration testing, white/black listing)
K0400	Knowledge of crisis action planning for cyber operations
K0413	Knowledge of cyber operation objectives, policies, and legalities
K0415	Knowledge of cyber operations terminology/lexicon
K0436	Knowledge of fundamental cyber operations concepts, terminology/lexicon (i.e., environment preparation, cyberattack, cyber defense), principles, capabilities, limitations, and effects
K0416	Knowledge of cyber operations
K0424	Knowledge of denial and deception techniques
K0442	Knowledge of how converged technologies impact cyber operations (e.g., digital, telephony, wireless)
K0465	Knowledge of internal and external partner cyber operations capabilities and tools
K0494	Knowledge of objectives, situation, operational environment, and the status and disposition of internal and external partner collection capabilities available to support planning
K0495	Knowledge of ongoing and future operations
K0496	Knowledge of operational asset constraints
K0497	Knowledge of operational effectiveness assessment
K0498	Knowledge of operational planning processes
K0499	Knowledge of operations security
K0503	Knowledge of organization formats of resource and asset readiness reporting, its operational relevance, and intelligence collection impact

(continued)

Acquisition Management

KSA ID	Description
K0519	Knowledge of planning timelines adaptive, crisis action, and time-sensitive planning
K0572	Knowledge of the functions and capabilities of internal teams that emulate threat activities to benefit the organization
K0585	Knowledge of the organizational structure as it pertains to full-spectrum cyber operations, including the functions, responsibilities, and interrelationships among distinct internal elements
K0588	Knowledge of the priority information requirements from subordinate, lateral, and higher levels of the organization
K0589	Knowledge of the process used to assess the performance and impact of operations
K0593	Knowledge of the range of cyber operations and their underlying intelligence support needs, topics, and focus areas
K0594	Knowledge of the relationships between end states, objectives, effects, lines of operation, and so forth
K0613	Knowledge of who the organization's operational planners are, how and where they can be contacted, and their expectations
S0030	Skill in developing operations-based testing scenarios
S0055	Skill in using knowledge management technologies
S0061	Skill in writing test plans
S0082	Skill in evaluating test plans for applicability and completeness
S0104	Skill in conducting test readiness reviews

Cyber Policy and Strategy Management

K0065	Knowledge of policy-based and risk-adaptive access controls
K0191	Knowledge of signature implementation impact
K0248	Knowledge of strategic theory and practice
K0288	Knowledge of industry standard security models

(continued)

Acquisition Management

KSA ID	Description
K0311	Knowledge of industry indicators useful for identifying technology trends
K0335	Knowledge of current and emerging cyber technologies
K0412	Knowledge of cyber lexicon/terminology
K0435	Knowledge of fundamental cyber concepts, principles, limitations, and effects
K0454	Knowledge of information needs
K0504	Knowledge of organization issues, objectives, and operations in cyber as well as regulations and policy directives governing cyber operations
K0521	Knowledge of priority information, how it is derived, where it is published, how to access, and so forth
K0526	Knowledge of research strategies and knowledge management
K0535	Knowledge of strategies and tools for target research
K0566	Knowledge of the critical information requirements and how they're used in planning
S0018	Skill in creating policies that reflect system security objectives
S0145	Skill in integrating and applying policies that meet system security objectives
S0146	Skill in creating policies that enable systems to meet performance objectives (e.g., traffic routing, SLAs, CPU specifications)
A0034	Ability to develop, update, and/or maintain standard operating procedures (SOPs)

Cyber Threat Analysis

K0426	Knowledge of dynamic and deliberate targeting
K0430	Knowledge of evasion strategies and techniques
K0453	Knowledge of indications and warning
K0469	Knowledge of internal tactics to anticipate and/or emulate threat capabilities and actions
K0474	Knowledge of key cyber threat actors and their equities
K0533	Knowledge of specific target identifiers and their usage

(continued)

Acquisition Management

KSA ID	Description
K0536	Knowledge of structure, approach, and strategy of exploitation tools (e.g., sniffers, keyloggers) and techniques (e.g., gaining backdoor access, collecting/exfiltrating data, conducting vulnerability analysis of other systems in the network)
K0540	Knowledge of target communication tools and techniques
K0546	Knowledge of target list development (i.e., RTL, JTL, CTL)
K0548	Knowledge of target or threat cyber actors and procedures
K0549	Knowledge of target vetting and validation procedures
K0551	Knowledge of targeting cycles
K0603	Knowledge of how targets or threats use the Internet
K0612	Knowledge of what constitutes a "threat" to a network
S0022	Skill in designing countermeasures to identify security risks
S0044	Skill in mimicking threat behaviors
S0052	Skill in the use of social engineering techniques
S0109	Skill in identifying hidden patterns or relationships

Cyber Security Management

KSA ID	Description
K0147	Knowledge of emerging security issues, risks, and vulnerabilities
K0173	Knowledge of operations security
K0242	Knowledge of organizational security policies
K0502	Knowledge of organization decision support tools and/or methods

Forensics Analysis

KSA ID	Description
K0017	Knowledge of concepts and practices of processing digital forensics data
K0118	Knowledge of processes for seizing and preserving digital evidence (e.g., chain of custody)
K0119	Knowledge of hacking methodologies in Windows or Unix/Linux environment

(continued)

Acquisition Management

KSA ID	Description
K0133	Knowledge of types of digital forensics data and how to recognize them
K0134	Knowledge of deployable forensics
K0184	Knowledge of anti-forensics tactics, techniques, and procedures
K0185	Knowledge of common forensics tool configuration and support applications (e.g., VMware, Wireshark)
K0268	Knowledge of forensics foot-print identification
K0433	Knowledge of forensics implications of operating system structure and operations
K0449	Knowledge of how to extract, analyze, and use metadata
K0573	Knowledge of the fundamentals of digital forensics to extract actionable intelligence
S0047	Skill in preserving evidence integrity according to standard operating procedures or national standards
S0065	Skill in identifying and extracting data of forensic interest in diverse media (i.e., media forensics)
S0069	Skill in setting up a forensic workstation
S0071	Skill in using forensic tool suites (e.g., EnCase, The Sleuth Kit, FTK)
S0075	Skill in conducting forensic analyses in multiple operating system environments (e.g., mobile device systems)
S0087	Skill in deep analysis of captured malicious code (e.g., malware forensics)
S0088	Skill in using binary analysis tools (e.g., hexedit, xxd command code, hexdump)
S0120	Skill in reviewing logs to identify evidence of past intrusions
S0175	Skill in performing root-cause analysis
A0010	Ability to analyze malware
A0043	Ability to conduct forensic analyses in and for Windows and Unix/Linux environments

(continued)

Acquisition Management

KSA ID	Description

Identity Management

K0007	Knowledge of authentication, authorization, and access control methods
K0033	Knowledge of host/network access control mechanisms (e.g., access control list)

Incident Response

K0041	Knowledge of incident categories, incident responses, and timelines for responses
K0042	Knowledge of incident response and handling methodologies
K0145	Knowledge of security event correlation tools
K0150	Knowledge of enterprise incident response programs, roles, and responsibilities
K0193	Knowledge of advanced data remediation security features in databases
K0230	Knowledge of cloud service models and possible limitations for an incident response
K0317	Knowledge of procedures used for documenting and querying reported incidents, problems, and events
K0381	Knowledge of collateral damage and estimating impact(s)
S0054	Skill in using incident handling incident response methodologies
S0080	Skill in performing damage assessments
S0098	Skill in detecting host and network-based intrusions via intrusion detection technologies
S0173	Skill in using security event correlation tools
A0025	Ability to accurately define incidents, problems, and events in the trouble ticketing system

APPENDIX 4

Resource Library

This resource library provides documentation, standards and frameworks on many IT-security related subject that can help security professionals to understand the technology and how to secure them. As new technologies are being developed, methods to secure them also changes. Please find the latest version of this list in `https://github.com/IT-Security-Controls/Documents/`.

> NIST SP 800-53 Rev. 5 Security and Privacy Controls for Information Systems and Organizations
>
> This publication provides a catalog of security and privacy controls for information systems and organizations to protect organizational operations and assets, individuals, other organizations, and the Nation from a diverse set of threats and risks, including hostile attacks, human errors, natural disasters, structural failures, foreign intelligence entities, and privacy risks. The controls are flexible and customizable and implemented as part of an organization-wide process to manage risk. The controls address diverse requirements derived from mission and business needs, laws, executive orders, directives, regulations, policies, standards, and guidelines. Finally, the consolidated control catalog addresses security and privacy from a functionality perspective (i.e., the strength of functions and mechanisms provided by the controls) and from an assurance perspective (i.e., the measure of confidence in the security or privacy capability provided by the controls). Addressing functionality and assurance helps to ensure that information technology products and the systems that rely on those products are sufficiently trustworthy.

© Virgilio Viegas and Oben Kuyucu 2022
V. Viegas and O. Kuyucu, *IT Security Controls*, https://doi.org/10.1007/978-1-4842-7799-7

NIST SP 800-53 Rev. 5 Control Catalog Spreadsheet

The entire security and privacy control catalog in spreadsheet format.

Mappings between 800-53 Rev. 5 and other frameworks and standards (NIST Cybersecurity Framework and NIST Privacy Framework; ISO/IEC 27001)

The mappings provide organizations a general indication of SP 800-53 control coverage with respect to other frameworks and standards. When leveraging the mappings, it is important to consider the intended scope of each publication and how each publication is used; organizations should not assume equivalency based solely on the mapping tables because mappings are not always one-to-one and there is a degree of subjectivity in the mapping analysis.

NIST SP 800-53A Rev. 5 Assessing Security and Privacy Controls in Information Systems and organizations

This publication provides a set of procedures for conducting assessments of security controls and privacy controls employed within federal information systems and organizations. The assessment procedures, executed at various phases of the system development life cycle, are consistent with the security and privacy controls in NIST Special Publication 800-53, Revision 4.

NIST SP 800-53B Control Baselines for Information Systems and Organizations

This publication provides security and privacy control baselines for the Federal Government. There are three security control baselines (one for each system impact level—low-impact, moderate-impact, and high-impact), as well as a privacy baseline that is applied to systems irrespective of impact level. In addition to the control baselines, this publication provides tailoring guidance and a set of working assumptions that help guide and inform the control selection process. Finally, this publication provides guidance on the development of overlays to facilitate control baseline customization for specific communities of interest, technologies, and environments of operation.

NIST SP 800-37 Rev. 2 Risk Management Framework for Information Systems and Organizations: A System Life Cycle Approach for Security and Privacy

This publication describes the Risk Management Framework (RMF) and provides guidelines for applying the RMF to information systems and organizations. The RMF provides a disciplined, structured, and flexible process for managing security and privacy risk that includes information security categorization; control selection, implementation, and assessment; system and common control authorizations; and continuous monitoring. The RMF includes activities to prepare organizations to execute the framework at appropriate risk management levels. The RMF also promotes near real-time risk management and ongoing information system and common control authorization through the implementation of continuous monitoring processes; provides senior leaders and executives with the necessary information to make efficient, cost-effective, risk management decisions about the systems supporting their missions and business functions; and incorporates security and privacy into the system development life cycle. Executing the RMF tasks links essential risk management processes at the system level to risk management processes at the organization level. In addition, it establishes responsibility and accountability for the controls implemented within an organization's information systems and inherited by those systems.

NIST Cybersecurity Framework

Framework is voluntary guidance, based on existing standards, guidelines, and practices for organizations to better manage and reduce cybersecurity risk. In addition to helping organizations manage and reduce risks, it was designed to foster risk and cybersecurity management communications amongst both internal and external organizational stakeholders.

NIST SP 800-181 Rev. 1 Workforce Framework for Cybersecurity (NICE Framework)

This publication from the National Initiative for Cybersecurity Education (NICE) describes the Workforce Framework for Cybersecurity (NICE Framework), a fundamental reference for describing and sharing information about cybersecurity work. It expresses that work as Task statements and describes Knowledge and Skill statements that provide a foundation for learners including students, job seekers, and employees. The use of these statements helps students to develop skills, job seekers to demonstrate competencies, and employees to accomplish tasks. As a common, consistent lexicon that categorizes and describes cybersecurity work, the NICE Framework improves communication about how to identify, recruit, develop, and retain cybersecurity talent. The NICE Framework is a reference source from which organizations or sectors can develop additional publications or tools that meet their needs to define or provide guidance on different aspects of cybersecurity education, training, and workforce development.

NIST SP 800-63-3 Digital Identity Guidelines

These guidelines provide technical requirements for federal agencies implementing digital identity services and are not intended to constrain the development or use of standards outside of this purpose. The guidelines cover identity proofing and authentication of users (such as employees, contractors, or private individuals) interacting with government IT systems over open networks. They define technical requirements in each of the areas of identity proofing, registration, authenticators, management processes, authentication protocols, federation, and related assertions.

NIST SP 800-81-2 Secure Domain Name System (DNS) Deployment Guide

This document provides deployment guidelines for securing DNS within an enterprise, extensive guidance on maintaining data integrity and performing source authentication, guidelines for configuring DNS deployments to prevent many denial-of-service attacks that exploit vulnerabilities in various DNS components.

NIST SP 800-161 Supply Chain Risk Management Practices for Federal Information Systems and Organizations, 2nd Draft

This publication provides guidance to federal agencies on identifying, assessing, and mitigating ICT supply chain risks at all levels of their organizations. This publication integrates ICT supply chain risk management (SCRM) into federal agency risk management activities by applying a multitiered, SCRM-specific approach, including guidance on supply chain risk assessment and mitigation activities.

NIST SP 800-115 Technical Guide to Information Security Testing and Assessment

The purpose of this document is to assist organizations in planning and conducting technical information security tests and examinations, analyzing findings, and developing mitigation strategies. The guide provides practical recommendations for designing, implementing, and maintaining technical information security test and examination processes and procedures.

NIST SP 800-137 Information Security Continuous Monitoring (ISCM) for Federal Information Systems and Organizations

The purpose of this guideline is to assist organizations in the development of a continuous monitoring strategy and the implementation of a continuous monitoring program providing visibility into organizational assets, awareness of threats and vulnerabilities, and visibility into the effectiveness of deployed security controls. It provides ongoing assurance that planned and implemented security controls are aligned with organizational risk tolerance as well as the information needed to respond to risk in a timely manner should observations indicate that the security controls are inadequate.

NIST SP 800-55 Rev. 1 Performance Measurement Guide for Information Security

This document provides guidance on how an organization, using metrics, identifies the adequacy of in-place security controls, policies, and procedures. It provides an approach to help management decide where to invest in additional security protection resources or identify and evaluate nonproductive controls.

NIST SP 800-60 Vol. 1 Rev. 1 Guide for Mapping Types of Information and Information Systems to Security Categories

This document contains the basic guidelines for mapping types of information and information systems to security categories.

NIST SP 800-60 Vol. 2 Rev. 1 Guide for Mapping Types of Information and Information Systems to Security Categories: Appendices

The appendices of NIST SP 800-60 Vol. 1 Rev.1

NIST SP 800-144 Guidelines on Security and Privacy in Public Cloud Computing

This publication provides an overview of the security and privacy challenges pertinent to public cloud computing and points out considerations organizations should take when outsourcing data, applications, and infrastructure to a public cloud environment.

NIST SP 800-145 The NIST Definition of Cloud Computing

This publication provides the NIST definition of cloud computing.

NIST SP 800-146 Cloud Computing Synopsis and Recommendations

This document reprises the NIST-established definition of cloud computing, describes cloud computing benefits and open issues, presents an overview of major classes of cloud technology, and provides guidelines and recommendations on how organizations should consider the relative opportunities and risks of cloud computing.

NIST SP 800-132 Recommendation for Password-Based Key Derivation: Part 1: Storage Applications

This Recommendation specifies techniques for the derivation of master keys from passwords or passphrases to protect stored electronic data or data protection keys.

NIST SP 800-135 Rev. 1 Recommendation for Existing Application-Specific Key Derivation Functions

This Recommendation provides security requirements for application-specific Key Derivation Functions (KDFs).

NIST SP 800-45 Version 2 Guidelines on Electronic Mail Security

The purpose of the publication is to recommend security practices for designing, implementing, and operating email systems on public and private networks.

NIST SP 800-56A Rev. 3 Recommendation for Pair-Wise Key-Establishment Schemes Using Discrete Logarithm Cryptography

This Recommendation specifies key-establishment schemes based on the discrete logarithm problem over finite fields and elliptic curves, including several variations of Diffie-Hellman and Menezes-Qu-Vanstone (MQV) key establishment schemes.

NIST SP 800-56B Rev. 2 Recommendation for Pair-Wise Key-Establishment Using Integer Factorization Cryptography

This Recommendation specifies key-establishment schemes using integer factorization cryptography (in particular, RSA). Both key-agreement and key transport schemes are specified for pairs of entities, and methods for key confirmation are included to provide assurance that both parties share the same keying material. In addition, the security properties associated with each scheme are provided.

NIST SP 800-56C Rev. 2 Recommendation for Key-Derivation Methods in Key-Establishment Schemes

This Recommendation specifies techniques for the derivation of keying material from a shared secret established during a key-establishment scheme defined in NIST Special Publications 800-56A or 800-56B.

NIST SP 800-58 Security Considerations for Voice Over IP Systems

This publication introduces VOIP, its security challenges, and potential countermeasures for VOIP vulnerabilities.

NIST SP 800-128 Guide for Security-Focused Configuration Management of Information Systems

The purpose of this document is to provide guidelines for organizations responsible for managing and administering the security of federal information systems and associated environments of operation.

NIST SP 800-92 Guide to Computer Security Log Management

This publication seeks to assist organizations in understanding the need for sound computer security log management. It provides practical, real-world guidance on developing, implementing, and maintaining effective log management practices throughout an enterprise. The guidance in this publication covers several topics, including establishing log management infrastructures, and developing and performing robust log management processes throughout an organization.

NIST SP 800-111 Guide to Storage Encryption Technologies for End User Devices

This publication explains the basics of storage encryption, which is the process of using encryption and authentication to restrict access to and use of stored information.

NIST SP 800-130 A Framework for Designing Cryptographic Key Management Systems

This Framework for Designing Cryptographic Key Management Systems (CKMS) contains descriptions of CKMS components that should be considered by a CKMS designer and specifies requirements for the documentation of those CKMS components in the design.

NIST SP 800-52 Rev. 2 Guidelines for the Selection, Configuration, and Use of Transport Layer Security (TLS) Implementations

This publication provides guidance to the selection and configuration of TLS protocol implementations while making effective use of Federal Information Processing Standards (FIPS) and NIST-recommended cryptographic algorithms.

NIST SP 800-78-4 Cryptographic Algorithms and Key Sizes for
Personal Identity Verification

This document contains the technical specifications needed
for the mandatory and optional cryptographic keys specified in
FIPS 201-2 as well as the supporting infrastructure specified in
FIPS 201-2 and the related NIST Special Publication 800-73-4,
Interfaces for Personal Identity Verification [SP800-73], and
NIST SP 800-76-2, Biometric Specifications for Personal Identity
Verification [SP800-76], that rely on cryptographic functions.

NIST SP 800-164 (Draft) Guidelines on Hardware-Rooted Security
in Mobile Devices

The guidelines in this document are intended to provide
a common baseline of security technologies that can be
implemented across a wide range of mobile devices to help secure
organization-issued mobile devices as well as devices brought
into an organization, such as personally owned devices used in
enterprise environments (e.g., Bring Your Own Device, BYOD).

NIST SP 800-41 Rev. 1 Guidelines on Firewalls and Firewall Policy

This publication provides an overview of several types of firewall
technologies and discusses their security capabilities and their
relative advantages and disadvantages in detail.

NIST SP 800-34 Rev. 1 Contingency Planning Guide for Federal
Information Systems

This publication assists organizations in understanding the purpose,
process, and format of information system contingency planning
development through practical, real-world guidelines. This guidance
document provides background information on interrelationships
between information system contingency planning and other types
of security and emergency management-related contingency plans,
organizational resiliency, and the system development life cycle. This
document provides guidance to help personnel evaluate information
systems and operations to determine contingency planning
requirements and priorities.

NIST SP 800-83 Rev. 1 Guide to Malware Incident Prevention and Handling for Desktops and Laptops

This publication provides recommendations for improving an organization's malware incident prevention measures.

NIST SP 800-84 Guide to Test, Training, and Exercise Programs for IT Plans and Capabilities

This publication seeks to assist organizations in designing, developing, conducting, and evaluating test, training, and exercise (TT&E) events to aid personnel in preparing for adverse situations involving information technology (IT).

NIST SP 800-94 Guide to Intrusion Detection and Prevention Systems (IDPS)

This publication seeks to assist organizations in understanding intrusion detection system (IDS) and intrusion prevention system (IPS) technologies and in designing, implementing, configuring, securing, monitoring, and maintaining intrusion detection and prevention systems (IDPS).

NIST SP 800-123 Guide to General Server Security

The purpose of this document is to assist organizations in understanding the fundamental activities performed as part of securing and maintaining the security of servers that provide services over network communications as a main function.

NIST SP 800-70 Rev. 4 National Checklist Program for IT Products: Guidelines for Checklist Users and Developers

This document contains instructions or procedures for configuring an information technology (IT) product to an operational environment, for verifying that the product has been configured properly, and/or for identifying unauthorized changes to the product.

NIST SP 800-47 Rev. 1 Managing the Security of Information Exchanges

This publication focuses managing the protection of the information being exchanged or accessed before, during, and after the exchange rather than on any particular type of technology-based connection or information access or exchange method and thus provides guidance on identifying information exchanges, considerations for protecting exchanged information, and the agreement(s) needed to help manage protection of the exchanged information.

NIST SP 800-77 Rev. 1 Guide to IPsec VPNs

This publication provides practical guidance to organizations on implementing security services based on IPsec so that they can mitigate the risks associated with transmitting sensitive information across networks.

NIST SP 800-113 Guide to SSL VPNs

This document seeks to assist organizations in understanding SSL VPN technologies.

SP 800-40 Rev. 4 (Draft) Guide to Enterprise Patch Management Planning: Preventive Maintenance for Technology

This publication frames patching as a critical component of preventive maintenance for computing technologies—a cost of doing business, and a necessary part of what organizations need to do in order to achieve their missions. This publication discusses common factors affecting enterprise patch management and recommends creating an enterprise strategy to simplify and operationalize patching while also improving reduction of risk.

NIST SP 800-116 Rev. 1 Guidelines for the Use of PIV Credentials in Facility Access

This recommendation provides a technical guideline to use Personal Identity Verification (PIV) Cards in facility access; enabling federal agencies to operate as government-wide interoperable enterprises. These guidelines cover the risk-based strategy to select appropriate PIV authentication mechanisms as expressed within Federal Information Processing Standard (FIPS) 201.

NIST SP 800-96 PIV Card to Reader Interoperability Guidelines

The purpose of this document is to present recommendations for Personal Identity Verification (PIV) card readers in the area of performance and communications characteristics to foster interoperability.

NIST SP 800-76-2 Biometric Specifications for Personal Identity Verification

This document contains technical specifications for biometric data. These specifications reflect the design goals of interoperability and performance of the Personal Identity Verification (PIV) Card. This specification addresses image acquisition to support the background check, fingerprint template creation, retention, and authentication.

NIST SP 800-79-2 Guidelines for the Authorization of Personal Identity Verification Card Issuers (PCI) and Derived PIV Credential Issuers (DPCI)

The purpose of this SP is to provide appropriate and useful guidelines for assessing the reliability of issuers of PIV Cards and Derived PIV Credentials.

NIST SP 800-85B-4 (Draft) PIV Data Model Test Guidelines

This Personal Identity Verification (PIV) test guide addresses test requirements for the interface to the PIV card and test requirements for the PIV data model.

NIST SP 800-122 Guide to Protecting the Confidentiality of Personally Identifiable Information (PII)

The purpose of this document is to assist organizations in protecting the confidentiality of personally identifiable information (PII) in information systems.

NIST SP 800-160 Vol. 1 Systems Security Engineering: Considerations for a Multidisciplinary Approach in the Engineering of Trustworthy Secure Systems

This publication addresses the engineering-driven perspective and actions necessary to develop more defensible and survivable systems, inclusive of the machine, physical, and human components that compose the systems and the capabilities and services delivered by those systems.

NIST SP 800-126 Rev. 3 The Technical Specification for the Security Content Automation Protocol (SCAP): SCAP Version 1.3

This publication, along with its annex (NIST Special Publication 800-126A) and a set of schemas, collectively define the technical composition of SCAP version 1.3 in terms of its component specifications, their interrelationships and interoperation, and the requirements for SCAP content.

NIST SP 800-57 Part 1 Rev. 5 Recommendation for Key Management: Part 1 – General

This Recommendation provides cryptographic key-management guidance.

NIST SP 800-131A Rev. 2 Transitioning the Use of Cryptographic Algorithms and Key Lengths

NIST Special Publication (SP) 800-57, Part 1, Recommendation for Key Management: General, includes a general approach for transitioning from one algorithm or key length to another. This Recommendation (SP 800-131A) provides more specific guidance for transitions to the use of stronger cryptographic keys and more robust algorithms.

NIST SP 800-147 BIOS Protection Guidelines

This document provides guidelines for preventing the unauthorized modification of Basic Input/Output System (BIOS) firmware on PC client systems.

NIST SP 800-82 Rev. 2 Guide to Industrial Control Systems (ICS) Security

This document provides guidance on how to secure Industrial Control Systems (ICS), including Supervisory Control and Data Acquisition (SCADA) systems, Distributed Control Systems (DCS), and other control system configurations such as Programmable Logic Controllers (PLC), while addressing their unique performance, reliability, and safety requirements.

NIST SP 800-18 Rev. 1 Guide for Developing Security Plans for Federal Information Systems

This document offers guidance on preparing, reviewing, and approving system security plans.

NIST SP 800-35 Guide to Information Technology Security Services

This guide helps with the selection, implementation, and management of IT security services by guiding organizations through the various phases of the IT security services life cycle.

NIST SP 800-12 Rev. 1 An Introduction to Information Security

This publication introduces the information security principles that organizations may leverage to understand the information security needs of their respective systems.

NIST SP 800-50 Building an Information Technology Security Awareness and Training Program

This document provides guidance for building an effective information technology (IT) security program.

NIST SP 800-114 Rev. 1 User's Guide to Telework and Bring Your Own Device (BYOD) Security

This publication provides recommendations for securing BYOD devices used for teleworking and remote access, as well as those directly attached to the enterprise's own networks.

NIST SP 800-46 Rev. 2 Guide to Enterprise Telework, Remote Access, and Bring Your Own Device (BYOD) Security

This publication provides information on security considerations for several types of remote access solutions, and it makes recommendations for securing a variety of telework, remote access, and BYOD technologies.

NIST SP 800-142 Practical Combinatorial Testing

This publication provides a self-contained tutorial on using combinatorial testing for real-world software, including how to use it effectively for system and software assurance.

NIST SP 800-95 Guide to Secure Web Services

This document describes how to implement security mechanisms in Web services. It also discusses how to make Web services and portal applications robust against the attacks to which they are subject.

NIST SP 800-121 Rev. 2 Guide to Bluetooth Security

This publication provides information on the security capabilities of Bluetooth and gives recommendations to organizations employing Bluetooth wireless technologies on securing them effectively.

NIST SP 800-124 Rev. 1 Guidelines for Managing the Security of Mobile Devices in the Enterprise

The purpose of this publication is to help organizations centrally manage and secure mobile devices against a variety of threats.

NIST SP 800-97 Establishing Wireless Robust Security Networks: A Guide to IEEE 802.11i

This report provides readers with a detailed explanation of next generation 802.11 wireless security. It describes the inherently flawed Wired Equivalent Privacy (WEP) and explains 802.11i's two-step approach (interim and long-term) to providing effective wireless security.

NIST SP 800-98 Guidelines for Securing Radio Frequency Identification (RFID) Systems

This publication seeks to assist organizations in understanding the risks of RFID technology and security measures to mitigate those risks.

NIST SP 800-218 Secure Software Development Framework (SSDF) Version 1.1: Recommendations for Mitigating the Risk of Software Vulnerabilities

This document recommends the Secure Software Development Framework (SSDF) – a core set of high-level secure software development practices that can be integrated into each SDLC implementation.

NIST SP 800-213 IoT Device Cybersecurity Guidance for the Federal Government: Establishing IoT Device Cybersecurity Requirements

This publication contains background and recommendations to help organizations consider how an IoT device they plan to acquire can integrate into a system.

NIST SP 800-210 General Access Control Guidance for Cloud Systems

This document presents cloud access control characteristics and a set of general access control guidance for cloud service models: IaaS (Infrastructure as a Service), PaaS (Platform as a Service), and SaaS (Software as a Service).

NIST SP 800-207 Zero Trust Architecture

This document contains an abstract definition of zero trust architecture (ZTA) and gives general deployment models and use cases where zero trust could improve an enterprise's overall information technology security posture.

NIST SP 800-190 Application Container Security Guide

This publication explains the potential security concerns associated with the use of containers and provides recommendations for addressing these concerns.

NIST SP 800-167 Guide to Application Whitelisting

This publication is intended to assist organizations in understanding the basics of application whitelisting.

NIST SP 800-153 Guidelines for Securing Wireless Local Area Networks (WLANs)

The purpose of this publication is to help organizations improve their WLAN security by providing recommendations for WLAN security configuration and monitoring.

NIST SP 800-150 Guide to Cyber Threat Information Sharing

This publication provides guidelines for establishing and participating in cyber threat information sharing relationships.

NISTIR 7864 The Common Misuse Scoring System (CMSS): Metrics for Software Feature Misuse Vulnerabilities

This report defines proposed measures for CMSS and equations to be used to combine the measures into severity scores for each vulnerability. The report also provides examples of how CMSS measures and scores would be determined for selected software feature misuse vulnerabilities.

NISTIR 7694 Specification for Asset Reporting Format 1.1

This interagency report describes the Asset Reporting Format (ARF), a data model for expressing the transport format of information about assets and the relationships between assets and reports.

NISTIR 7511 Rev. 5 Security Content Automation Protocol (SCAP) Version 1.3 Validation Program Test Requirements

This report defines the requirements and associated test procedures necessary for products or modules to achieve one or more Security Content Automation Protocol (SCAP) validations.

NISTIR 7275 Rev. 4 Specification for the Extensible Configuration Checklist Description Format (XCCDF) Version 1.2

This report specifies the data model and Extensible Markup Language (XML) representation for the Extensible Configuration Checklist Description Format (XCCDF) Version 1.2.

CIS Critical Security Controls Version 8

CIS Critical Security Controls are prioritized set of actions to protect organizations and data from cyber-attack vectors.

HIPAA (Health Insurance Portability and Accountability Act of 1996)
Also, HIPAA Administrative Simplification
HIPAA Administrative Simplification, Regulation Text 45 CFR Parts 160, 162, and 164 Unofficial Version, as amended through March 26, 2013.

Framework for SCADA Security Policy

The SCADA policy framework has been developed to make it easier to create a SCADA security policy. Using a framework allows authors to apply a systematic approach that ensures that policy addresses all critical topics adequately.

COBIT Control Objectives

COBIT provides management and business process owners with an IT governance model that helps deliver value from IT and understand and manage the risks associated with IT. COBIT helps bridge business requirements, control needs, and technical issues. It is a control model to meet the needs of IT governance and ensure the integrity of information and information systems. It is available for purchase from ISACA.

PCI DSS - Payment Card Industry Data Security Standard v3.2.1

The Payment Card Industry Data Security Standard (PCI DSS) was developed to encourage and enhance cardholder data security and facilitate the broad adoption of consistent data security measures globally. PCI DSS provides a baseline of technical and operational requirements designed to protect account data. PCI DSS applies to all entities involved in payment card processing—including merchants, processors, acquirers, issuers, and service providers. PCI DSS also applies to all other entities that store, process or transmit cardholder data (CHD) and/or sensitive authentication data (SAD).

PCI DSS - The Prioritized Approach

Prioritized Approach provides six security milestones that will help merchants and other organizations incrementally protect against the highest risk factors and escalating threats while on the road to PCI DSS compliance.

SANS Security Policy Templates

SANS developed SANS has developed set of security policy templates.

COVID-19 Security Resource Library

Useful tools and updated information on current scams, cyber threats, remote working, disaster relief, and more.

OWASP Top Ten

The OWASP Top 10 is an awareness document for developers and web application security. It represents a broad consensus about the most critical security risks to web applications.

CVE List

The mission of the CVE Program is to identify, define, and catalog publicly disclosed cybersecurity vulnerabilities.

Index

A

Access control, 24, 25, 70, 89, 93
Access control lists (ACLs), 143
Accredited Standards
    Committee (ASC), 326
Active Directory (AD), 117
Advanced Encryption Standard (AES),
    46, 67, 163
Advanced persistent threats (APTs),
    3, 92, 139, 201, 295
Adversary emulation, 275
Annualized loss expectancy (ALE), 181
Annualized rate of occurrence (ARO), 181
Antivirus software, 39, 49, 123
Application control, 25, 105, 124, 125
Application layer attacks, 52, 116
Application Security Life Cycle (ASLC),
    see Software development life
    cycle (SDLC)
Approved Scanning Vendors (ASV), 57
Asset management, 24, 89, 204
  configuration, 205
  media sanitation, 204
  security architecture, 206, 208
Attack simulation tools, 263
Attribute-based access control, 144
Authentication Header (AH), 112
awesome-osint, 265

B

Bank Identification Code (BIC), 61
Bank Identification Number (BIN), 45
Banking Regulatory and Supervisory
    Authority (BDDK), 99
Baseline cybersecurity, 91, 92
Benchmarks, 68, 148
Bluetooth Attacks, 284
Bluetooth Low Energy Attack tool
    (BLEAH), 284
BobCat, 271
Brazil, 94
Breach and Attack Simulation, 275
Bringing your own device (BYOD), 104
British Standards Institution (BSI), 18
    BS 7799, 18
Broken access control, 144
Business continuity, 14, 29, 71, 156
Business email compromise (BEC), 134
Business impact analysis (BIA), 156
Business networks, 159

C

Center for Internet Security (CIS), 88, 90,
    148, 340
Centralized endpoint management, 118
Centralized management, 160

D

J

K

L

M

Printed in the United States
by Baker & Taylor Publisher Services